The Great Yazoo Lands Sale

LANDMARK LAW CASES
&
AMERICAN SOCIETY

Peter Charles Hoffer
N. E. H. Hull
Williamjames Hull Hoffer
Series Editors

For a complete list of titles in the series go to www.kansaspress.ku.edu

CHARLES F. HOBSON

The Great Yazoo Lands Sale

The Case of

Fletcher v. Peck

UNIVERSITY PRESS OF KANSAS

Published by the University Press of Kansas (Lawrence, Kansas 66045), which was
organized by the Kansas Board of Regents and is operated and funded by Emporia
State University, Fort Hays State University, Kansas State University, Pittsburg State
University, the University of Kansas, and Wichita State University

Library of Congress Cataloging-in-Publication Data

Names: Hobson, Charles F., author.
Title: The great Yazoo lands sale : the case of Fletcher v. Peck /
Charles F. Hobson.
Description: Lawrence, Kansas : University Press of Kansas, 2016.
Series: Landmark law cases & American society.
Includes bibliographical references and index.
Identifiers: LCCN 2016023592
ISBN 9780700623303 (hardback) | ISBN 9780700623310 (paperback)
ISBN 9780700623327 (ebook)
Subjects: LCSH: Fletcher, Robert, of Amherst, in the District of New-
Hampshire—Trials, litigation, etc. | Peck, John, of Newton, in the District of
Massachusetts—Trials, litigation, etc. | Yazoo Fraud, 1795. | Contracts—United
States—History—19th century. | Public land sales—Georgia—History—18th
century. | Georgia Mississippi Company—Trials, litigation, etc. | New England
Mississippi Land Company—Trials, litigation, etc. | BISAC: HISTORY / United
States / Revolutionary Period (1775–1800). | LAW / Constitutional. | POLITICAL
SCIENCE / Government / National.
Classification: LCC KF228.F55 H63 2016 | DDC 346.7304/4—dc 3
LC record available at https://lccn.loc.gov/2016023592.

British Library Cataloguing-in-Publication Data is available.

Printed in the United States of America

10 9 8 7 6 5 4 3 2 1

The paper used in this publication is recycled and contains 30 percent postconsumer
waste. It is acid free and meets the minimum requirements of the American National
Standard for Permanence of Paper for Printed Library Materials z39.48-1992.

For Ann

CONTENTS

Rarely can one say that a study of a case is definitive. Charles Hobson's study of *Fletcher v. Peck* (1810) is the exception to this rule. It is difficult to see how it can be surpassed.

The case itself is a tangle of land speculation, state building, corruption, and ambition that is worthy of study in itself and opens a window on land transactions, Indian relations, and politics in the early nation. The scene shifts from the frontier to the courtroom and from Georgia to New England, as it seemed the entire nation had a financial interest in the Yazoo lands.

Hobson's mastery of the details of the litigation is matched by his intimate understanding of the Marshall Court. His exposition of the legal story is both clear and technically accurate. A leading student of Marshall, Hobson presents a cast of characters that also includes sharp dealers like Robert Morris, hot-headed politicians like James Jackson, and able counsel like John Quincy Adams to tell a story full of dramatic twists and fascinating turns.

The case is surely a landmark worthy of a first-rate study. It established judicial review of state legislative proceedings, provided a gloss on the contract clause of the Constitution (extending it to acts of states themselves), and established the preeminent role of the High Court in private law matters. As Hobson concludes, "Yet *Fletcher*, like *Marbury*, transcended its peculiar circumstances to become the foundation for the Marshall Court's effort to fashion the contract clause into an effective instrument to restrain the legislative powers of the states."

This is must reading for any student of our early law and our early politics.

ACKNOWLEDGMENTS

The idea for this book arose around the turn of the present century when I learned of the University Press of Kansas series Landmark Law Cases and American Society. A few years earlier the press had published *The Great Chief Justice: John Marshall and the Rule of Law*, which included a chapter on Marshall's contract clause opinions. In response to my inquiries, editor-in-chief Michael Briggs informed me that series editors Peter Hoffer and N. E. H. Hull were open to my participation and that I could choose the contract case or cases I preferred to write on.

This was in May 2000. In what proved to be an ominous pattern, I set the matter aside, mostly out of sight though not entirely out of mind. After a lapse of more than two years, Mike Briggs inquired if I was still interested and would be willing to put together a proposal, assuring me there was "no rush." This gentle prodding succeeded in eliciting a proposal, which I submitted early in 2003. After review, the proposal was accepted and I signed a contract in May of that year with Fred M. Woodward, then director of the press. In signing, I agreed to deliver a manuscript by August 2006. Publication was scheduled for fall 2007. The irony of failing to fulfill the strict terms of a contract for a book on the contract clause has weighed heavily on me. It is some consolation that actual publication has occurred less than ten years after the stipulated date.

With great forbearance the press granted me successive reprieves on hearing my pleas that ongoing professional commitments prevented my timely compliance. I thank Mike Briggs in particular for his kindly indulgence over the years when I had to give primary attention to two scholarly editions: first, *The Papers of John Marshall*, the twelfth and final volume of which was published in 2006; then three volumes of *St. George Tucker's Law Reports and Selected Papers*, published in 2013. By the latter date I had no more excuses. That year Charles T. Myers introduced himself as the new director of the press and as having taken over responsibility for the Landmark Law Cases series. I was much gratified (and relieved) by his warm encouragement and willingness to work with me. Like Mike Briggs he has shown tact and patience in coaxing me to the finish line.

I chose *Fletcher v. Peck* as my contribution to the series because of its undoubted landmark status as the first case to expound the contract clause and as the first application of judicial review to a state law. In both these respects the case provided the occasion for Chief Justice Marshall to shape the development of American constitutional law. *Fletcher* also had a decided narrative advantage in having as its "backstory" Georgia's land sales of 1795, perhaps the most infamous land-speculating venture in American history. The law case grew out of and was part of the broader episode known as "Yazoo," which roiled the politics of the new nation for nearly two decades. Another consideration was that no general work on the subject had appeared since 1966. In the ensuing decades a proliferation of studies has significantly enriched our knowledge and understanding of American constitutional history and law. The time seemed right to look at this case anew, aided by the perspectives of recent scholarship.

My indebtedness to this scholarship should be evident in the appended bibliographical essay. At an early stage I had the benefit of valuable comments and suggestions from two readers of the original proposal. At a late stage Chuck Myers read the manuscript with the critically discerning eye one would expect from the head of a university press. Besides catching errors, he identified passages that needed clarification and revision.

I would like to recognize persons and institutions who aided my research. Walter Hickey, archives specialist with the National Archives at Boston (now retired), supplied copies of the records and proceedings of *Fletcher v. Peck* as heard in the U.S. Circuit Court from 1803 to 1807. These records were particularly valuable for identifying the lawyers who represented Fletcher and Peck. Frank C. Mevers, then archivist of the state of New Hampshire, sent me information about Robert Fletcher not otherwise easily accessible. Melissa Bush of the University of Georgia's Hargrett Rare Book and Manuscript Library made copies of that institution's New England Mississippi Land Company Records, much of it relating to Perez Morton's tenure as the company's agent.

For more than three decades I had a congenial academic home

at the College of William and Mary, both as member of the staff of the Omohundro Institute of Early American History and Culture and as a resident scholar at the William and Mary School of Law. The Swem Library and the Wolf Law Library were indispensable to my research, not only for their holdings of actual books and other sources but also and more importantly for giving access to a vast virtual archive of online databases.

I am deeply grateful to my wife, Ann, for many years of love and companionship. She cheerfully lifted depressed spirits and sent me back to the writing table with renewed conviction that I was equal to the task.

The Great Yazoo Lands Sale

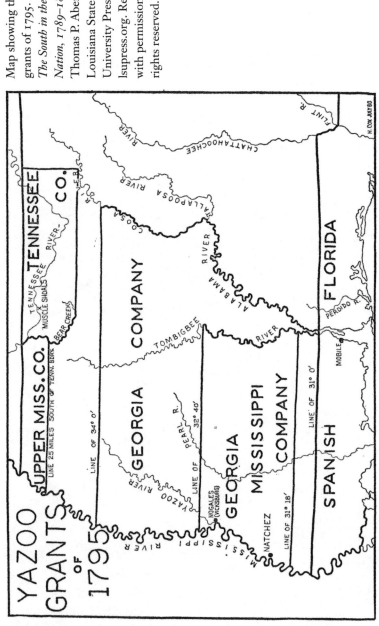

Map showing the Yazoo grants of 1795. From *The South in the New Nation, 1789–1819* by Thomas P. Abernethy, Louisiana State University Press, lsupress.org. Reprinted with permission.

Introduction

The case of *Fletcher v. Peck* (1810) is a landmark of American constitutional law for two reasons: It was the first time the Supreme Court invalidated a state law as contrary to the Constitution and the first time the Court applied the clause of the Constitution that prohibits the states from impairing the "Obligation of Contracts." Although in *Marbury v. Madison* (1803) the Court had struck down a portion of a federal statute, the practice of what came to be known as "judicial review" had its true beginnings with the exposition of the contract clause in *Fletcher*. Ideas about the judiciary's authority to void legislative acts were still in flux at the time of this decision, with jurists appealing to extraconstitutional principles as well as specific provisions of the Constitution. Chief Justice John Marshall interpreted the contract clause in a way that resolved this debate in favor of invoking the written constitutional text, a development of great significance in consolidating the practice of judicial review.

Marshall served as chief justice of the United States from 1801 to 1835, longer than any other chief justice to date. During his tenure the contract clause emerged as the constitutional expression of the doctrine of "vested rights," which held that rights acquired by individuals under law—most importantly, the right to the security and free enjoyment of property—were to be regarded as inviolable, not to be infringed by governmental power. Vested rights, in the words of twentieth-century scholar Edward S. Corwin, became "the basic doctrine of American constitutional law." Through much of the nineteenth century the contract clause was the Supreme Court's principal weapon to restrain state interference with the vested rights of property. *Fletcher* established a precedent for an expansive reading of the clause that brought under judicial scrutiny a wide spectrum of state laws. It established the principle that public as well as private contracts were protected against impairment and extended the meaning of contract to include grants of land. In subsequent cases the Court voided a New Jersey law repealing a tax exemption on land formerly belonging to Indians, struck down New Hampshire's laws radically modifying Dartmouth College's colonial charter, and overruled Kentucky's occupying-claimant laws. The term "contract" was further broadened to embrace corporate charters and compacts entered into between two states. In cases between private persons, the Court invalidated a New York bankruptcy statute discharging a previously contracted debt. However, a closely divided Court later upheld a bankruptcy law that discharged a debt contracted after the law's enactment.

In its last decade the Marshall Court sustained state laws challenged under the contract clause, including a Rhode Island tax on a bank chartered by the state. These later decisions modified but did not repudiate the broad reading first articulated in *Fletcher*. The Supreme Court continued to apply the clause robustly to protect property rights against state interference throughout the chief justiceship of Roger B. Taney (1836–1864). In the late nineteenth century the contract clause began to lose its high standing in constitutional law, superseded by the far more comprehensive due process clause of the Fourteenth Amendment. Although the contract clause in our own time has largely receded into insignificance, the broader purposes of constitutional law that it served have proved enduring.

The ruling in *Fletcher v. Peck* did not actually prevent a state from impairing vested rights the Supreme Court deemed to be protected by the Constitution, though it did contribute indirectly to bringing about a partial redress for this infraction. The Court in 1810 held that a law enacted in 1796 by the legislature of Georgia was unconstitutional, by which time the proscribed act had long since achieved its purpose and was well on its way to becoming a revered milestone of state sovereignty. In *Fletcher*, Chief Justice Marshall could do no more than demonstrate the contract clause's great potential to be an effective restraint upon the state legislatures.

The case had its beginnings in January 1795, when the state of Georgia sold its western lands, encompassing most of present-day Alabama and Mississippi, to four land companies for $500,000. Then inhabited by the Choctaw, Chickasaw, Creek, and Cherokee tribes of

Native Americans, this territory was commonly called "Yazoo," after the river that flows into the Mississippi River near Vicksburg. The Yazoo sale earned a dubious reputation as the greatest land-speculation venture in American history, perhaps unsurpassed in the scale of its operations, in the mania generated by its promise of untold wealth, in the pervasiveness of corruption attending the sale, and in the political and legal reverberations radiating from it.

The next year, in February 1796, a newly elected Georgia legislature, reacting to charges of bribery and corruption, revoked this sale and all contracts made under it and reclaimed the lands. Six years later, in 1802, Georgia ceded these lands to the United States for $1,250,000, more than twice the amount paid by the land companies. In the meantime, however, the companies had sold the lands to third-party purchasers in the northeast, many of them residing in New England. By this time the Yazoo sale became embroiled in national politics, as the New England claimants, once it was clear they would not obtain actual possession of the lands, looked to the federal government for compensation. For nearly two decades they doggedly pursued their case in Congress. The lawsuit brought by Robert Fletcher of New Hampshire against John Peck of Massachusetts in 1803 and culminating in the Supreme Court's decision in 1810 was inseparably connected with this political goal.

Ostensibly a legal dispute between private parties, *Fletcher v. Peck*, as C. Peter Magrath observed a generation ago, provides a case study of the interplay of law and politics in the Early Republic. From the nation's beginning, organized interest groups have looked to government to accomplish their ends—typically, to ensure the success of an investment in a commercial enterprise. Courts no less than the political branches of government have been vital to this process, of which *Fletcher* furnishes an early prototype. A central player in this case, though not an actual party, was the New England Mississippi Land Company, which simultaneously pursued its interests in Congress and in the federal courts.

More than is usual for a case that makes constitutional law, *Fletcher* has the attraction of being an integral part of a fascinating episode of our early national history. Beneath its dry legal pleadings lay a tale of bribery and collusion, featuring vivid incidents and a colorful cast of characters. More than an engaging story, the controversy over the Yazoo lands draws within its narrative such resonant themes as land speculation, westward expansion and settlement, republicanism, party politics, and relations with the Native American tribes. Beyond its political and legal aspects, Yazoo had a moral dimension that transformed it into a battle for the republican character of the citizens and government of the new nation.

The founding of the colonies was the first speculation in North America's "vacant" lands, and many more would follow. From the onset of colonization, governments relied on companies of investors to purchase large tracts and sell them in smaller parcels to settlers. Speculation was a routine and indeed essential part of the process of opening and settling new lands. It provided an outlet for private ambition to serve public ends. This "public good" aspect was present in attenuated form even in the Yazoo sale act, which was blandly (and misleadingly) cast as an appropriation of "unlocated territory" for paying state troops and defending the state's frontiers. Georgia's western lands sale shared features of earlier speculative land ventures, differing mostly in degree rather than in kind. The term "speculator" applied to a wide variety of persons, from the modest investor seeking to enlarge his holdings to the "jobber" who bought land for no other purpose but to "flip" it for a quick profit. Few equaled George Washington in accumulating lands over a lifetime, but he denied that he was "a monopolizer, or land-jobber." One who did surpass Washington in the avidity and extent of his speculations was Robert Morris, at heart a jobber with no intention of holding lands for long.

Great land-speculating enterprises that preceded Yazoo, such as those formed to purchase the Northwest Territory and western New York, were accompanied by genuine attempts to colonize and settle the lands. A distinguishing feature of the purchase of Georgia's western lands was that it was conceived and executed not to settle the lands but to resell them immediately. The sale originated in the particular circumstances of Georgia's postwar history as a thinly populated settlement on the margins of the new nation. Alone among those states with western land claims, Georgia had not ceded its claims to Congress before 1789. The state's continued possession of vast reaches of territory west of the Chattahoochee River mostly inhabited by Indian tribes was costly and ineffectual. After two earlier attempts to dispose of the lands, the Georgia legislature approved a sale to a consortium of land companies headed by James Gunn, then a U.S. senator. Gunn was a representative type of postwar land speculator: a Continental army officer of modest origins who parlayed successful military service into political prominence, which in turn provided a platform to launch ambitious land schemes. A believer in the politics of interest and influence, Gunn skillfully pushed the Yazoo sale through, even resorting to bribing potentially friendly legislators with shares in the companies. In his mind such tactics were an acceptable, even necessary, means of influencing the legislature. Gunn gained his grand prize but seriously miscalculated the degree to which revelations of bribery and corruption would provoke popular revulsion and bring forth a political movement dedicated to undoing the Yazoo sale.

As Gunn was the mastermind of the sale, so James Jackson, Georgia's other U.S. senator, was the guiding genius who brought about its revocation. To this task he brought a crusading zeal that aimed to restore and preserve the republican character of Georgia. In a series of published letters he spelled out the principles of a populist constitutionalism subsequently embodied in one of the most extraordinary laws enacted by an American legislature. The rescinding act of 1796 aimed not just to repeal but to declare the sale act and all rights derived from it "null and void." It further ordered the "usurped act" to be expunged from the public records. Before adjourning, the anti-Yazoo legislators staged a public burning of the reviled act, a ritual purging by fire designed to remove all traces of the state's infamous descent into corruption.

Before these events had transpired, the two largest Yazoo companies—the Georgia Company and the Georgia Mississippi Company—hastily sold their lands, mostly to purchasers in New England. The New Englanders were eager buyers, who pushed the price steadily upward until the bubble burst with news that Georgia had revoked the sale. Many of the purchasers resided in Boston, where Yazoo fever ran high. They included John Peck, who was among the most conspicuous investors in Georgia lands, accumulating large tracts in his own name and as a principal in the N.E.M. Land Co., formed early in 1796 to purchase the Georgia Mississippi Company's tract. For the next two decades Peck was an influential participant in the company's affairs and actively engaged on his own behalf. He was by no means a nominal party to the case that bears his name.

Even if Georgia had allowed the Yazoo sale to stand, the federal government was prepared to intervene to prevent any immediate colonizing or settlement plans that third-party purchasers might have contemplated. Alarmed about the sale's potential to provoke conflict with the Indian tribes, the Washington administration referred the matter to Congress. The upshot was a report presented by the attorney general in April 1796 on land claims in the Southwest. This report prepared the way for legislation in 1798 establishing the Mississippi Territory and authorizing negotiations with Georgia for ceding the lands reclaimed by the rescinding act. Around this time arguments began to surface in Congress contending that title to all or part of the Mississippi lands actually belonged to the United States. Yazoo purchasers, who bought on the assurance that Georgia had complete authority to sell its western lands in 1795, viewed this development with alarm. Indeed, they perceived the assertion of a U.S. title to be a greater threat to their titles than the rescinding law. Two pamphlets published in 1797 defending the Yazoo title focused primarily on refuting the case for a U.S. title.

As purchaser of an extensive Yazoo tract, the N.E.M. Land Co. soon evolved into an organization dedicated to asserting its title, directing its attention to the federal government, which so far had been more inclined to delay or block than facilitate the interests of the New England claimants. As early as 1798 the company joined with others in a memorial to the president, complaining that the governor of the newly created Mississippi Territory would not let them take steps to settle their lands. The company then still intended to colonize the territory, but it soon became evident that the government would not allow private settlement for fear of provoking hostilities with the Indians. In 1800 U.S. commissioners, then negotiating with Georgia for a cession of its western lands, were empowered to allow private claimants to submit compromise proposals. The New England claimants now abandoned their colonizing plans and shifted their attention to obtaining the best possible indemnity from the government.

After Georgia ceded its Mississippi lands in 1802, the U.S. commissioners presented a report to Congress in February 1803. Much to the claimants' disappointment, the commissioners asserted that titles derived from Georgia's 1795 sale act could not "be supported." At the same time, they acknowledged "equitable considerations" rendering it "expedient" to compromise on "reasonable terms." They proposed to compensate the claimants out of 5 million acres set aside in the cession compact with Georgia, though that agreement said nothing about claims based on the act of 1795. Rather than adopt the commissioners' plan, Congress in March 1803 postponed consideration of these claims until the next session without giving them any specific recognition. Nonetheless, the New England purchasers remained optimistic that Congress would act promptly and favorably on their behalf.

From 1803 onward, the N.E.M. Land Co. devoted all its attention and considerable resources to lobbying Congress for an act to indemnify the New England claimants for their investments in Yazoo lands. It hired lawyers to draw up memorials and serve as agents on the spot in Washington. As part of this campaign, the company in June 1803 instituted the lawsuit between Fletcher and Peck in the U.S. circuit court at Boston. The law case and the political lobbying were directed at the single aim of obtaining compensation. It was understood that a Supreme Court decision upholding the title would not put the claimants in possession of lands in Mississippi but might well induce Congress to provide them monetary relief.

How to get the nation's highest court to give a decision on the Yazoo title was no simple matter. By this time it was more or less settled that the Supreme Court would decide only cases or controversies; it would not give advisory opinions unconnected with adjudicating a legal dispute. The problem for the company's lawyers was to devise a case that would in effect produce an advisory opinion. *Fletcher v. Peck* was the result of shrewd and painstaking deliberation about all aspects of the case, including the type of legal action, the parties, and most importantly the pleadings, which were carefully crafted to bypass a jury and produce only legal issues for the court to decide. Everything about the case bespoke its feigned character, provoking charges that it was not a true adversarial case and that the Supreme Court should not have agreed to hear it.

If Congress had settled quickly with the claimants, there would have been no need for the law case. This possibility was soon foreclosed, however, when fierce resistance to the Yazoo claims arose in the House of Representatives, led by the redoubtable John Randolph of Virginia. Randolph combined deft political tactics with ideological passion that adamantly opposed compromise with the claimants as sanctioning vile corruption. He made Yazoo a test of Republicans' loyalty to party principles, turning it into a battle to preserve true republicanism. The ensuing debate was unmatched for intemperate language and vituperative personal attacks, exposing a division in the party between unbending purists and moderates willing to accommodate principle to expediency. Despite an apparent majority disposed toward compromise, Randolph and his followers maintained the upper hand for years by exploiting delaying tactics to prevent votes from taking place or postponing the subject to the next session or to a new Congress. Repeated frustration did not deter the claimants, who matched their adversaries in stubborn pursuit of their interests.

Anticipating timely approval of a compensation bill, the N.E.M. Land Co. let *Fletcher* languish in the U.S. circuit court for several years, not bothering to obtain a judgment. By June 1807, Congress's inaction prompted a renewal of proceedings, and judgment for Peck was entered in October of that year without arguments of counsel, jury deliberations, or opinion of the judges. The judgment was a mere formality, allowing Fletcher to bring a writ of error as expeditiously as possible. He filed his appeal with the Supreme Court in February 1808, which put the case on the docket for argument at the February 1809 term.

The Supreme Court was then less than a decade into the tenure of John Marshall as chief justice—before it had become the "Marshall Court." Thanks to his moderate temperament and sound political instincts, Marshall had successfully navigated the turbulent years of Thomas Jefferson's first administration, which included *Marbury v. Madison*, the repeal of a Federalist judiciary act, and the impeachment of federal judges. Although he did not shy away from conflict, Marshall sought accommodation by means of a strategic retreat from politics, reserving for the judiciary department the authority to decide only matters of law. By the time *Fletcher* was first argued in 1809, the Supreme Court had emerged from crisis and confrontation to a state of mutual respect if not harmony with the other branches of government. Chief Justice Marshall had begun to shape the institution and define the office in certain characteristic ways, such as adopting the practice of a single majority opinion and promoting institutional unity by bringing the justices together in the same boardinghouse during court terms.

Fletcher v. Peck was argued over four days in early March 1809 but without any decision on the merits. In fact, the Court ruled against Peck on a technical point, meaning that the pleadings had to be amended and the case reargued at the next term. But this concern for technical propriety also provided a cover for the justices' reluctance to decide a case so obviously made up to extract an advisory opinion from the Court. No doubt the chief justice and his brethren aired this matter in conference before agreeing that despite its feigned aspects the case presented a legal issue appropriate for judicial decision. The rehearing of *Fletcher* in 1810 required only one day. As expected, the Supreme Court upheld Peck on all counts, most importantly in ruling that Georgia held rightful title to the Yazoo lands in 1795 with full authority to sell them and that Georgia's rescinding act of 1796 was invalid. Despite this victory in the courtroom, Peck and the other New England claimants were denied immediate satisfaction in the halls of Congress. Anti-Yazoo Republicans, now led by Georgia's George M. Troup, continued to block compromise in the House. Yet with the onset of the War of 1812, their ideological grip on the party was weakening. More Republicans came round to the view that indemnifying the claimants was not a betrayal of republican principles but an honorable and just measure that served the true interests of the United States. The Supreme Court's decision of 1810 appears to have had a real though indeterminate influence in tilting opinion in the claimants' favor and bringing about the Yazoo compensation act of 1814.

Whatever effect it had in settling the Yazoo controversy, *Fletcher v. Peck* marked a critical step toward making good the Supreme Court's claim to enforce the law of the Constitution, to interpret and adjudicate this law as it did any other law. No part of the Constitution proved to be more important than the contract clause in establishing the Supreme Court as a tribunal for deciding on the validity of state legislative acts. That *Fletcher* became the first contract clause case was largely the doing of Chief Justice Marshall. Until his opinion, the clause had not figured centrally in the debates and commentary provoked by Georgia's revocation of the Yazoo sale. "Natural justice" and general principles of law took precedence over the contract clause in denying the validity of the rescinding act. Marshall recognized the opportunity to show how the text of the Constitution, through its prohibition against impairing the obligation of contract, could be an effective means of enforcing the limits on the legislative powers of a state.

The contract clause had its origins in the reaction to the excesses committed by the state legislatures during the 1780s. As James Madison acutely pointed out, the laws enacted by these faction-ridden assemblies often reflected the selfish interests of popular majorities who proved only too willing to sacrifice the private rights of individuals and minorities. Anxiety about the security of private rights in the republican governments of the new nation was a strong impetus to the reform movement that resulted in the Federal Convention of 1787. Madison went so far as to propose a federal "negative" or veto on the acts of the state legislatures. The Convention rejected this radical measure but not the idea behind it, choosing instead to enumerate certain prohibitions on the states in the text of the Constitution. Protecting private rights against state infringement was thus entrusted to the federal judiciary.

For Marshall the meaning and intent of the contract clause was essentially the same as what Madison hoped to accomplish with his negative, to provide a comprehensive check on the state legislatures that embraced not only past and present but also unanticipated mischiefs that might arise. He adopted a broad construction of the contract clause in the confident belief that the framers intended the Constitution to serve as a charter of rights for protecting the American people from the acts of their state governments. As Marshall observed in *Fletcher*, "the constitution of the United States contains what may be deemed a bill of rights for the people of each state."

CHAPTER ONE

Georgia Sells Its Western Lands

Georgia's massive Yazoo land sale of January 1795 was the culmination of a successive wave of land speculations dating from the early eighteenth century that looked to the vast and fertile territory beyond the Appalachian (then called the Allegheny) Mountains, seeking to exploit the relentless westward movement of an ever-expanding North American population. After Yazoo, there was less enthusiasm for large-scale enterprises of the kind that proliferated in the postrevolutionary years. Many land company investors had been disappointed in their expectations of great profits; not a few found themselves overextended, unable to meet their obligations, and endured bankruptcy and ruin. The failure of Robert Morris, resulting in his imprisonment for debt, was an object lesson in the perils of land speculation.

Optimistic by nature, speculators were not easily deterred, and traffic in buying and selling lands would revive and flourish again at various times in American history. In the nineteenth century there were several surges of speculation in public lands, as enterprising opportunists succeeded in manipulating a national land system that was designed to sell in small parcels at cheap prices. Notable speculation episodes were triggered by the discovery of gold in California in 1848 and by land grants to encourage the building of railroads. In the early twentieth century there was the Florida land boom and bust, and in our own time the real estate bubble whose bursting set off the "Great Recession" of 2007.

Investment in land took firm root in the British American colonies, which were founded as speculative ventures undertaken by profit-seeking companies of gentlemen and adventurers. In the New World land came to be prized not merely because of the potential wealth to be extracted from the soil but also because uncultivated and unexploited land was itself a valuable commodity to be bought and sold. Trading in land was attractive because it could be bought cheaply and resold at a higher price as population increased. "Speculative commercial operations," Bernard Bailyn has written, "had been part and parcel" of the earliest settlement of North America. "There was never a time in American history when land speculation had not been a major preoccupation of an ambitious people." The speculative spirit spread throughout the populace, affecting not only the great and powerful but also the humbler sorts aspiring to improve their lot. According to Bailyn, "[e]very farmer with an extra acre of land became a speculator—every town proprietor, every scrambling tradesman who could scrape together a modest sum for investment."

Enterprising Americans embraced trafficking in land while not thinking of themselves as "speculators" in the pejorative sense as "jobbers," who regarded land solely as a means to turn a quick profit with the smallest possible expenditure. Those who engaged in land speculation did so with varying degrees of motivation and participation, from the prudent investor seeking a supplemental source of income to the risk-taking adventurer in pursuit of a great fortune. Because of its seemingly limitless potential as a pathway for bold and resourceful persons—even of modest background and means—to amass great wealth, investment in land attracted a disproportionate share of reckless opportunists.

The peopling of early America and the expansion of settlement westward produced a conjunction of interests between governments and land speculators, particularly those who purchased large tracts. Land speculation served as an outlet for personal gain while also serving the needs of government and public policy. Lacking the money and administrative machinery to attract settlers to take up vacant lands and transform them into productive farms, governments allowed "wholesale" purchase by speculators who in turn would "retail" the land in smaller parcels to settlers. Governments thereby received immediate revenue for various public exigencies while being spared the expense of settling their public lands.

A French traveler to the United States in the 1790s noted the pressure on governments to accommodate large purchasers, even to the point of ignoring the law:

But the states, more taken up with the desire of obtaining the money, of which they stood in need, than of that of speedily covering those lands with cultivators; and thinking, besides, that great proprietors would be excited by their interest to parcel them out with more promptitude than a state could do, readily consented to sell them in large masses, in opposition to the law which, in many of the states, limited the number of acres that would be sold to any one person to five or six hundred." Much earlier, a Virginia colonial governor pointed out the advantages of granting large tracts to "men of substance" in settling the colony. In counties that were "seated in small parcells," he remarked, population growth was sluggish compared to those where the "greatest tracts have been granted and possessed." The great proprietors encouraged "the meaner sortof people to seat themselves as it were under the shade and protection of the greater.

The mutual needs and advantages of government and land speculators became even more evident after the Revolution. Both the state and Confederation governments were eager to sell off their "vacant" lands (still largely occupied by Indian tribes) as a means of retiring their massive debts incurred during the war. Lands could be purchased with depreciated public securities at face value, which meant that land selling at a dollar per acre could be bought for as little as ten or twenty cents an acre. With the prospect of relieving themselves of a crushing debt burden while shifting the costs of administering public lands to the purchasers, governments were even more inclined to sell on terms that favored purchase of large tracts by persons of means and influence.

No matter how selfish their motives, acquisitive, upwardly striving Americans who eagerly embraced land speculation could assure themselves they were advancing the public weal. They were promoting settlement, turning a wilderness into cultivation, and spreading "civilization" ever westward; they were expanding and strengthening the British Empire and its North American successor, the newly independent United States. Even Georgia's Yazoo sale in 1795, as brazen a land-jobbing scheme as there ever was, could be defended as enabling the state to meet a pressing public exigency, the payment of its troops and defense of its frontiers.

Colonial and Prerevolutionary Land Companies

From the outset in the colonial period, large-scale land speculation operated principally through joint-stock companies, associations of investors who pooled their capital and were assigned shares based on the proportion invested. These companies typically were composed of moneyed and well-connected persons who used their political influence to obtain vast tracts of vacant lands. By the mid-eighteenth century several groups of Virginia investors, organized as the Ohio Company, the Loyal Company, and the Greenbrier Company, had obtained large grants beyond the Alleghenies and penetrating deep into the Ohio Country, a territory occupied by Indian tribes and also claimed by France. The subsequent outbreak of the French and Indian War suspended these companies' operations. In an effort to make peace with the Indians in the area newly gained from France, the British Crown issued a royal proclamation in October 1763, which prohibited further English settlement west of a line separating lands whose waters flowed into the Atlantic from those whose waters flowed into the Mississippi River. The proclamation also barred private purchases of Indian lands, which henceforth were to be acquired solely by the Crown or with its approval.

British efforts to limit and control westward expansion by American colonists scarcely deterred speculation in western lands, as companies formed before the war revived their activities and were joined by new companies of adventurers seeking to establish extensive settlements and colonies in the Ohio and Mississippi Valleys. These companies included investors from Virginia, Pennsylvania, Maryland, and North Carolina and also a number of well-placed shareholders in England who could use their influence to persuade the government to relax strict enforcement of the Proclamation of 1763 and approve the requested grants or confirm purchases made directly from Indian tribes. None of these enterprises came to fruition, stifled by official opposition in London and eventually foundering with the outbreak of the War of Independence in 1775. Indeed, frustration with British western-land policy was one of the grievances that brought about the war.

One such disappointed investor and claimant was George Washington, a point man for western exploration and development since his days as a surveyor for Lord Fairfax in Virginia's Shenandoah Valley. Over his lifetime Washington shrewdly and aggressively acquired lands, in the West and elsewhere. He was a land speculator but denied that he was "a monopolizer, or land-jobber," who bought only to sell at a quick profit. Like his fellow American colonists, Washington regarded the Proclamation of 1763 as a temporary expedient to appease hostile Indian tribes, not a permanent barrier to settlement beyond the Alleghenies. In the same year as the proclamation, Washington became a shareholder in the Mississippi Company, an ambitious venture that envisioned a colony at the junction of the Ohio and Mississippi Rivers. This investment did not pan out because the Crown refused to approve the requested grant. Another source of vexation with British policy was the proclamation's ban against settlement by veterans who had been promised land as an incentive to enlist in the recent war. Through persistence and considerable political skill, Washington at length managed to secure the colonial governor's approval of grants on the Ohio and obtained patents for 20,000 acres of choice land for himself. However frustrated or unsympathetic he was with British western-land policy during the 1760s, as president three decades later he confronted the same problem of maintaining peace with the Indians in the face of relentless westward advancement by white settlers.

Another prerevolutionary land venture was the Grand Ohio Company (or Walpole Company), which numbered Benjamin Franklin among its shareholders and whose base was a group of Pennsylvania merchants. Better connected politically than Washington's Mississippi Company, this company in 1772 secured a grant south of the Ohio (in present-day West Virginia and eastern Kentucky) and planned a colony known as Vandalia. The company made no progress in realizing these plans before its operations shut down permanently with the coming of war. Other companies embarked on colonizing schemes after making direct purchases from the Indians in contravention of the proclamation. An association of North Carolina speculators under Richard Henderson formed the Transylvania Company early in 1775 and soon thereafter acquired 20 million acres

of Kentucky land from the Cherokee, with plans to establish a proprietary colony. In 1773 and 1774 Philadelphia merchants formed the
Illinois and Wabash companies to purchase Indian lands in the upper
Mississippi Valley (called the Illinois Country). These companies, as
well as Henderson's associates, apparently acted under the belief that
a widely circulated British legal opinion of 1757 sanctioned direct
purchase from the Indians. In fact, that opinion concerned only India and the East India Company, but as circulated in 1773 the text
was heavily edited—undoubtedly to promote land speculation—to
remove all such references.

Although their grand hopes were never realized, many of the land
companies formed prior to the Revolution continued to press their
claims and interests after Independence in the legislatures and courts
of the new United States. Speculators first directed their appeals to
Virginia, which claimed much the largest share of the lands between
the Alleghenies and the Mississippi. Of the Virginia companies obtaining grants before the French and Indian War, the Ohio Company petitioned unsuccessfully in 1778 to have patents issued to the
amount of the grant to the remaining shareholders. The Loyal and
Greenbrier companies, on the other hand, had their surveys confirmed and obtained patents for their lands. The state was particularly unreceptive to land companies that were based outside Virginia
and founded their claims on Indian purchases. In 1778 the legislature
declared the Transylvania Company's claim void, though Henderson
and his associates were awarded a smaller tract in Kentucky as compensation for their trouble and expense.

Virginia perceived a more serious threat to its sovereign jurisdiction in the West from the Indiana Company and the Illinois and
Wabash companies. The former company later merged its interests
with the Grand Ohio Company but retained its separate identity
and claim to a tract along the Ohio (in present West Virginia) acquired in 1768 from the Iroquois. The Illinois and Wabash companies combined in 1779 to form the United Illinois and Wabash Land
Company. Among the shareholders of the new company were James
Wilson and Robert Morris, who thus embarked on their fateful ventures in land speculating. After Virginia rebuffed their claims, the Indiana and Illinois-Wabash companies shifted their focus to Congress,

which despite intense lobbying also failed to recognize the validity of their purchases. The Indiana Company's final defeat came in 1798, when its suit against Virginia in the Supreme Court was dismissed following ratification of the Eleventh Amendment. The Illinois-Wabash Company made one last attempt to gain legal recognition of its Indian purchases of 1773 and 1775 in the form of a lawsuit brought by the heirs of a company shareholder. In the 1823 appeal of this case, *Johnson v. McIntosh*, Chief Justice Marshall denied the validity of private purchases of Indian lands. The Yazoo speculators were to prove no less tenacious than the Indiana and Illinois-Wabash companies in pursuing their claims in the halls of Congress and in the federal courts.

Postrevolutionary Land-Speculating Enterprises

With the Revolution, American land speculation entered a new and more prolific era, as the removal of barriers to western settlement imposed by the British crown opened up numerous opportunities for the enterprising and adventurous to exploit. The new states, particularly those with claims to western lands, actively engaged in the business of selling lands, their principal asset for retiring the enormous debts incurred during the War of Independence. Even states without western claims had plenty of acreage to dispose of within their boundaries. The Confederation government, too, became a major source of land sales after the state cessions of claims northwest of the Ohio River. Congress adopted ordinances in 1785 and 1787 that provided for surveying and subdividing the lands in rectangular parcels and for establishing territorial governments in what became the Northwest Territory.

Many of the new land companies that came into being after the war were composed of former Continental Army officers eager to embrace the risks and rewards of investing in land. They were particularly well placed to traffic in the land bounties given to soldiers as an inducement to enlist for extended terms. Warrants issued by governments to military veterans could be used to locate, survey, and patent lands in the West. Virginia, for example, set aside large districts in

Kentucky and Ohio (as a condition of its Northwest cession) to satisfy military claims. Military warrants were transferable and could be divided or combined as the holder or purchaser desired. They were accordingly a particularly attractive investment and not surprisingly fell into the hands of speculators, who purchased them from soldiers having little interest in settling in the West and willing to sell at a discount for ready money.

Although the land policies established by both the state and general governments aspired to sell surplus lands cheaply to actual settlers, the same circumstances that during the colonial period made it more convenient to sell in large tracts to companies continued to exist. For example, Congress's 1785 land ordinance contained a provision for individuals of modest means to purchase lots instead of whole townships. But initial sales were disappointing, and Congress was impatient to generate revenue or at least reduce the massive public debt incurred during the war. It accordingly adopted a policy favorable to entrepreneurs with sufficient capital to make large purchases and assume the expense of administering large sections of the national domain. Terms for purchasing public lands were highly advantageous to speculators, who could pay in installments and in depreciated public securities at par value. Thus land offered at a dollar an acre could actually be bought for 10 cents an acre. The prospect of reaping great profits with comparatively little outlay brought about the first large sale of the national domain to the Ohio Company of Associates in 1787.

The Ohio Company was founded in Boston in 1786 by a group of Continental Army officers who sought land on the Ohio that would attract emigrants from New England, particularly war veterans. The articles of association envisioned a genuine colonizing scheme, limiting stock ownership to discourage speculators, allowing small investors to purchase jointly, and setting aside funds to aid poorer emigrants. In 1787 the company secured from Congress a contract for 1 million acres and a year later sent a group of emigrants who established the first permanent white settlement in the Northwest Territory at Marietta. For all its noble and visionary aims, the Ohio Company's need to raise capital attracted investors whose interests turned more toward speculation—buying and selling stock—than to settling and developing land. In negotiating its contract with Congress, company officers associated themselves with William Duer, the influential secretary of the Board of Treasury, whose activities as a land and securities speculator eventually landed him in debtors' prison. Ultimately, the Ohio Company was unable to pay the second of two installments on its purchase and had to settle for half the land it had contracted to buy.

In 1788 Congress made a second large sale of the Northwest Territory, 1 million acres in the southwestern section of what became the state of Ohio. The purchasers were a group of New Jersey associates, including present and former members of Congress, headed by John Cleves Symmes. A Revolutionary veteran, Symmes soon moved to Ohio and became a judge of the territorial court. The Symmes purchase was on the same terms as that of the Ohio Company, payable in depreciated public securities that made the real cost less than 10 cents an acre. Both sales illustrated the reciprocal relationship between Congress, with its prize asset of the Northwest Territory, and the large investors seeking to profit from ownership of a sizable portion of this asset. Like the Ohio Company, Symmes was genuinely interested in promoting western settlement with emigrants principally drawn from the ranks of military veterans. However, like others who ventured into the land business, he overextended himself, even to the point of selling land he did not own. Despite his services in settling and administering the Northwest Territory, Symmes's speculating schemes eventually earned him a reputation as "the greatest landjobber on the face of the earth."

The states as well as Congress had abundant lands to sell to adventurers in search of a cheap investment promising great dividends. One of the prime areas of land speculation in the postrevolutionary era was western New York, much of which remained unsettled because of Indian occupancy and conflicting claims to ownership between New York and Massachusetts. In 1786 Massachusetts ceded sovereignty to New York in return for the right to sell the land, subject to the Indian title. This agreement cleared the way for Massachusetts's sale in 1788 of the right to purchase some 6 million acres to a syndicate formed by two notable politicians and businessmen, Oliver Phelps and Nathaniel Gorham. The price was $1 million, payable in three installments in depreciated Massachusetts scrip at an actual cost of about 25 cents an acre. Through negotiations with the Indians Phelps cleared title to more than 2 million acres of the tract. A Connecticut native of humble origins, Phelps was representative of that class of ambitious strivers who ventured into large-scale land speculation after the Revolution. Like others of this group, he was a Continental Army officer. His activities in the commissary department brought him into contact with Robert Morris, the great financier of the war effort. This connection and others aided his rise to business and political prominence in Massachusetts. Although the purchase with Gorham was the principal investment of his remarkable business career, Phelps was also deeply involved in two other major land enterprises. He was the chief organizer and subscriber to the company that in 1795 purchased the "Western Reserve," that portion of northeastern Ohio claimed by Connecticut. At the same time he plunged headlong into buying and selling Yazoo lands, including a tract sold to John Peck that gave rise to *Fletcher v. Peck.*

Yet for all his Yankee shrewdness, Phelps ultimately failed, brought down by miscalculation, overextension, and bad luck. After initial success in selling his New York lands at a higher price than he bought them, sales did not keep pace with his payment obligations, forcing him to dispose of the remainder to Robert Morris in 1790. He borrowed heavily to finance his subsequent Western Reserve and Yazoo speculations, evidently in a futile attempt to recoup his finances. Although he was indeed a land speculator with large ambitions, Phelps was no land-jobber. He combined the pursuit of profit with a genuine desire to settle and develop the lands he bought and sold. He himself settled in New York, where he was a judge and served a term in Congress. He was a benevolent citizen who supported education and whose indulgence to those whose mortgages he held contributed to his own financial ruin.

Robert Morris entered big-time land speculating with his purchase of Phelps's western New York lands. Before the Revolution, Morris had amassed a vast fortune as a Philadelphia shipping merchant. During the war he mixed private mercantile activities with public services in supplying the army, often financing government purchases with his personal credit. As superintendent of finance from 1781 to 1784, he continued to use his private credit to support the Confederation government while working toward establishing its long-term credit. Morris's wealth and financial reputation were so high during the 1780s that his personal promissory notes circulated as common currency.

Despite serious business setbacks in the late 1780s, Morris retained abundant confidence in his ability to assume huge risks and turn them to great profit. Seeming to embody the speculating mania that reached its peak in the last decade of the eighteenth century, he made land contracts of such magnitude and dizzying complexity as to be unmanageable. At heart he was a jobber, who bought lands not to hold for any length of time but to sell quickly for a profit. Not content with his initial success in disposing of New York lands, Morris avidly plunged more deeply into the land market, borrowing heavily in the belief that sales would enable him to meet his obligations and increase his wealth. In 1795 he and two partners formed the North American Land Company, reputed to be the largest real estate trust established in America, consisting of some 6 million acres in seven states from New York to Georgia and in the District of Columbia. Perhaps because he was already overextended, Morris evidently did not participate, at least directly, in Georgia's Yazoo sale in 1795, though he invested heavily in other Georgia lands known as the Pine Barrens. A huge debt burden, economic recession, sluggish sales, costly litigation, and, ironically, a restoration of public credit that increased the market value of public securities pledged as payment for land purchases—all contributed to Morris's eventual ruin and imprisonment for debt in 1798.

Concurrent with sales by Congress and northern states of lands in the Northwest Territory and in western New York were sales by southern states of western lands south of the Ohio River. After ceding its claims northwest of the Ohio, Virginia held on to Kentucky and successfully asserted jurisdiction over this district until its admission as a state in 1792. When North Carolina finally ceded its western claims in 1790, Congress established the Southwest Territory, which was admitted to the union as the state of Tennessee in 1796.

As elsewhere, adventurers, former military officers, and influential politicians associated to acquire large tracts at bargain rates to sell higher to intermediate purchasers or actual settlers.

With the collapse of Henderson's Transylvania project, the settlement of Kentucky came under control of Virginia, which like other states looked to land sales to retire its war debts, including land bounties promised to soldiers. Although providing means by which squatters could acquire title to homestead-size tracts, Virginia's land laws favored the interests of large purchasers. The state parceled out Kentucky in large tracts, mostly in excess of 100,000 acres. By 1792, twenty-one individuals or partnerships held title to nearly a quarter of the state. These included prominent members of Virginia's political elite and merchant class, most of whom had little intention of moving to Kentucky. One Virginian who did emigrate was Thomas Marshall, father of the future chief justice, who with his sons received military warrants for Kentucky land and purchased additional warrants from other veterans. Although absentee purchasers held much of Kentucky, actual settlers were also drawn into the speculative process by acquiring and selling preemption rights to additional acreage for making improvements. Settlers could enhance their individual holdings and further enrich themselves by teaming with absentee purchasers seeking to meet the law's nominal requirements. In a short time, speculation transformed Kentucky into a maze of overlapping and conflicting land claims, spawning a mass of litigation in the courts of Virginia and Kentucky that continued until well into the nineteenth century.

North Carolina never had more than a tenuous control over its western district, unable to prevent clashes between settlers and the Cherokee or provide military assistance to distant outposts. Settlers in the region responded to an indifferent government far to the east by forming self-governing associations, culminating in the "State of Franklin" under the leadership of John Sevier, whose exploits as a soldier, Indian fighter, and land speculator won him a reputation as Tennessee's founding father. Never recognized by North Carolina or by Congress, Franklin came into being in 1784 after North Carolina ceded its western lands to Congress. The state responded to the breakaway movement by rescinding its cession later the same year and reasserting jurisdiction over the area. Unable to get recognition and beset by factionalism and recurrent warfare with the Cherokee, Franklin effectively ceased to exist by early 1789, and its leaders swore allegiance to North Carolina. For all the fractious relations between the government and its western settlers, North Carolina proved to be a hospitable environment for acquiring large tracts of western land.

A key operator at the nexus of politics and land speculation was William Blount, a paymaster and commissary during the war who afterward served in the North Carolina legislature, the Confederation Congress, and the Federal Convention of 1787. He was appointed governor of the Southwest Territory in 1790 and in 1796 was elected as one of Tennessee's U.S. senators. As a state legislator, he secured passage of acts opening the state's western lands to settlement, making soldiers eligible for grants, and ceding the western district to Congress. Although this cession was soon repealed, North Carolina made a second cession in 1789 after ratification of the new Constitution. By then influential politicians and speculators had concluded that a stronger central government would pacify the Cherokee and thereby enhance the value of their investments in land. Blount and his brothers purchased more than 2 million acres of western lands, mostly on credit, leaving them overextended when the market dropped sharply in the mid-1790s. In a desperate attempt to recover, Blount hatched a plan to allow Great Britain to gain control of Florida and Louisiana so that Americans could have free access to New Orleans and the Mississippi River. Exposure of this "conspiracy" led to Blount's expulsion from the Senate in 1797.

Georgia's Sale of 1789

Alone among the "landed" states, Georgia did not cede its claims after the war but continued to hold onto the vast area west of the Chattahoochee River and extending to the Mississippi. In its first two decades as an independent state, Georgia was centrally engaged in attempts to turn this asset to profitable account, to join other states and Congress in the seemingly inexhaustible bonanza of land sales to eager purchasers. In the immediate postwar years, however, Georgia's western lands appeared to hold little promise of becoming a coveted object of land speculation.

The territory was largely a wilderness, occupied by Native American tribes, the Creeks in what is now Alabama, the Choctaw in the southern two-thirds of present-day Mississippi, and the Chickasaw in the northern third. The Cherokee also held a small portion on the Tennessee River in northern Alabama. Spain held Louisiana and also claimed territory east of the Mississippi as far north as the Ohio, not recognizing Great Britain's cession to the United States of the lands above the thirty-first parallel. In particular, Spain contended that the northern boundary of its West Florida province extended above the thirty-second parallel. This included Natchez, where English colonists had settled during Great Britain's possession of West Florida. Another English settlement had grown up around the lower Tombigbee River in southern Alabama. As of 1783, these two widely scattered districts constituted the extent of white settlement in the western territory claimed by Georgia. "No one could say what was the value of Georgia's title," wrote Henry Adams, "for it depended on her power to dispossess the Indians; but however good the title might be, the State would have been fortunate to make it a free gift to any authority strong enough to deal with the Creeks and Cherokees alone."

With their ingrained optimism, prospective adventurers were inclined to gloss over the obstacles to opening the western territory to emigration and settlement. They were animated by rosy visions of a healthy and temperate climate, with well-watered lands whose soil was rich and fertile, as set forth in works such as Thomas Hutchins's *Historical Narrative and Topographical Description of Louisiana and West-Florida* (1784). They assured themselves that the removal of the Spanish and the extinguishment of Indian titles were inevitable, if not immediately in prospect. In the meantime, they saw an opportunity to buy cheaply with the certainty that land values would rise even if settlement was retarded in the short run. In addition to the Natchez and Tombigbee districts, land speculators envisioned two other areas of potential settlement. One was Walnut Hills, the present site of Vicksburg, where the Yazoo River flows into the Mississippi. That tributary's evocative name soon became the shorthand designation for Georgia's western lands, referring to the indefinite extent of territory above and below the "Yazoo line," running from the mouth of the Yazoo due east to the Chattahoochee. Great Britain had made this line the northern boundary of its West Florida province. The other prospective settlement was at Muscle Shoals, in present-day Alabama, where the Tennessee River bends northward toward the Ohio.

Although claiming its western territory on the basis of its colonial charter, Georgia was too weak to establish jurisdiction over this immense and distant region. Indeed, the settled portion of the state far to the east was itself a frontier, situated on the periphery of the United States, surrounded by Indian tribes and Spanish Florida. In 1783 Georgia contained two thinly populated tiers of counties extending from the principal town of Savannah. One proceeded south along the Atlantic to the St. Marys River; the other ran northwest up the Savannah River past the town of Augusta. Several more counties were created during the 1780s, but in 1790 white settlers and their slaves inhabited only about a third of the land within the state's present boundaries. The remainder was occupied by the Creeks to the west and south and the Cherokee in the northwest. White population grew rapidly after the Revolution, mostly by emigration from Virginia and North Carolina. Still, in 1790, whites in Georgia numbered only a little more than 50,000 and held another 30,000 enslaved persons.

In the coastal tidewater large-scale plantations engaged in rice and sea island cotton cultivation predominated, while the upland counties consisted mostly of small farms whose principal crop was tobacco. Although sectional distinction promoted political division among Georgians, a historian of postrevolutionary Georgia notes that until well into the 1790s politics in this frontier society was characterized by "personal factionalism, unencumbered by either ideology or formal party organization." The newly independent state confronted two dominant and interconnected issues, land policy and defense against Indian attacks. Georgia's politicians agreed that the state's exposed position on the periphery required a constant influx of new settlers who would provide a buffer against Indian incursions and keep the militia well supplied with fighting men.

In response to a flood of immigrants into the state after the war, Georgia opened a land office and enacted legislation to dispose of land to war veterans and other prospective settlers in newly formed counties. Although the land laws restricted the number of acres an individual could acquire to 1,000, enterprising purchasers managed to circumvent this restriction by exploiting a decentralized system that placed approval of grants in the hands of local surveyors. Georgia was thus no more successful than other states in preventing land speculation from gaining a foothold. It too bowed to expediency in acquiescing in proposals for large purchases as a way of meeting pressing financial exigencies. The legislature was particularly receptive to schemes involving the western territory, which was too wild and remote for the state to extend its administrative control.

One such plan was to colonize the Muscle Shoals region at the bend of the Tennessee River, for which purpose William Blount, John Sevier, and other North Carolinians formed a company in 1783. The company purchased the Cherokee claim to the area and in 1784 obtained an act from Georgia establishing a county and opening the land between the river and North Carolina's southern boundary to settlement. Although this project came to naught with the rise of the state of Franklin, speculation in the Muscle Shoals would revive as part of the Yazoo sales of 1789 and 1795. In 1785 the Georgia legislature erected Bourbon County, embracing settlements along the Mississippi south of the Yazoo, which included the Natchez District. This attempt to establish Georgia's jurisdiction in an area controlled by Spanish civil and military authorities was woefully ineffectual and was quietly dropped a few years later in the face of Spanish resistance and opposition from Congress. No land office was created by the act, but it provided that when an office opened actual settlers would have preference to purchase at 25 cents an acre. In 1786 a trader residing in the area acquired from the Choctaws a tract of some 2–3 million acres, which included Walnut Hills at the mouth of the Yazoo. Although a plan to settle Walnut Hills with colonists from Kentucky failed of execution, the Choctaw purchase was sold to a group of speculators who would revive this colonizing project in an enlarged scheme presented to the Georgia legislature in 1789.

Confronting the obstacles posed by Spanish claims to and actual control of key areas and by Indian occupation of the interior, Georgia by the late 1780s felt increasing pressure to rid itself of an unmanageable burden by disposing of its western territory on receiving the first good offer. One possibility was to bargain with Congress. Early in 1788 the legislature authorized its delegates in Congress to cede a portion of the state's territorial claims to the United States on certain conditions. Congress rejected the conditions, noting that the proposed cession (essentially the southern half of the state's western claim) would be too remote from the union's other public lands "to be of any immediate advantage." Congress also refused to accept Georgia's insistence on guaranteeing its remaining territorial rights and its request to be credited on future federal requisitions for money expended by the state in dealing with Indian hostilities. Congress made a counteroffer: the state should cede all its claims west of the Chattahoochee, drop the proviso for guaranteeing remaining territorial rights, and have credit for sums spent on Indian hostilities only on present requisitions and on its account with the United States for money loaned. Georgia declined this offer and soon after took up proposals from private land companies to purchase large areas of the western territory.

These proposals were presented to the Georgia legislature in November 1789, first by the South Carolina Yazoo Company, headed by Thomas Washington (alias Walsh), who had already acquired a reputation in Georgia as a notorious promoter and speculator. He was joined by three South Carolina partners, including William Moultrie, a Revolutionary War general and a past and future governor of his state. The legislature also received petitions from the Virginia Yazoo Company, composed of Patrick Henry and seven other Virginians active in land dealings, and from what became the Tennessee Yazoo Company, whose principal partner was Zachariah Cox, a Georgia land surveyor who had recently explored the Muscle Shoals area on behalf of Blount and Sevier. Cox had access to legislators and government officials as an assistant clerk of the lower house.

The applicants made glowing representations of the great benefits Georgia would gain by selling them large tracts. The state not only would receive greater financial remuneration than Congress had previously offered but also would be relieved of the burden of extinguishing Indian claims and providing protection for the settlers. Moreover, the cultivation of the lands sold to the companies would enhance the value of that remaining in Georgia's hands, thus doubly benefiting the state. With such flattering arguments along with a skillful use of political influence, the land companies obtained passage of a bill, though not without opposition, on December 21. The South Carolina Yazoo Company obtained 10 million acres between the Mississippi and Tombigbee Rivers, including Walnut Hills, for $67,000. The Virginia Yazoo Company received 11 million acres north of the South Carolina company's tract for $94,000; the Tennessee Yazoo Company was granted 4 million acres around Muscle Shoals for $47,000. The act stipulated that payment be made within two years and that the companies were to refrain from hostile attacks on Indian tribes and bear the expense of preserving peace and of extinguishing Indian claims.

The land sale act provoked immediate protest from the legislative minority, who complained that it slighted the rights of Georgia citizens to become purchasers, particularly in rejecting an offer made late in the session by a Georgia company that appeared to be a much better bargain for the state. Grand juries in several counties urged repeal of the act. As it turned out, the companies purchasing under the 1789 act ultimately failed to obtain grants because of opposition from the federal government and subsequent action taken by the Georgia legislature. Concerned that the proposed settlements under the act might disturb relations with the Cherokee, Choctaw, and Chickasaw nations, President Washington issued a proclamation in August 1790 to warn citizens against violating treaties with those tribes and to enforce the act regulating Indian trade and intercourse. Since the Virginia Yazoo Company had no immediate plans to promote settlement, this warning was intended to curb the activities of the other two companies, neither of which was deterred. The South Carolina Yazoo Company and its agent James O'Fallon, a reckless adventurer and intriguer, aggressively pursued an ambitious scheme to colonize Walnut Hills on the Mississippi, even to the point of enlisting recruits for a military expedition that threatened to upset relations with the Indians and Spain. In March 1791 the president issued a proclamation aimed at O'Fallon, which effectively brought an end to this project. Soon thereafter a band of Cherokee forced Cox and his associates of the Tennessee Yazoo Company to abandon their settlement at Muscle Shoals, evidently with the support of Cox's erstwhile associate William Blount. As governor of the Southwest Territory, Blount was under instructions to enforce federal Indian policy.

By this time all three companies were embroiled in a dispute with Georgia over the terms of paying for the Yazoo lands. In June 1790 the legislature adopted a resolution prohibiting the state treasurer from accepting anything but gold or silver (or state paper money until August 1790) in payment of debts owed the state. The sale act of the preceding December specified only the dollar amounts without saying anything about the mode of payment. In their petitions presented prior to the passage of the act, the companies indicated that they expected to pay in Georgia currency or in audited certificates of the state's Revolutionary debt, worth about one-eighth of the nominal amount. The upshot was that they failed to pay the full specie amount within the two-year deadline and thus did not obtain grants for their lands. Complaining bitterly of the state's bad faith, the companies later sought redress from the federal government. In 1797 the South Carolina Yazoo Company sued Georgia in the U.S. Supreme Court, only to have its case (*Moultrie v. Georgia*), like that of the Indiana Company, dismissed after ratification of the Eleventh Amendment.

––––––

Georgia's Sale of 1795

The failure of the 1789 Yazoo sale underlined the inherently volatile nature of land speculation in Georgia, where the opportunities for enrichment were abundant but where public reaction to the practice could suddenly shift. Those who trafficked in Georgia lands had to design proposals that promised great public benefits while holding out inducements to influential persons to facilitate the often tortuous path through to legislative consummation. No matter how well planned and executed, any sale of Georgia's public lands was bound to be controversial. There would surely be an outcry against selling so vast a region (more than twice the area of Georgia's settled limits) at any price to private companies. And the many more who did not object in principle to such a sale would most likely never be satisfied that the price was the best that could be obtained. Disappointed speculators whose proposals had been rejected would of course join in opposition to the sale.

Such considerations by no means discouraged interest in the Yazoo lands, which continued to percolate among speculators and politicians poised to try again at the most favorable opportunity. That moment arrived in the fall of 1794, when the legislature convened at the temporary capital in Augusta. Adventurers and moneyed persons, mutually attracted to one another, crowded the town's streets in anticipation that a second Yazoo sale was imminent. Plans for such an event had been forming for months, as pressure on Georgia to dispose of its western territory was mounting. Beset with the expenses of chronic warfare with the Creeks on the borders of the "home" counties, the state had never established effective sovereignty over the area west of the Chattahoochee. By 1794 it seemed increasingly clear that only the federal government, empowered to regulate trade with the Indians and negotiate with Spain, could rightfully assume this responsibility. To some this circumstance showed that the United States had a better claim to the region than Georgia, however good the state's title appeared to be on paper. In any event, the general government was clearly better positioned than it had been in 1788 to prescribe the terms of a cession of the territory. Not wanting to let slip away what might be the state's last chance to reap some value from its title, the Georgia legislature was only too ready to consider anew a sale to private companies. The land companies also felt a sense of urgency to buy while the price of Georgia's western lands remained low. If pending negotiations with Spain succeeded in opening the navigation of the Mississippi and establishing the thirty-first parallel as the United States' southern boundary, there was likely to be a sharp increase in the price of those lands.

Credit for engineering the second Yazoo sale belongs principally to James Gunn, then a U.S. senator, who skipped the session in Philadelphia in order to be in Augusta for the meeting of the Georgia legislature. A Virginia native of modest origins, Gunn as a member of his state's Continental line had served in Georgia during the war. He later settled in Savannah, practiced law, took up planting, served in the militia, and entered politics. With a bent for dueling and brawling (which probably helped his popularity among Georgians), Gunn was a forceful personality blessed with leadership and organizing skills. He was a Federalist who like Alexander Hamilton believed in attracting the support of the wealthy and influential to achieve great political ends.

At the legislative session that began in November and adjourned in early January 1795, Gunn single-mindedly and relentlessly pursued his goal, determined above all to avoid the fiasco that brought about the reversal of the 1789 sale. A few days into the session, the legislature reelected him to the U.S. Senate by a wide margin. Confident as he was that the Georgia General Assembly was amenable to selling the Yazoo lands and was favorably disposed toward him, Gunn nonetheless understood that obtaining approval of his and his associates' particular proposals was fraught with difficulties at each stage of the legislative process. Knowing that others were also interested in purchasing Yazoo lands, he sought cooperation among a large group of speculators who would organize themselves into separate companies and bid for tracts that did not overlap with each other.

Late in November 1794 Gunn and two associates, styling themselves the Georgia Company, entered the most ambitious Yazoo proposal to date: a purchase embracing nearly half of present-day Alabama and Mississippi, including most of the old South Carolina Yazoo grant. Their application was accompanied by another from Thomas Glascock and others on behalf of what became the Georgia Mississippi Company. The juxtaposition of these two proposals suggests that Gunn and Glascock, a militia general and resident of Augusta, had previously agreed to coordinate their bids for western lands. For Gunn, an alliance with a group of investors based in the upcountry would facilitate his efforts to obtain broad support in the legislature. Glascock's group proposed to buy a tract immediately below that of Gunn's company, including that part of the old South Carolina Yazoo grant embracing Walnut Hills on the Mississippi, and extending eastward as far as the Tombigbee. The purchase price offered by Gunn and Glascock together came to just over $400,000, with one-fifth of that amount to be a down payment.

At the time he submitted the Georgia Company's bid, Gunn was negotiating with John B. Scott, agent for the Virginia Yazoo Company, who was in Augusta seeking to revive his company's 1789 proposal. The two made an agreement whereby Gunn's company adjusted its boundaries so as not to conflict with those of the Virginia company. Gunn also no doubt made overtures to Zachariah Cox, who was in Augusta seeking to renew the Tennessee Yazoo Company's 1789 grant. Cox soon became an associate of the Georgia Company, perhaps an indication of a deal he made with Gunn. Another investor who became a Georgia Company associate was Gunn's friend Wade Hampton, a wealthy South Carolina planter and politician, who had recently purchased a partnership in the Virginia Yazoo Company.

Gunn, in short, took care to create a union of interests among the four companies, so that the legislature would consider their separate petitions as parts of a single grand purchase. Each of the companies adopted the terms offered by the Georgia Company: a purchase price of 2.33 cents per acre, a down payment of one-fifth of the total purchase price, and the balance payable by November 1, 1795. This date, not coincidentally, was the last day of the term of the current legislature. Gunn clearly expected (or hoped) that a completed sale could not be undone by a succeeding legislature. To avoid the ambiguity about the means of payment that doomed the 1789 sale, Gunn's group stipulated to pay in specie, United States bank bills, and certain warrants of the state of Georgia. On December 8, a joint committee of the legislature reported favorably on the propositions of the four companies, though not excluding "the legislature from receiving and acceding to other proposals which may be deemed more advantageous to the state, should any such be made during the passage of the bill." Gunn then sweetened the Georgia Company's offer by proposing to reserve 1 million acres of its grant for Georgia citizens. The other companies agreed to reserve the same proportion of their grants, making a total reservation of 2 million acres.

The offers of the four companies were embodied in a bill "declaring the right of this State to the unappropriated territory thereof, for appropriating a part of the same, for raising a fund for the extinguishment of Indian claims: for the protection and support of the frontiers of this State and for other purposes." After the bill had passed two readings, a rival group of speculators, styling themselves the Georgia Union Company, submitted a proposal that directly threatened Gunn's plans. Building on petitions presented earlier by individuals outside Gunn's group, the Georgia Union Company proposed to pay $500,000 for all the lands sought by Gunn and Glascock (nearly $100,000 more than they had offered) and to reserve 5 million acres for Georgia citizens. This newly formed company was a late entry in the competition for Georgia lands, however, and could scrape together only $5,000 as a deposit. The house soon thereafter approved by a vote of seventeen to eleven the bill appropriating the western lands to Gunn, Glascock, and the Virginia and Tennessee companies. While the bill was pending in the senate, the Georgia Union Company substantially increased its down payment offer to $21,000, a sum that still fell far short of that offered by Gunn's group. On December 20 the Senate passed the bill by a narrower margin, ten to eight, and sent it on to Governor George Mathews.

To Gunn's dismay, Governor Mathews vetoed the bill on December 29. Among his reasons for dissenting was that the total sum offered was "inadequate to the value of the lands"; that the quantity of lands reserved for Georgia citizens was too small; and that granting so large an extent of territory to private companies would create "monopolies which will prevent or retard settlement, population, and agriculture." The governor observed that if public notice had been given of the sale, "the rivalship in purchasers would most probably have increased the sums offered."

The governor's veto put in jeopardy Gunn's carefully laid plans and set off a flurry of intense negotiation and lobbying inside and outside the legislative hall. Immediately on receipt of the veto message, the house appointed a committee of five to "confer with" Governor Mathews "on the subject matter of his dissent." This committee held two conferences with the governor, the upshot of which was a revised bill that was approved by both houses early in January 1795—the house by a vote of nineteen to nine and the senate by a vote of ten to eight. The key feature of the revised bill was that it engrafted the sale bill with an act previously adopted "for appropriating a part of the unlocated territory of this State for payment of the late State troops, and for other purposes therein mentioned." The revised bill recast the Yazoo sale as a "supplement" to the state troops act. Its full title was "An Act supplementary to an act, entitled 'An act for appropriating a part of the unlocated territory of this State for the payment of the late State troops, and for other purposes therein mentioned,' declaring the right of this State to the unappropriated territory thereof, for the protection and support of the frontiers of this State, and for other purposes." The bill's promoters clearly hoped to forestall opposition by attaching it to such undeniably patriotic ends as paying the state troops and defending the state's frontiers. The supplemental bill's title went even further than the original in concealing the bill's principal object—the sale of millions of acres of Georgia's western lands between the Chattahoochee and the Mississippi to four private land companies.

The supplementary bill did strengthen the state troops act by appropriating additional money, drawn from the land companies' deposits, for paying long-promised bounties to soldiers who had fought against the Creeks. The special committee that met with the governor insisted that the state troops act was "so intimately connected" with the land sale bill that it could not "be separately carried into effect without a dangerous anticipation of funds" or a "derangement" of the state's finances. Whether true or not, this argument was sufficient to persuade Governor Mathews to sign the "supplementary act" on January 7. As an old soldier, a Continental Army veteran and forceful defender against Indian hostilities, Mathews found himself in the awkward dilemma that if he vetoed the Yazoo sale a second time he would be denying much-needed funds for paying the troops and bolstering frontier defenses. Even if (as is likely) the governor still had misgivings about the sale, he now could persuade himself that public duty required his signature to the second bill. This action cost him his political life and brought charges that he was a knowing participant in the corruption that allegedly brought the sale to consummation. Mathews had a solid reputation for honesty and integrity, however, and the worst that could be said of him was that he allowed himself to be swayed by persons of lesser stature.

Before the supplementary bill became law, the Virginia Yazoo Company withdrew its offer. The company's agent then formed a new concern called the Upper Mississippi Company in partnership with two others. This company's bid for a smaller tract within that of the Virginia Yazoo Company was incorporated into the supplementary act. The total purchase price stipulated by the four companies came to $500,000, divided as follows: Georgia Company, $250,000; Georgia Mississippi Company, $155,000; Upper Mississippi Company, $35,000; and Tennessee Company, $60,000. The amount deposited as a down payment was $98,000. The Upper Mississippi Company deposited $5,000, which was one-seventh of its total, as opposed to one-fifth paid by the other companies. The act did not specify the number of acres allotted to each company, but a Georgia Company document drawn up shortly after the act's passage shows that Gunn and his partners estimated their tract to consist of 10,762,000 acres. This quantity presumably represented half the total estimated acreage purchased by the four companies: 21.4 million acres, making a purchase price of 2.33 cents per acre. This estimate turned out to be well below the actual total, however, which came to about 35 million acres or 1.4 cents per acre.

While the supplementary bill was pending in the legislature, the Georgia Union Company made a final bid, this time proposing to purchase all the territory sought by the other four companies for $800,000, to reserve 4 million acres for Georgia citizens and another 4 million to the state to be disposed of as the legislature saw fit, and to increase its deposit to $40,000. The house rejected this proposal, reportedly by the close vote of fourteen to twelve. The refusal to accept the Georgia Union Company's offer, the spurning of $300,000 in additional funds for the state treasury and more generous concessions to Georgia citizens, would soon be frequently cited as unequivocal proof that the Yazoo sale was accomplished by corrupt means. Yet the company's deposit remained less than half the amount put down by Gunn's consortium. Defenders of the Yazoo sale countered that the smallness of the deposit showed that the Georgia Union Company could not raise the full amount promised and never intended to, and that its bid was a mere ploy to defeat the sale to the four companies.

If the dismissal of the Georgia Union Company's eleventh-hour application could be defended as sound policy, still a suspicion that the Yazoo sale was rife with dishonesty and bad faith hovered over the proceedings in Augusta. Soon the entire state would be in an uproar over charges that the people's representatives had succumbed to corruption, fraud, and bribery—had in effect engaged in public plunder for personal enrichment. "Yazoo" swiftly emerged as a galvanizing issue that transformed and indelibly stamped Georgia politics for generations to come. "Yazoo" also entrenched itself in the national political consciousness and permanently entered the language as a byword for venality and betrayal of the public trust. Indeed, it came to occupy a singular place in the annals of American land speculation, unprecedented for its audacity and presumed villainy.

CHAPTER TWO

Georgia Rescinds the Yazoo Sale

Georgia's sale of its western lands in 1795 was unmatched in the sheer magnitude of the enterprise, the imperial scale of a purchase of a land mass nearly equal to that of Great Britain. It was national in scope, attracting investment capital from Savannah northward to Charleston, Philadelphia, New York, and Boston. Where earlier land speculations involved plans (some more serious than others) to settle the purchased lands with emigrants, the purchase of Georgia's western lands from the outset was an unabashed land-jobbing scheme. The traffic, the buying and rapid resale, was not in the lands themselves but in the preemption rights to lands occupied by Indian tribes, whose claims supposedly would soon be "extinguished."

If Yazoo stands apart, it was not so much because "corruption" was its defining essence as because the corruption seemed to reach a new level and was widely documented. The best evidence of how Gunn and his associates tried to influence the Georgia legislature came from the Georgia Company itself, in articles of agreement drawn up on January 1, 1795, while the revised bill was pending in the legislature. The company, according to the articles, found it "expedient to dispose of a considerable quantity" of the lands it sought "to divers persons, for the purpose of raising a fund to effect the purchase the same." It was also found "necessary to distribute to a variety of" Georgians "certain sub-shares . . . in order that the benefit of such purchase, if any there be, should be as generally diffused as possible." After the act passed, the company annexed a schedule of those who purchased "money shares" for a cash advance and those who received sub-shares payable in seven months. Heading the list of twenty persons who advanced money was Supreme Court Justice James Wilson; for £25,000 he purchased ten shares, or 750,000 acres.

Of greater interest is the list of seventy-five persons who received sub-shares of 56,000 acres. At 2.33 cents per acre, the cost of a sub-share came to just over $1,300, which was payable in August 1795, seven months after the passage of the act. Among the influential Georgians with sub-shares in the Georgia Company were twenty-nine legislators, including two who did not vote on the bill. A similar schedule issued by the Tennessee Company also shows the names of a number of legislators who held certificates of shares, which were payable in seven months. This evidence was presented in 1803 to the federal commissioners examining the Yazoo claims. As their report dryly noted, a comparison of the names of shareholders with the vote tally shows that all the members of the house and senate who voted for the bill "were, with one single exception . . . interested in, and parties to, the purchase."

Gunn and agents of all four companies were ubiquitous at the session, mingling with members of the legislature in the statehouse lobby, in taverns, and in boardinghouses, urging the great advantages to the state to be gained by the sale. At the same time they offered legislators who were favorably disposed the opportunity to buy into the companies. As one company principal reportedly said, if a member "thought it right to sell the lands, he should not be precluded from having a share, although a member, for that the companies had made provision for shares for all the members, provided they thought fit to take them." As Gunn no doubt calculated, once word spread that a member who expressed support for the sale could get a share, the effect would be to bring others in. Thus the offer of a share became indistinguishable from an inducement to bring about support.

Legislators who accepted shares would have to pay for them eventually, but at least some of them appear to have specially benefited from the brisk trafficking in shares that took place while the bill was under consideration. They in effect became speculators, with a chance to sell their shares at a greater price than they had contracted to pay and without having to advance any of their own money. At worst, if the legislature failed to approve the Yazoo sale, they could return the money paid to them. Otherwise, a sale might provide them with enough money to cover the cost of their shares and reap a tidy profit. Augusta at the time was swarming with persons eager to make contracts with legislators who held shares. According to one hostile witness, providing shares to well-disposed members amounted to "indirect bribery."

Gunn clearly believed that distributing shares in the companies was an acceptable, even necessary, means of influencing the legislature. He acted openly, seemingly without concern that his actions might produce an angry popular backlash. Indeed, his greater fear was that the grand prize might be lost if he did not do all in his power to bring about the desired result. He placed great faith in his strategy of creating an "interest" in the Yazoo sale among influential Georgians inside and outside the legislature, so that its benefits might be "as generally diffused as possible." As a lawyer, he no doubt reckoned that the Yazoo sale, once safely enacted into law, would acquire all the legitimacy it needed, that it was a contract that could not be undone.

As the bill made its fitful progress through the legislature, Gunn remained in a state of high anxiety, particularly in regard to the senate, where the margin was so narrow that a single vote might decide the question. Increasingly worried that his close majority in that chamber could slip away, he was apparently not unwilling to use stronger means of inducement. Much of the subsequent testimony about legislative corruption centered on efforts to keep one wavering senator in line, allegedly by buying back his company shares at a handsome price. There were also alleged promises of payoffs to those who successfully persuaded an opposition senator to go home before the final vote.

In the emerging debate, Yazoo defenders strove to divert attention away from faithless, perhaps corrupt legislators, indeed, to treat the entire matter of "corruption" as essentially irrelevant to the question of whether Georgia's sale of its western lands was valid. They showed little enthusiasm for representing the majority as honorable and faithful public servants, admitting that legislators who held shares were guilty of an "impropriety" and "acted imprudently, and probably corruptly." If corruption had any bearing on the legitimacy of the Yazoo sale, they insisted that it had to be established by strict legal evidence admissible in a court of law. They denied that the ex parte depositions and hearsay testimony collected and published as part of a campaign to discredit the sale and bring the legislators into disrepute met this standard. In any case, so they argued, it was improper for a court of law to inquire into the motives of individual legislators in determining the validity of a law.

As much as defenders of the sale law tried to shift the focus from corruption, their opponents were equally determined to make it the central issue in overturning the law. During the next two decades, Americans would passionately and exhaustively contest the Yazoo question in legislative halls and courtrooms, in newspaper articles and pamphlets, in petitions and memorials, offering up abundant material for observing the interplay of law and politics in the new nation. More than any other great public dispute of the day, Yazoo compelled a republican citizenry to grapple with the competing claims of popular government and the rule of law, to determine what limits if any there were to the people's sovereign will as expressed through their legislatures. Alongside this debate raged a battle for the nation's republican soul, forcing Americans to confront a seemingly unresolvable tension between maintaining republican principles and making concessions to political expediency.

From the moment Governor Mathews put his signature to the act, the Yazoo sale sparked an intense controversy that dominated Georgia politics during the next year, culminating in an act declaring the sale null and void. The sale act also provoked an early and anxious reaction from the federal government. As in 1789, President Washington looked askance at this second sale of Georgia's western lands and its potential for disturbing his administration's policy of maintaining peaceful relations with the Indian tribes. In February 1795, barely a month after its enactment, the president laid this act and also the state troops act before Congress, noting that they "embrace an object of such magnitude and in their consequences may so deeply affect the peace and welfare of the United States." Echoing the president's alarm, a House committee report foresaw "great danger to peace" posed by a sale dependent on the extinguishment of Indian titles and consequently tending "to embroil the Government with the neighboring Indians, in hope of their extinction or banishment."

In early March the House passed a bill authorizing the president to obtain Georgia's cession of its claim to lands "within the present Indian boundaries." The brief debate on this bill exposed contrasting opinions about Georgia's right to the lands, with one member urging

Congress "to declare at once, that the lands belong to the United States." This prompted a response from Robert G. Harper of South Carolina, who as a politician, pamphleteer, and lawyer played a leading role in defending the Yazoo purchasers and claimants. Owner of a share and sub-share in the Georgia Company, Harper "went into a long historical detail to prove that Georgia actually has a right to the lands in question." He recommended that once the companies completed their payments, the United States should "repurchase from them." The bill as passed by the House contained no language about the companies, but in the Senate James Jackson of Georgia was able to block a third reading. Jackson would later return home to lead the fight against the Yazoo sale. The only action taken by Congress was a resolution requesting the president to direct the U.S. attorney general to "to collect, digest, and report" all the documents relating to the title to lands in the Southwest and "claimed by certain companies" under the Georgia act of January 1795. Jackson tried unsuccessfully to strip the resolution of any references to the companies and was one of just two senators to vote against it.

Congress adjourned on March 3, effectively postponing any action on Georgia's sale until the next session. Both of the state's senators were concerned about federal intrusion in the matter, Jackson that Congress would strengthen the hand of the Yazoo speculators and Gunn that the assertion of a U.S. claim to the lands would hinder his efforts to make the final payments for the lands. In the meantime, the growing agitation in Georgia against the Yazoo sale posed a much more serious threat to the purchasers. The anti-Yazoo campaign had begun with a series of grand jury presentments, a common means employed by Georgians to register their opinions about public measures. This was succeeded by a statewide petitioning movement urging the forthcoming constitutional convention to overturn the sale.

The convention met at the new capital in Louisville, just southwest of Augusta, in May 1795. Despite the popular clamor, the convention delegates were not of a mind to revoke the Yazoo sale, having been elected at the same time as the legislature that approved the sale. A motion to this effect was defeated, giving the Yazoo proponents a victory that proved to be short lived. The convention deferred consideration of Yazoo to the next meeting of the General

Assembly, set for early January 1796, and at the same transmitted all the petitions and memorials on the subject that had been submitted. Although widespread, anti-Yazoo sentiment had so far been largely ineffectual in the absence of a leader who could transform it into a formidable political movement. Senator Jackson had expected to be in Louisville for the convention but bad weather forced him to turn back northward to Philadelphia in order to attend a special Senate session in June 1795.

Back in Georgia later that summer, Jackson finally assumed leadership of the movement to reverse the western lands sale. His aim was not just to dethrone his rival James Gunn as the arbiter of Georgia politics but to purge the state of the noxious taint of Yazooism. A native of England who landed in Savannah at age fifteen, Jackson, like Gunn, overcame humble origins and used his Revolutionary military experience as a springboard to wealth and prominence. Like Gunn, he practiced law, acquired plantations, served as a militia general, and had a warm temper that got him into brawls and duels —all of which served him well in the rough-and-tumble politics of this frontier state. The rivalry between Jackson and Gunn dated from the 1780s, when the two clashed over militia policies, and in the next decade their relationship continued to fester.

After 1789, both Georgians served in the U.S. Congress, Jackson in the House of Representatives and Senate and Gunn in the Senate. Jackson quickly aligned himself with the opposition to Hamilton's financial program, believing that it furthered the interests of speculators and a moneyed aristocracy. Gunn, too, initially opposed the secretary of the treasury's policies, but in foreign affairs he ultimately cast his lot with the administration and the Federalists. In June 1795 the Senate narrowly agreed to ratify the controversial treaty with Great Britain, known as the Jay Treaty, with Jackson voting against and Gunn one of only two southern senators to vote in favor. This vote further undermined Gunn's popularity in Georgia, already damaged by Yazoo, so much so that a public meeting of Savannah citizens burned him in effigy. Reports circulated (with some foundation) that Gunn gave his treaty vote for assurances of administration support for his great land purchase.

With Gunn's star falling, Jackson chose an opportune moment to launch his anti-Yazoo crusade in August 1795. During the next several months, he organized a political movement centered on Yazoo but also exploiting popular dissatisfaction with the federal government, not only because of the administration's domestic and foreign policies but also and more importantly because of what Georgians perceived to be the government's lax efforts in extinguishing Creek Indian claims within the state and opening these lands to settlement. Jackson's genius was to fuse these elements together to establish and consolidate a party machine under the banner of Jeffersonian Republicanism. Although his enemies denounced his attack on Yazoo as motivated by personal and political ambitions, Jackson was genuinely opposed in principle to the western lands sale. He never caught the land-speculating fever, evidently content with the ample lands granted him for his military service, which he turned into profitable rice and cotton plantations.

From the outset, Jackson expressed deep alarm about the policy and constitutionality of the sale of Georgia's western lands. Commenting on the impending passage of the Supplementary Act in January 1795, he likened it to "a confiscation Act of the rights of your Children & mine, & unborn Generations, to supply the rapacious graspings of a few sharks." "Our Constitution," he continued, "breathes Republican & equality principles—Our Legislature, acting under it, establishes Aristocratic Bodies, in those Speculating companies." He predicted that "the day will come when another and more pure & virtuous Legislature, will make null & void *this Sale of birthright*—for in my opinion the Legislature will constitutionally have a right to do so." Here in a nutshell was the populist constitutionalism he laid out eight months later in "Letters of Sicilius" and subsequently had codified in Georgia's rescinding act of February 1796. On the one hand he argued that a republican legislature was strictly bound by constitutional limits; on the other he acknowledged virtually unlimited power of a succeeding "virtuous" legislature to undo the acts of a corrupt predecessor.

"Letters of Sicilius," first appearing in newspapers and then as a separate pamphlet in the fall of 1795, was a passionate denunciation of the "monstrous grant" contained within a constitutional and legal treatise replete with quotations from such luminaries of the law as Grotius, Vattel, Montesquieu, Burlamaqui, and Blackstone. The author founded his argument on the notion that the true spirit of republicanism was a "democratic equality" that rejected concentration of power and wealth in the hands of a few. He also posited a sharp distinction between the "transcendent authority" of the people as embodied in their constitution and the "supreme governing power" or legislature. In this understanding of republican constitutionalism, a legislature was a decidedly subordinate creature of the constitution, strictly bound by implied and express restraints and unable to act without "express authority." The Georgia legislature, he wrote, was "no more than the agent or attorney" under the constitution's grant, and "so far as this grant or constitution expressly warrants, they may go, but no further."

Sicilius devoted his longest letter to showing that Georgia's constitution did not authorize the General Assembly to grant monopolies of land that benefited only a few individuals. The instrument itself restricted the legislature to enacting only those laws that were "necessary and proper for the good of the state." The legislators who enacted the Yazoo sale, he contended, considered not "the good of the state" but "the good of their own private interests." Their selfish act was thus "unconstitutional, and a mere nullity." Aside from his contention that the Yazoo grant was repugnant to the constitution's requirement that laws must be for the "good of the state," Sicilius rested his case on the absence of any constitutional warrant for an act of such magnitude as selling the greater part of the state's public lands.

Sicilius adduced numerous other points to arraign the Yazoo sale act—the enormous waste of giving away an immense and valuable property for a trifling sum, the consequent loss of a certain and steady source of revenue, the malignant effects of monopoly in making the people subservient to an aristocracy of a "few Nabobs," and the likelihood of promoting civil discord—all to buttress his principal argument that the act was manifestly contrary to the "good of the state." Sicilius was a master of invective, who used language to good effect to rouse the Georgia citizenry to a high pitch of indignation and revulsion. "The corruptions of a Walpole, the squanderings of a Pitt, and the extravagancies of a Marie Antoinette, are all eclipsed by this abominable act," he wrote. With an eye to the approaching elections, he exhorted the people to instruct their representatives to adopt sweeping measures of redress, warning that "in so flagrant a breach of the principles of democratic government; so violent an attack on the rights of equality; so wanton a dissipation of the public property; and so evident an intention of destruction to your liberties; and the raising a well-born aristocracy on their ruins—patience and moderation are no longer virtues, but the most infamous offices, and will be detested, with their owners, as the sycophants of a venal day."

Sicilius took no notice of the cases of individual legislators having been bribed with shares in the companies. Indeed, in his telling it was not the overt instances of corruption as detailed in numerous affidavits and published in the newspapers that invalidated the Yazoo sale act. Rather, that act was on its face unconstitutional and illegal, its very terms proof of the corruption of the legislature that enacted it. "This unparalleled speculation" was "a manifest robbery" of the people's "birthright," he wrote, echoing the point Jackson had previously expressed in private correspondence. In short, Sicilius took the position that alienation of the state's western lands on such a massive scale to private companies could not be lawful even if no bribery or corruption occurred. He dismissed the precedents of land speculations in other states as "mere bagatelles to our sale of Nations." As to Georgia's Yazoo sale of 1789, he had "ever viewed that law as unconstitutional, as the present, and a majority of that legislature, which refused to renew it, considered it in the same light."

Jackson's "Letters of Sicilius" offered a principled and passionate critique of the Yazoo sale that resonated deeply with the citizens of Georgia. The pamphlet circulated widely as a campaign document in the fall elections to the General Assembly. At the urging of his constituents, Jackson himself became a candidate, resigning from the U.S. Senate to take personal command of the movement to overturn the Yazoo sale. As the point man in this political contest, Jackson led the anti-Yazoo forces to a decisive victory, with many of the newly elected legislators pledged to declare the "usurped act" null and void.

The key to Jackson's political triumph was his knack for explaining the Yazoo episode in clear and simple terms as a radical deviation from the republican principles of "democratic equality" and aversion to "aristocracy." Jackson infused anti-Yazooism with a revolutionary fervor and apocalyptic urgency, transforming the election into the higher cause of restoring Georgia to republican virtue. No opportunity was missed to portray the 1795 sale of the western lands in the most lurid colors, as a heinous crime against Georgians that called for sweeping remedial action. He offered a compelling narrative of recent history in which the "spirit of speculation had invaded our happy land" in consequence of evasion and manipulation of the laws and constitution. Speculation and its insidious corrupting influences soon pervaded the legislature, formerly "pure and undefiled," resulting in the sale of 1789. Virtue returned briefly with the repeal of that law, only to be replaced by the "infamous scheme" of 1795. To Georgia's shame, the "love of virtue and democracy" were "destroyed," "speculation, monopoly, and aristocracy" were "triumphant," and the "democratic republic" was "on the point of being utterly undone." The message was clear: Yazooism—Resistancethe toxic spirit of land speculation—Resistancehad to be rooted out once and for all so that the virtuous democratic republic, which "your fathers bled for, and many of yourselves fought for," could be restored and established on a permanent foundation.

Against this ideologically charged appeal to the people, defenders of the Yazoo purchase found themselves on the defensive. The sensational charges of bribery and corruption, however exaggerated and based on one-sided testimony, had severely damaged the reputations of Gunn and the other principals of the land companies. Gunn in particular must have been disconcerted by this sudden turn of the tide, having calculated that the support of men of standing and influence would command proper deference from the populace. Perhaps for this reason he was unable to mount an effective counter-campaign to persuade Georgians that the sale of the western lands benefited the many, not just the few. One tactic frequently employed by Gunn and his allies was to discredit Jackson, portraying him as a revenge-seeking party man motivated solely by ambition and political aggrandizement. In an attempt to show that "disappointed avarice," not principle, was behind the opposition, Yazoo proponents lost no opportunity to point out that members of the Georgia Union Company were prominently allied with Jackson in seeking to nullify the sale. Jackson and his anti-Yazoo cause proved remarkably resistant to such charges, however.

Even as the political landscape was tilting against them, Yazooists believed that the western lands sale had the sanction of law and could not be reversed—indeed, that as a matter of law their case was virtually unassailable. They affirmed two principal points: that the January 1795 act was constitutional and that the proposed act to declare it null and void was unconstitutional. On the former point, they contended that Georgia's legislature had proper constitutional authority to alienate the state's public domain and had exercised this power prior to 1795 without objection. No one, for example, questioned the 1788 act authorizing Georgia's delegates in Congress to cede the state's western lands. And the objections to the 1789 Yazoo sale act did not raise the issue of constitutionality. The Yazooists also closely examined particular provisions of the constitution, dismissing Sicilius's strained readings as contrary to the rules of legal construction. In regard to corruption, they denied that this could affect the question of constitutionality since the evidence presented did not meet the standards of legal proof. In any case, the judiciary, not the legislature, was the proper organ to conduct an inquiry into corruption.

Confident as they were that the 1795 act was constitutional, Yazooists were equally emphatic that a succeeding legislature could not declare it null and void. To do so would itself be an unconstitutional act, they explained, as amounting to an "ex post facto" law or law impairing the obligation of contract, both of which were prohibited by the U.S. Constitution. But critics of the proposed rescinding act relied much less on the Constitution than on the broader principles of constitutionalism and maxims of law that proscribed retrospective laws—laws that extend back in time and take effect before passage of the act—as exceeding the boundaries of legislative power. A legislative act, they repeatedly insisted, declares what the law shall be and can operate only prospectively. In voiding the Yazoo sale, the Georgia legislature would be assuming the judicial power to expound the law, contravening the principle of separation of powers embedded in republican constitutionalism. Legislatures, they conceded, could repeal laws adopted by their predecessors, but this repealing power extended only to laws of general application, in which the state was the sole party. It did not extend to a different class of laws—contracts in which there were two parties and in which rights were acquired and vested. Public contracts, like private contracts between individuals, could not be abrogated or annulled by one of the parties without violating "natural justice."

Arguments of this kind, couched in the technical language of the law of contracts and vested rights, had little purchase in the highly charged political climate of Georgia in 1795. To a populace righteously indignant at what was perceived to be an atrocious fraud perpetrated against the state, Yazooists were manipulating law, raising it as a barrier to prevent the people from taking remedial action against massive wrongdoing. Even though the sale of Georgia's western domain was made by a faithless and corrupt legislature for the enrichment of a few rapacious land speculators, the law declared this to be an irrevocable contract fully protected against infringement. Law, so it seemed, was being invoked to protect rights founded on fraud, and the people were powerless to do anything about it.

Jackson and his followers vehemently dismissed what they perceived to be a perversion of law while insistently claiming that they themselves were faithful adherents of law and constitutionalism. The anti-Yazoo leader was himself a proficient lawyer, conversant with the principles of English common law and equity and of the law of nations, who could hold his own in discussing rights and obligations arising from the law of contract. But the essential premise of his campaign to overturn Georgia's western lands sale was that this was a public transaction of deep constitutional significance that could not be assimilated to the ordinary law of contract as applied to private contracts between individuals. Indeed, in his view the Yazoo sale had brought the state to the point of crisis—it was not simply a violation of the constitution but a mortal threat to Georgia's republican character. To meet this challenge he turned to the populist constitutionalism he had set forth in "The Letters of Sicilius" and to which he would give practical application in Georgia's rescinding law of 1796.

Jackson employed populist constitutionalism as a means to buttress the republican values of democratic equality and opposition to aristocracy, to give primacy to the rights of the community, and to provide remedial action when those rights were injured. His notion of the legislature as the people's "agent or attorney" foresaw the representative body as acting in two capacities. On the one hand it was an ordinary lawmaking body, confined to the exercise of powers expressly warranted by the constitution. On the other the legislature was the institution for enforcing the republican constitution, in which capacity it was empowered to take radical corrective action. The legislature could act in the latter capacity only in exceptional circumstances, in situations of dire emergency, in which republican government was usurped by a corrupt aristocracy that committed a great wrong against the people.

A legislature acting as the savior of the republic had to differentiate itself from its customary role as a legislative body composed of competing political factions. Those elected to such an assembly had to be seen as representing not a temporary majority faction but in fact the unambiguous will of the whole people, with a clear mandate to repair the breach in the constitutional fabric and restore the state to its true republican character. Such a representative assembly, brought into being at a time of acute crisis, was vested with plenary authority, not bound by such conventional maxims as the separation of powers or the inviolability of vested rights. The only maxim that applied in this case was "salus populi suprema lex": the good of the people is the supreme law.

Jackson succeeded brilliantly in persuading Georgians that the Yazoo sale had produced this very situation of extreme peril to the state, demanding swift and sweeping action to redress the injury to the rights of the people. With most of the newly elected members, including Jackson, pledged to revoke the Yazoo sale, the legislature that convened in Louisville in January 1796 proceeded to carry out its appointed mission. Early in the session Governor Mathews, whose term of office was about to expire, sent a message to the General Assembly expressing doubt "whether a law can be constitutionally made to repeal another that has been so fully carried into effect as the one now in question." He also forcefully defended his ultimate approval of the sale act of the preceding January and requested that a committee be appointed to examine into his conduct. But the governor's cautionary words and exculpatory remarks went unheeded. Immediately after the reading of the message, the assembly elected

Jared Irwin to replace Mathews as governor and on the following day appointed a committee to inquire into the validity and constitutionality of the sale act.

Jackson was chairman of this committee, to which were submitted all the petitions forwarded from the preceding May's constitutional convention, together with additional petitions and grand jury presentments addressed to the present legislature. His report for the committee, presented on January 22, echoed the language of Sicilius: "It appears to your committee, that the public good was placed entirely out of view, and private interest alone consulted; that the rights of the present generation were violated, and the rights of posterity bartered, by the said act; and that by it, the bounds of equal rights were broken down, and the principles of aristocracy established in their stead." While deploring "the utmost depravity in the majority of the late Legislature" and acknowledging "with shame and confusion . . . that such a Legislature . . . should have existed in Georgia," the chairman was gratified to report that there were "sufficient grounds" to pronounce the Yazoo sale act "a nullity in itself, and not binding or obligatory on the people of this State." He then proposed that a declaration to this effect should be embodied in a legislative act, which he believed would have the salutary purpose of checking "that rapacious and avaricious spirit of speculation, which has in this State overleaped all decent bounds, and which, if it were to continue, would totally annihilate morality and good faith from among the citizens of the State." There could be no better expression of Jackson's hopes not merely of righting a constitutional wrong but of reforming—or more precisely, restoring—Georgia's republican honor.

The report concluded with a bill declaring the sale act void and "expunging" it "from the face of the public record." After moving quickly through the legislature, the bill became law on February 13, having passed the house by a vote of forty-four to three and the senate fourteen to four—an overwhelming display of the Assembly's intention to crush the pernicious spirit of Yazooism. Commonly known as the "rescinding act," this law became a seminal document in the history of Georgia and ranks among the most extraordinary legislative acts in American history, virtually without precedent or successor. The text, three-fourths of which is preamble recapitulating the constitutional views of Sicilius, clearly identifies Jackson as the author.

The evident purpose of the lengthy preamble was to codify the essential points of populist constitutionalism and its accompanying narrative and explanation of the sale of Georgia's western lands. After premising that Georgia's "free citizens" were "essentially the source of the sovereignty of the state," that the constitution was "the only existing legal authority derived" from that source and "the only foundation of the legislative power or government thereof," and that any exercise of power beyond what the constitution "expressly warrants" was "of no binding force . . . but null and void," the preamble declared that the preceding legislature, "not confining itself" to its constitutionally vested powers, "did usurp a power" to pass the act of January 1795 selling the western lands. The evocative word "usurp" was carefully chosen to conjure an image of the Yazoo legislature as having by a sudden coup overthrown the state's republican constitution and bartered away the people's rights. Henceforth, Yazoo opponents ritually referred to the infamous measure as the "usurped act" to underscore its utter lack of validity and binding authority from the moment of enactment.

Most of the remainder of the preamble recited the ways in which the Yazoo sale violated the general principles and specific provisions of the constitution. It then declared that Georgia's western territory "attempted to be disposed of by the said usurped act," remained "vested in the state and people thereof," and could not be alienated except by a convention called "for that express purpose" or by some constitutional power "delegating such express power to the legislature." Finally, the preamble turned to the means of remedying the wrong committed against the people of Georgia as a result of the fraud used to obtain the "usurped act." Invoking the "fundamental principle both of law and equity, that there cannot be a wrong without a remedy," it nonetheless denied that redress could be obtained in a regular court of law. There was "no court existing, if the dignity of the state would permit her entering one," for remedying "so notorious and injury." Unstated but understood was that if Georgia subjected itself to the rules of law and equity that ran in the ordinary court system, the Yazoo sale would be upheld as a binding contract that could not be revoked—a point its defenders had steadfastly insisted upon.

If conventional law provided no means for Georgians to reclaim their rights, then their proper recourse was to seek a remedy in the law that ran in a higher court, namely, "the representatives of the people chosen by them, after due promulgation" by grand juries and remonstrances "setting forth the atrocious speculation, corruption and collusion, by which the said usurped act and grants were obtained." Implicit in the preamble's narrative was that the rescinding law was enacted by the legislature acting in its capacity as guardian of the state's republican constitution, possessing full authority to uphold the people's rights. Indeed, the legislature in this instance was scarcely different from a special convention of the people elected for the purpose of relieving the damage incurred by the Yazoo sale. After all, the convention of May 1795 had by resolution transferred the Yazoo matter to the present legislature, investing it by a kind of laying on of hands "with conventional powers, *quo ad hoc.*" This resolution thus bestowed "additional validity to legislative authority, were the powers of one legislature over the acts of another to be attempted to be questioned."

The preamble's primer on government and constitutionalism was followed by enacting clauses that further underlined the rescinding act's distinctive place in the annals of American legislation. As expected, the law declared the "usurped act" and any "grant or grants, right or rights, claim or claims, issuing, deduced, or derived therefrom" to be "null and void" and also declared the western territory "to be the sole property of the state." Not content with a mere declaration, the law took special care to expunge "from the face and indexes of the books of record of the state" all the official records, documents, and deeds relating to the sale. The "usurped act" was then to be "publicly burnt, in order that no trace of so unconstitutional, vile and fraudulent a transaction, other than the infamy attached to it by this law, shall remain in the public offices thereof." In addition, county clerks, on pain of loss of office and fine, were to "obliterate" any recorded documents concerning the sale under the "usurped act" and refuse to enter on record any document "relative to the said purchase under the said usurped act." Another provision prohibited the Yazoo act and related documents from being received as evidence in the state courts, "so far as to establish a right to the said territory, or any part thereof." The act also allowed persons who had "*bona fide*" deposited money in the state treasury in payment "of pretended shares of the said pretended territory" to be reimbursed. Applications for this purpose had to be made within eight months, after which any remaining money was to revert to the state.

Leaving nothing to chance in removing all traces of the reviled act from the official record, the rescinding law aimed at nothing less than to reverse history, to restore Georgia, at least in a legal sense, to a time preceding the Yazoo sale—as if the act and sale had never taken place. In a broader sense it sought to remove a stain on the state's republican reputation, so grievously sacrificed to the idol of speculation. The same day the act passed, February 13, the legislature appointed a joint committee to prescribe the mode of expunging the records and burning of the "usurped act." This committee's report of the next day was remarkable for its exact and minute instructions, including that to the clerks to cut out "the leaves of the book" containing the offending records, with "a memorandum . . . expressing the number of pages so expunged."

No less extraordinary were the committee's directions for burning the Yazoo act, which was to take place "in the square, before the State House," the fire "to be made in front of the State House door, and a line to be formed by the members of both branches [of the legislature] around the same." The secretary of state and the committee were to "produce the enrolled bill and usurped act" from the state archives and deliver them to the senate president and to the house speaker for each to examine. The speaker would then deliver them to the house clerk, who was "to read aloud the title of the same" and deliver them to the house messenger, "who shall then pronounce: 'God save the state, and long preserve her rights; and may every attempt to injure them perish as these corrupt acts now do!'"

The solemn ceremony accordingly took place in the state house square in Louisville on February 15, 1796. Except for the script prescribed by the committee report, there is no contemporary description of what surely must have been an astonishing spectacle. In the popular and undocumented telling and retelling of the story, the fire that destroyed the condemned "usurped act" was not lit in the usual way but ignited by drawing the sun's rays through a magnifying glass. The detested act thus appropriately met its end not by earthly fire but by "fire from heaven . . . consumed as by the burning rays of the lidless eye of Justice." Even without this colorful detail, the scene, in the words of a nineteenth-century Georgia historian, "was sufficiently striking and impressive." The public burning of the notorious act and accompanying records was a singular act of purgation, "not only never beheld in Georgia before, but unknown to any Assembly on this continent." It was indicative of "the intense sense of indignation at the dishonor cast upon the State, and the equally intense desire to burn out the infamy; purifying, as by fire, the archives of the State from such fraud-begotten records." A historical marker with the heading "Yazoo Fraud" stands on the grounds of the old state house in Louisville, commemorating the events of this day and serving as a permanent testament to the rescinding law's honored place in the state's history.

In the immediate aftermath of its passage, however, the rescinding law remained controversial, provoking heated opposition, though political control of Georgia remained decisively in the hands of Jackson and his party. Perhaps uneasy at the repeated attacks on the law as itself an unconstitutional exercise of legislative power, Jackson at Georgia's constitutional convention of 1798 sought to give it a firmer and more permanent foundation by writing its principles into the new state constitution. One section, for example, declared the western territory to be "now, of right, the property of the free citizens of this State, and held by them in sovereignty, inalienable but by their consent." It further declared that "monopolies of land by individuals" were "contrary to the spirit of our free government" and prohibited land sales "to individuals or private companies," except where counties had first been laid off and Indian rights extinguished. A subsequent section noted that in consequence of Georgia's having declared its right to the western territory, "the contemplated purchases of certain companies of a considerable portion thereof are become constitutionally void."

The 1798 constitution perhaps gave finality to the rescinding law as far as Georgia was concerned but only stoked the raging controversy over Yazoo that had spread beyond the state's borders to the country at large. During the year preceding the February 1796 rescinding law, a large portion of the Yazoo purchase was bought up by New England investors, many of them concentrated in the Boston area. After passage of that law foreclosed likelihood of legal redress from Georgia, these purchasers organized themselves into an effective interest group for asserting their rights and claims before the federal government. The contest between competing visions of law and constitutionalism, having concluded with a decisive victory for the anti-Yazoo party in Georgia, now moved to the national arena, where it proved strikingly resistant to resolution during the next two decades.

CHAPTER THREE

New England Purchasers Become Yazoo Claimants

The Speculative Spirit in New England

Nothing else so clearly illustrates the land-jobbing nature of the Yazoo sale as the rapid turnover of the Georgia lands from the original grantees to third-party purchasers, who in turn sold their holdings to others, launching a speculative bubble that continued throughout 1795 and into early 1796. To meet the November 1, 1795, deadline for paying the purchase balance, the Yazoo companies immediately set about selling their lands at a price that would cover the balance and return a handsome profit. They accordingly sent their agents to where the concentration of money and speculating enthusiasm was highest—to the northeastern states, particularly New England. The agents who flocked to the northeast represented the two largest companies, the Georgia Company and the Georgia Mississippi Company, each of which received a title deed from Governor Mathews in the winter of 1795 after making their respective down payments.

The Georgia Company, headed by Senator Gunn, disposed of a large share of its grant in a sale to James Greenleaf in August 1795. A Boston native, Greenleaf was then, at age thirty, well launched on an extraordinary if ultimately unsuccessful career in land speculation. Earlier he had prospered as an import merchant in New York and spent a few years in Amsterdam promoting purchase of U.S. securities among Dutch capitalists. On his return to America in 1793, Greenleaf abandoned trade for real estate investment, becoming deeply involved in the purchase of lots in the new Federal City that was to become Washington, D.C. Having previously associated himself with Robert Morris and John Nicholson in a mammoth land trust known as the North American Land Company, Greenleaf brought these Pennsylvanians in as partners in his Washington venture. The scheme proved costly, however, and eventually soured Greenleaf's relations with Morris and Nicholson, both of whom eventually went bankrupt and entered debtor's prison.

Already overextended in his purchase of Washington lots, Greenleaf plunged headlong into the Yazoo speculation, hoping to extricate himself from impending insolvency. Greenleaf paid $225,000 to Gunn and his associates, of which $200,000 was immediately required to enable the Georgia Company to pay its balance to the state of Georgia. The tract conveyed to Greenleaf was an estimated 13,500 acres, of which he was directed to convey 1 million acres each to James Wilson and Zachariah Cox, who were principals in the Georgia Company. A yellow fever outbreak in the fall of 1795 made money tight in Philadelphia, New York, and Baltimore, effectively forcing Greenleaf (as he claimed in a later statement) to pay nearly double to meet that engagement. Between September and November 1795 Greenleaf sold off the greater part of his purchase from the Georgia Company. In September 1796 he conveyed the unsold residue "in trust for the payment of a very large amount" due to his creditors.

Greenleaf sold 2.8 million acres of his Georgia Company purchase to New York merchants Nathaniel Prime and Samuel Ward Jr. in September 1795 for $180,000. Prime, who had recently moved to New York after serving as an apprentice to a Boston broker, soon began selling numerous Yazoo tracts in Boston and other New England towns. One subsequent purchaser under the conveyance from Greenleaf to Prime and Ward was John Peck of Boston. Prime and Ward sold an unspecified amount of this land to Oliver Phelps, a Connecticut speculator of vast extent, in February 1796. Phelps, in turn, sold 400,000 acres to Peck and an associate in December 1800. Out of this tract, Peck sold 15,000 acres to Robert Fletcher in May 1803, the transaction that gave rise to *Fletcher v. Peck*. In November 1795 Greenleaf sold 5 million acres to a number of Boston investors, including Peck, at 13 cents per acre. Peck's direct purchase from Greenleaf came to 320,000 acres.

Peck and other New England speculators were also deeply involved in the tract conveyed to the Georgia Mississippi Company.

An agent of the company, William Williamson, traveled to Boston in the summer of 1795 to obtain a sale of the company's lands. He entered negotiations with George Blake, a Boston lawyer who had been associated in land speculations with Oliver Phelps. Blake agreed to procure a company to buy the lands, and soon a contract was opened to sell by subscription the tract estimated at 11.38 million acres at 10 cents an acre. The subscription filled quickly, and Williamson returned to Georgia in August to get a "good and sufficient deed." In December 1795 the Georgia Mississippi Company conveyed its tract to Williamson and Amasa Jackson as coagents to sell the lands. In Boston, on February 13, 1796—as it happened, the same day that Georgia enacted its rescinding law—Williamson and Jackson delivered this deed to trustees of the New England purchasers, who had organized themselves as the New England Mississippi Land Company. Under the terms of the contract as finally settled, the purchasers paid an additional 1 cent per acre, making a total purchase price of $1,250,000. They paid down $340,000, and the balance was secured by promissory notes, for which the individuals giving the notes, not the company, were responsible.

Peck was one of twenty-nine proprietors, mostly Boston residents, who subscribed to eighteen "Articles of Association and Agreement Constituting the New-England Mississippi Land Company" on February 11, 1796. Then only twenty-six, Peck was among the most active New England speculators in Yazoo lands. From his initial purchase of 320,000 acres from Greenleaf in November 1795 he would eventually accumulate tracts amounting to nearly 2 million acres, of which he sold about 1.5 million, exclusive of lands held under the N.E.M. Land Co. As a charter member of the company, he subscribed for four shares amounting to 1 million acres. He was also one of the company's seven original directors. During the next dozen years Peck for himself and as a company director signed memorials, propositions, and other documents presented to Congress on behalf of the Yazoo claimants.

Peck, like Greenleaf, Prime, and Blake, belonged to a younger generation of land speculators who came of age in the postrevolutionary years. A portrait executed around the time of the 1795 Yazoo sale reveals a young man brimming with confidence. He came from an established Boston family of tradesmen and merchants. His father entered trade, probably under the direction of a wealthy uncle who was also his guardian, before joining the Continental Navy as a midshipman. During the summer of 1779 nine-year-old John Peck served with his father as "mizzen top boy" on a Continental frigate. The father continued to serve in the navy until his death at Charleston in July 1780. John also continued as a ship's boy on various privateers until the end of the war and was twice captured by the enemy. His mother's remarriage in 1782 to a trader in public securities enabled John Peck to get into the brokerage business when he was only seventeen.

On his stepfather's death in 1789, Peck carried on the business, advertising his services at his office on Marlborough Street, "opposite the State Treasurer's Office." According to newspaper advertisements, he offered cash for Rhode Island "state notes," military bounty rights, Massachusetts lottery lands, and Ohio Company rights. In 1794 his interests shifted to real estate development and land speculation. Marriage into the wealthy Gilman family in 1801 substantially increased his prospects. Soon after, he began constructing a large house in Newton, about ten miles from Boston, with a commanding "view not to be surpassed in the United States." In addition to his Yazoo speculation, Peck pursued land closer to home, acquiring townships in the district of Maine that he then offered for sale. Peck was also actively involved with other wealthy proprietors in developing the site of Boston's millpond. In time, he suffered financial reversals and was forced to sell his "elegant country seat" in 1814. By 1817 he had moved from Boston and was residing in Lexington, Kentucky, where he reinvented himself and lived until his death in 1847.

Like Peck, many New Englanders caught the speculative fever in Yazoo lands that swept through the region in 1795 and 1796. "On this ocean of speculation," wrote Yale president Timothy Dwight, "great multitudes of sober, industrious people launched the earnings of their whole lives; and multitudes became indebted for large sums which they never possessed." A French traveler in Boston at the time remarked that "speculation is the favourite passion of the inhabitants of New-England," affecting all classes, "even watchmakers, hair-dressers, and mechanics of all description." The citizens of Boston, he added, had "sunk above two millions of dollars" in "sales and sub-sales without number." Many eager buyers imprudently entered into contracts "on the bare security of titles," without stipulating any responsibility on the seller's part. Company agents exploited "this inconceivable infatuation" by raising "the price each day, often twice in the day," exciting hasty purchases before the price rose again. Some "artful, interested agents," a Boston newspaper reported, induced "industrious people" to purchase by showing fictitious lists of "respectable citizens" who had supposedly already subscribed.

This unbridled pursuit of Georgia lands left its mark on the New England consciousness, inspiring native playwright Royall Tyler to write "The Georgia Spec; or, the Land in the Moon." Tyler was the acclaimed author of the "The Contrast" (1787), a comedy that was the first American play to be performed in public by professional actors. "The Georgia Spec," now lost, was a "comedy in three acts" performed at the Haymarket Theatre in Boston in October 1797. It was said to be "the best production that has flowed from the ingenious pen of R. Tyler, Esq. It contains a rich diversity of national character and native humour, scarcely to be found in any other drama in the language."

By the time the play opened, the Yazoo bubble had long since burst. Word of Georgia's impending passage of the rescinding act reached Boston in late February 1796, and the fact was confirmed in mid-March. The immediate effect was a precipitous drop in Georgia land prices. Tracts that had sold as high as 13–16 cents per acre, recalled a director of the N.E.M. Land Co., were "so materially affected, that sales could not afterwards have been made at any price." A mock obituary notice announced the "SUDDEN DEATH" by "legislative stroke" of *Miss Georgia Purchase*, aged one Year only. Yet so extravagant were her nurses, that drafts, bonds and notes, to near one million of dollars have been given and accepted, and must be paid by the child's friends in this town. The child was very feeble from its birth, being born of depraved parents."

The news from Georgia provoked alarm throughout New England, as investors in Yazoo lands not only saw their hopes of future wealth suddenly dashed but, worse, faced imminent financial hardship if not ruin. "The shock produced by [the rescinding] act," wrote

Dwight, "cannot be described. The speculating Croesus in a moment became a beggar, while the honest purchaser, stripped of his possessions, was left to meet old age without property, consolation, or hope." The typical purchase contract was partly in cash and partly in promissory notes payable in installments. Many purchasers bought beyond their means, counting on their landed assets rising in value and enabling them to pay off their notes when they came due.

One reaction among Yazoo subscribers was to refuse to honor their notes, claiming release from their contracts because the consideration for which they promised to pay was now virtually worthless. One such disappointed buyer was Benjamin Weld, one of many Bostonians who purchased tracts from Nathaniel Prime in January 1796. Weld placed a "caution" notice in the newspapers, warning the public not to receive his notes, "as he intends, by every legal means, to avoid the payment thereof." The intent was to keep these notes in the seller's hands, so the purchaser could contest the notes directly with the party who sold the lands. In fact, however, as the French traveler noted, these promissory notes in many instances had already passed from the seller to others, "wholly unconnected with that speculation, and who cannot be excluded from payment without a most glaring act of injustice." In those cases where the notes remained with the seller, many purchasers were able to compromise by paying cash immediately for their notes discounted at 50 percent.

Some Early Cases Arising from the Yazoo Sales

Several lawsuits in state and federal courts arising from contested promissory notes attracted notice in New England. One case arose from a February 1796 sale of 1 million acres from Nathanial Prime to three buyers in the Boston area, one of whom was Samuel Dexter, later a member of President Adams's cabinet. Prime's associates in this sale were William Payne of Boston and three New Yorkers, all of whom signed a bond for $300,000 as security for the deed to the land. In consideration of this bond Dexter and the other buyers gave promissory notes for $220,000 payable in installments. In this case the buyers had prudently insisted on a bond requiring the sellers to provide authentic copies of the Yazoo sale act and the grant pursuant to that act and also certificates from Georgia officials attesting to the recording of the conveyance according to Georgia law. The rescinding act made it virtually impossible for the sellers to meet the conditions of the bond.

Perhaps in anticipation of legal action against them on the promissory notes, Dexter and the other buyers brought an action on the bond in January 1797 against Payne in a Massachusetts court. They ultimately obtained judgment on that bond in March 1798 in the Supreme Judicial Court of Massachusetts. Payne satisfied this judgment by surrendering the notes given to him by Dexter and others, evidently preferring to settle rather than continue expensive litigation. This case, then, did not bring into question the constitutionality of Georgia's rescinding law. Had he chosen to contest the action against him on that ground, Payne might have prevailed in the Massachusetts court or, if he lost there, he could have taken an appeal to the U.S. Supreme Court.

In some instances purchasers aggressively responded to legal action by bringing their own suits against sellers in courts of chancery, seeking to void their contracts on account of fraud. This occurred in Connecticut, for example, in cases arising from a sale to a group of New Haven buyers in October 1795. The sellers were Phineas Miller and John C. Nightingale, New Englanders who had moved to Georgia. Miller, a Connecticut native, and Nightingale, originally from Rhode Island, were connected to the family of the late Revolutionary general Nathanael Greene, whose widow continued to live on the Georgia plantation given to him for his war services. In the early 1790s Miller was instrumental in bringing Eli Whitney to the Greene plantation, where he invented the cotton gin. A partnership with Whitney in patenting and manufacturing the gin proved financially disastrous for Miller, which led him to join the Yazoo speculation in hopes of making a quick recovery. He was the author of an early pro-Yazoo pamphlet, *State of Facts. Shewing the Right of Certain Companies to the Lands Later Purchased by Them from the State of Georgia* (1795), defending the right of the companies to the lands sold under the act of January 1795.

To Miller and Nightingale no legal adversaries proved more vexatious and combative than the brothers Abraham and John Bishop, who were among the largest purchasers at the New Haven sale. Although Miller compromised with some of the New Haven buyers after passage of the rescinding law, the Bishops refused his terms. He and Nightingale accordingly brought suit on several of the Bishops' outstanding notes in April 1797 in the U.S. Circuit Court for Connecticut. The Bishops thereupon pressed their own suit against Miller and Nightingale on the chancery side of the federal court. A Yale graduate and lawyer, Abraham Bishop was later active in his state's Republican politics. Perhaps prompted by the lawsuit brought on his notes, Bishop wrote an angry pamphlet, *Georgia Speculation Unveiled* (1797), denouncing the Yazoo sale as fraudulent and urging his fellow purchasers not to pay off their notes. The litigation finally concluded in 1805, evidently by mutual consent. By this time Miller and John Bishop had died, and Nightingale died soon after. Abraham Bishop ultimately returned most of the land he and his brother had bought in 1795 to the heirs of Miller and Nightingale. He retained 50,000 acres, for which he received $5,700 on a final settlement of Yazoo claims in 1818. In this case, as in that between Payne and Dexter, there was no court pronouncement on the validity of Georgia's rescinding law.

Many sellers apparently preferred to compromise with buyers rather than exact full payment on the promissory notes, which they presumably might have done if the courts held that the Georgia rescinding law could not nullify contracts for Yazoo lands. Apart from not wanting to incur the expense of protracted litigation, sellers in time were more willing to receive lands back from their buyers. After an initial plummet, Yazoo land prices had begun to rise again, helped by the Senate's ratification of the treaty with Spain, which established the thirty-first parallel as the southern boundary between the United States and Spain and guaranteed both nations navigation of the entire length of the Mississippi River. Land values rose as well because of the likelihood that Georgia would cede its Mississippi lands to the United States, potentially clearing the way for a settlement with the Yazoo claimants.

One case that did produce a decision on the Georgia rescinding law was mostly likely arranged for that very purpose. *Derby* v. *Blake* was heard in the Supreme Judicial Court of Massachusetts in August 1799. A report of the case based on a memorandum probably drawn up by defendant's counsel George Blake was published in the Boston *Columbian Centinel.* The newspaper noted that the report "contains the decided opinion of the highest judiciary of Massachusetts, relative to the memorable repealing Law of the Georgia Legislature; an Act which, however void and nugatory in itself, has nevertheless been attended with almost irreparable injury to very many worthy and respectable citizens of this and other States in the Union."

The case arose from a preliminary contract in January 1796 by which the agents of the Georgia Mississippi Company conveyed that company's grant to the subscribers who formed the N.E.M. Land Co. The facts were complicated, but the court's essential holding was that this contract "had not been legally affected by the *Repealing Act of Georgia.*" The Georgia law was "a mere nullity—as a flagrant, outrageous violation of the first and fundamental principles of social compacts." That law, the court added, was also "void" as being "directly repugnant" to the clauses in the U.S. Constitution prohibiting the states from passing ex post facto laws or laws impairing the obligation of contracts. According to George Blake's later statement, this 1799 decision "put at rest" the question of whether purchasers could continue to withhold payment of their notes. They "were then left to make the best terms they could" with the holders.

Although the collapse of the Yazoo bubble clearly caused financial hardship for purchasers lacking the funds to pay off their promissory notes, in time the shock and panic brought on by the Georgia rescinding act began to subside. In numerous instances buyers and sellers reached an accommodation, with the former canceling a portion of their notes and the latter returning an equivalent part of their lands. Rather than pursue costly litigation against each other, those caught up in the Yazoo speculation, sellers and buyers alike, began to perceive a common interest in asserting the validity of their title to Georgia's western lands notwithstanding the rescinding act. Throughout New England claimants to Georgia land organized themselves, held meetings, assessed taxes to defray expenses, and employed legal counsel. The N.E.M. Land Co., formed in 1796 to purchase the Georgia Mississippi Company's tract, met quarterly beginning in 1798. Purchasers under the Georgia Company also began to organize and appoint agents to act on their behalf. Many Massachusetts claimants, including John Peck, were members of both the N.E.M. Land Co. and one of the smaller groups claiming under the Georgia Company. In 1798 the N.E.M. Land Co. and other Massachusetts claimants joined together to present a memorial to the president of the United States.

The New Englanders were confident that law and justice were on their side; that the rescinding act, however much short-run damage it wreaked, could not destroy the validity of their title. As early as March 1796 a Connecticut newspaper observed, "The alarm is general but we think too great. So flagrant a violation of the Constitution cannot be suffered to pass into an effective law." Writing at the same time, a Yazoo seller acknowledged that the rescinding act had "created a violent alarm throughout the eastern States," but then added optimistically that the "most able counsel have given it as their opinion" that the Georgia law did "not in the least affect the validity of the former grants." Among those "able counsel" was Alexander Hamilton, who rendered professional advice to several large investors in Georgia lands, including James Greenleaf, Nathaniel Prime, and William Constable. In March 1796 Hamilton rendered a formal opinion for Constable that Georgia's rescinding act was void, in particular for being contrary to the Constitution's contract clause.

There was nothing novel in the opinion that the Georgia legislature could not revoke the Yazoo grant—a view that was frequently expressed by proponents of the sale well before the rescinding act was adopted. Arguments to this effect, however, primarily invoked general principles of law and "natural justice" rather than the Constitution. And when the Constitution was cited, either the ex post facto and contract clauses were linked together without discrimination or the latter was not even mentioned. (Not until *Calder v. Bull* in 1798 did the Supreme Court express the view that the ex post facto prohibition referred to criminal law.) Although he too pronounced Georgia's revocation act contrary "to the first principles of natural justice and social policy," Hamilton was the first to give specific attention to the prohibition against laws impairing the obligation of contract. That prohibition, he said, was "equivalent to saying no state shall pass a law revoking, invalidating, or altering a contract." He also made the crucial point that a grant, whether made by a state or an individual, was "virtually a contract that the grantee shall hold and enjoy the thing granted against the grantor, and his representatives."

Pamphlets Defending and Attacking the Yazoo Titles

Hamilton's opinion gained wide circulation after its publication in two pro-Yazoo pamphlets in 1797 and was no doubt known to the court that decided *Derby v. Blake* in 1799 and to Chief Justice Marshall when the Supreme Court decided *Fletcher v. Peck* in 1810. These pamphlets sought to persuade purchasers and prospective purchasers of Yazoo lands that the 1795 sale act was valid and that titles originating in that act were legally sound. They were directed not so much at Georgia's rescinding act, however, as at a new and potentially more serious threat to Yazoo claims arising from a report on land claims in the Southwest, submitted to Congress in April 1796 by Attorney General Charles Lee. Drawn in pursuance of a resolution Congress adopted shortly after receiving news of the Yazoo sale, the report digested numerous documents and arguments that supported the claims of both Georgia and the United States to this territory. The assertion of a U.S. right was particularly disturbing to Yazoo purchasers, for their title depended on Georgia's right to sell the lands. On this point the state of Georgia and those claiming lands under the sale of January 1795 were in complete agreement.

In the summer of 1796 Robert G. Harper wrote *The Case of the Georgia Sales on the Mississippi Considered . . .*, published in Philadelphia in February 1797. Then a member of Congress from South Carolina, Harper had supported Georgia's title in a brief debate on the question in March 1795. Although Phineas Miller's *State of Facts* (1795) had ably defended the Yazoo sale, Harper or those who employed him concluded that the attorney general's report appearing close on the heels of Georgia's rescinding act required a comprehensive restatement of the purchasers' case. Harper acted on behalf of prospective purchasers "of land on the Mississippi and Donbigby [Tombigbee], lately made from the state of Georgia." These lands most likely were in the southern third of the territory, to which the United States seemingly had its strongest claims as against those of Georgia. The Georgia Mississippi Company's grant and a portion of the Georgia Company's grant fell within this area. The argument was that Great Britain had extended the West Florida colony's northern boundary to just above the thirty-second parallel and that by the 1783 peace treaty establishing the United States' southern boundary as the thirty-first parallel the territory between the two parallels belonged not to Georgia but to the United States.

Harper devoted much the larger portion of his pamphlet to refuting this and other arguments in support of a U.S. claim to all or part of the western territory claimed by Georgia. This, he said, was "far the most extensive field of inquiry." In a shorter section on the rescinding act, Harper did not mention the contract clause except for a footnote reference to Hamilton's opinion, which he included as an appendix. He was content to restate arguments that the Georgia law violated the separation of powers principle by deciding a judicial question and that its abrogation of the sale contravened the "invariable maxim of law and of natural justice, that one of the parties to a contract, cannot by his own act, exempt himself, from its obligation."

Later in 1797 another defense of the Yazoo title was published in Boston by Jedidiah Morse, the noted geographer. In his *American Gazetteer* (1797) Morse had a long entry on the "Georgia Western Country" and an appendix, "Statement of the Claims upon the Georgia Western Territory." The entry and the appendix were subsequently published as a separate pamphlet, *A Description of the . . . Georgia Western Country*. Like Harper's *Case of the Georgia Sales*, Morse's pamphlet was intended to assure Yazoo investors that the title under the January 1795 sale remained valid against both the rescinding act and the assertion of U.S. claims. His detailed geographical survey, which included a map showing the boundaries of the four purchasing companies, was a fulsome account of the climate, soil, and water of a region that afforded "delightful situations for settlements." Mixing geography and politics, Morse closed his entry with a brief narrative of the Yazoo sale and the "unprecedented proceedings" that produced the rescinding act. That act, he said, had momentarily thrown the purchasers "into an unpleasant dilemma," though now their title had "been still further embarrassed by a claim brought forward in behalf of the United States." Morse accordingly added "a summary statement of the claims" to the Mississippi territory, though "foreign to the express design of this work."

Morse purported to give as "impartial a view of the conflicting claims" as he could from documents in his possession, though there was no mistaking his belief that the U.S. claim to the western territory was without merit. Like Harper, he took relatively brief notice of the rescinding act, remarking that it seemed "to be generally agreed among the informed part of the community" that the act was (quoting Harper) a "'contravention of the first principles of natural justice and policy,' and void." Morse also reprinted Hamilton's opinion that the rescinding act was unconstitutional, but his greater concern was to counter arguments supporting a U.S. title. Like Harper, he took special pains to deny U.S. ownership of the southern third of the territory based on the northward extension of the West Florida boundary. Morse was well aware that this claim was particularly disquieting to Boston and New England subscribers to the N.E.M. Land Co., which had purchased the Georgia Mississippi Company grant.

Late in 1797 New Englanders had an opportunity to purchase and ponder yet another pamphlet on the vexing question of the fate of their grand investment in Mississippi lands. Abraham Bishop's *Georgia Speculation Unveiled*, published in Hartford, appeared in two numbers followed by a second part of two more numbers and a conclusion in 1798. The title sufficiently captures the author's passionate anti-Yazoo stance and his aversion to land speculation and speculators. In sharp contrast to Harper and Morse, Bishop contended that the Yazoo title was worthless and that nothing could be done to restore it. For that reason, in a conclusion "addressed to the northern purchasers," he urged them to withhold payment of notes given for land purchases. He himself was one of those disappointed New England purchasers who tenaciously contested lawsuits to recover on their notes.

Bishop was a skilled polemicist, who combined colorful and biting prose with a mastery of law-learning to denounce the Yazoo sale as a clear fraud. The fraud, he reiterated time and again, was that the deeds purported to convey a title in "fee simple" (absolute ownership) but in fact conveyed only a worthless "preemption right" (right to buy). The "insertion of the word fee-simple," he wrote in a typical passage, was "a supreme instance of fraud, collusion and atrocious speculation, engendered between corrupt members of a legislature and corrupting purchasers, *for the express purpose of swindling.*" Those corrupt legislators and purchasers, he insisted, knowingly committed deception and falsehood by claiming that the state of Georgia owned "the right in fee" to the lands occupied by the Creeks, Choctaws, and Chickasaws. In fact, however, "the Indians were the first discoverers of this country, and if first discovery and continued occupation gives title according to the law of nature and nations, they had acquired an unquestionable title." Bishop's tract, among other things, was a powerful brief in favor of Native Americans' absolute ownership of the lands they occupied, directly challenging the prevailing theory that by European discovery and conquest Indians held nothing more than a mere temporary right of occupation.

Apart from "unveiling" the fraud in passing off a valueless preemption right as a fee-simple title, Bishop regarded Georgia's rescinding act as an expression of "the sovereignty of an independent state" and as such, uncontrollable. Although he approved of that act as reflecting the highest principles of law and equity, the main point he pressed upon northern purchasers was that nothing could be done to reverse it. It was an act of sovereign power beyond the reach of courts. Georgia as a sovereign state and contracting party had "*abundant power*" to reverse its grant and had actually done so. Bishop wholly endorsed the theory of legislative sovereignty espoused by Jackson and embodied in the rescinding act. The legislature alone had the right to judge the validity of its own laws. "Take this power from a legislature, and where is the sovereignty of the state?" he asked. He made no concession to this sovereignty despite Georgia's membership in a federal union bound by a federal Constitution. Neither Congress nor the Supreme Court "can control the state of Georgia in the enaction of their laws, or the management of their records."

Bishop, in short, dismissed the "miserable delusion" that the rescinding act was void, that a state as a party to a contract could not reverse that contract. But he was not satisfied to regard it as simply a fait accompli, an irresistible exercise of sovereign power. He repeatedly assured northern purchasers that common law and "equity" (a separate jurisdiction administered by courts of chancery that supplemented the common law and provided relief in cases not covered by common law remedies) were on their side. He exhorted them not to be "frightened by" law books and the army of lawyers employed by sellers who cited English cases as authorities for compelling payment of their notes. Although he countered with his own ample supply of English case law, Bishop ultimately questioned the applicability of that law to the unique circumstances arising from the Yazoo sale. English cases were "not mighty enough to decide a question depending solely on the law of nature and nations," he wrote, adding that they "never conceived of a pre-emptive right, and never heard of a sovereign independent state rescinding an act." Bishop, like Jackson, was an adamant defender of the legality and constitutionality of the rescinding act, and both were equally insistent that the technical doctrines of the law of contract and negotiable instruments founded on English cases did not apply to the speculative sale of an immense tract of American wilderness.

Bishop's pamphlet circulated outside New England and was known to Senator Jackson, who quoted it in 1805 at the height of the debate in Congress. Jackson and his party were surely gratified with Bishop's stinging censure of the Yazoo speculation and its robust defense of state sovereignty. Their enthusiasm must have been tempered, however, by the author's expansive notions of Indian sovereignty and ownership of the soil. In a state whose white inhabitants were impatient to remove the Creeks and Cherokees then occupying large swaths within Georgia's settled boundaries, such sentiments could not be countenanced. In time, New England philanthropy and missionary zeal would clash with Georgia's harsh policies toward its native population.

In New England, *Georgia Speculation Unveiled* was an attempt to drive a wedge between the large speculators and sellers of Yazoo lands and the mass of intermediate purchasers. To the latter Bishop delivered a harsh message: Your investment has wholly failed, your lands "are not worth one cent," and there is no prospect of recovery or reimbursement. He admonished them not to be flattered by hopes of obtaining confirmation of their titles in the event of a cession to the United States. "Shall every new position in which this floating bubble can be presented charm you with new colours and brighten your hopes?" In these circumstances he advised them that their only realistic course of action was to swallow the loss and prevent further damage by not paying off their outstanding notes.

Bishop and his brother boldly followed this course, at some cost, evidently, for John Bishop, who became bankrupt during the litigation with Miller and Nightingale and died in 1803. Abraham Bishop lived to a ripe age and died rich, overcoming whatever temporary damage he might have incurred as a result of his venture in buying Georgia lands. Few northern purchasers heeded Bishop's advice, however, unwilling to set aside hopes of eventually realizing something from their investment. Instead, these small investors, a numerous class "of sober, industrious people," formed the backbone of a large interest group in New England that refused to accept the verdict of Georgia's rescinding act and steadfastly held to the belief that their Yazoo titles remained good under the sale act of January 1795.

Many of the New England purchasers, like Bishop, were attracted to the Jeffersonian Republicans, regarding that party as open to the talents, ambition, and enterprise of the middling classes. This political migration added a new and complicating plotline to the Yazoo narrative. In its origins and early stages the Yazoo speculation had a "Federalist" cast about it, with prominent members of the party holding shares in the companies and wealthy capitalists associated with the party providing financial backing. As events were to show, however, Yazoo spilled across party lines, notably in New England. With the eclipse of Federalism in the wake of Jefferson's victory in 1801, James Jackson and other southern Republicans no doubt hoped that the spirit of Yazooism had been eradicated forever. To their dismay, they soon discovered that it not only had survived but had penetrated the ranks of their own party, posing a dire threat to Republican political and ideological unity.

The Creation of the Mississippi Territory and Georgia's Cession

Attorney General Lee's report on land claims in the Southwest, submitted in April 1796, resulted in a series of Senate resolutions and reports that two years later culminated in legislation settling the limits with Georgia and establishing the Mississippi Territory. These actions did little to relieve anxiety among purchasers under Georgia concerning U.S. assertions of title to all or parts of the western lands claimed by Georgia. A committee report of March 1797, for example, seemed to endorse the argument that by the Proclamation of 1763 the western lands came under the sovereignty of the British Crown and thus devolved on the United States. It further contended for U.S. jurisdiction and ownership of the southern portion (above the thirty-first parallel) formerly belonging to West Florida. "There can be no doubt," the report read, "that this territory did not revert to Georgia . . . and now belongs to the United States." Conceding, however, that the boundary had "never been ascertained" and that Georgia had "claimed and exercised jurisdiction over a great portion of this territory," the report proposed "an amicable and conciliatory plan of adjusting these adverse claims." It recommended that the president appoint three commissioners to meet with commissioners appointed by Georgia to adjust interfering claims and that the president, with Georgia's consent, authorize the establishment of a territorial government in the area similar to that in the Northwest Territory.

With Congress adjourning before taking any action on this report, the subject was renewed at the next Congress in January 1798. The Senate appointed a committee to inquire into what territory south and west of Georgia belonged to the United States and to report a plan for governing such territory as belonged to the United States. In February this committee reported a bill for "an amicable settlement of limits with Georgia, and authorizing the establishment of a government in the Mississippi territory." The Senate passed the bill on March 5 and sent it to the House, which over several days debated various provisions and proposed amendments. The first section authorized the president to appoint commissioners to meet with Georgia commissioners to adjust interfering claims and to receive proposals for the cession of the whole or part of the "territory claimed by or under the state of Georgia." John Milledge, one of Jackson's Georgia associates, moved to strike out "or under" as seeming "to sanction claims which had been declared not to exist, and would be offensive to the State of Georgia." Harper once again came to the aid of the Georgia claimants, though he wished his fellow House members to know that he himself no longer had an "interest" in the Yazoo claims, having given it up "when there was a prospect in the year 1795 of the business coming before Congress." He opposed the amendment, believing that it would be "good policy" to accommodate these "powerful" and numerous interested persons and enlist them on the side of obtaining a cession. These claims could be settled simply by dividing the lands, without "paying large sums of money," he explained, for he had "no doubt these persons would be glad to relinquish one-half or two-thirds of the country for an undisputed title to the rest." The amendment carried, however, and the words were struck out.

The bill's third section described the proposed Mississippi territory as bounded on the west by the Mississippi River, on the north by a line drawn from the junction of the Yazoo and Mississippi Rivers and extending due east to the Chattahoochee River, on the east by the Chattahoochee, and on the south by the thirty-first parallel. This was the area formerly belonging to West Florida to which a claim of U.S. ownership had been asserted. It included the Natchez District, where most of the inhabitants of the territory lived. Milledge also sought to amend this section by adding to the clause for establishing a provisional government in Natchez the words "as soon as the consent of the Legislature of Georgia shall be obtained." This prompted a debate over the competing claims of Georgia and the United States to the territory. Harper opposed the amendment on policy grounds, urging the immediate necessity of erecting a government in Natchez and pointing to the bill's express clause that establishing a government would not affect Georgia's rights of jurisdiction or soil to this territory. Contrary to what he had argued in *Case of the Georgia Sales*, Harper expressed his opinion that there was "the most undeniable evidence" of a U.S. right to the territory. The House ultimately rejected this amendment.

The bill provided that the government to be established was to be the same as that "now exercised" in the Northwest Territory, "excepting and excluding the last article" of the Northwest Ordinance. No one needed to be told that this article prohibited slavery. A Massachusetts member moved to strike out this clause, touching off a brief and fateful debate with some testy exchanges. When Harper said he did not believe this motion was "a proper mode of supporting the rights of man," another Massachusetts member retorted that "where there was a disposition to retain a part of our species in slavery, there could not be a proper respect for the rights of mankind." A South Carolina colleague of Harper's hoped that the Massachusetts member "would not indulge himself and others in uttering philippics against a practice with which his and their philosophy is at war." The debate brought forth the earliest articulation of the "diffusion" argument, the idea that as slavery expanded and spread over a large area, there was "a greater probability of ameliorating" the slaves' condition and in time making it safe to carry out emancipation plans. In the end the motion mustered only twelve votes in favor, with many northern representatives voting against it as well.

The bill for settling the limits of Georgia and establishing a government in the Mississippi territory became law in April 1798. The act stated that the establishment of this government "shall in no respect impair the rights of the state of Georgia, or of any person or persons either to the jurisdiction or the soil of the said territory." President Adams first nominated George Mathews, the erstwhile governor of Georgia who had signed the Yazoo sale act, to be the new territory's first governor. Mathews was then acting as agent for the N.E.M. Land Co., which claimed the territory now under U.S. jurisdiction and evidently was now making plans to colonize the area. The president soon withdrew this nomination in favor of Winthrop Sargent, a Massachusetts native, who was then secretary of the Northwest Territory. Despite his New England roots and his involvement in land speculation, Sargent showed no disposition to accommodate the N.E.M. Land Co.'s activities in Mississippi.

Soon after he arrived in Natchez in August 1798, Sargent received notice that "certain persons" had "presumed to make surveys upon the Lands of the United States, and also within the Indian Boundary . . . with a View to Settlement." On October 4 he issued a proclamation against such actions, threatening prosecution of those who remained illegally on the lands. Later that month Mathews on behalf of the N.E.M. Land Co. wrote to Sargent, asking the governor if he thought himself "bound to interfere with any disposition the Company may make of the lands in the territory." Sargent replied that he knew "of no *right* in any Company to Lands within the Mississippi Territory" and considered it his "duty to prevent all intrusion on the same." His opinion was that any rights of Georgia or of individuals claiming under the state were "suspended" pending negotiations by the commissioners provided under the 1798 act.

Soon thereafter the N.E.M. Land Co., as purchasers of the grant to the Georgia Mississippi Company, joined with Massachusetts purchasers of the grant to the Georgia Company in drawing up a memorial to the president of the United States. This was the first in a series of memorials the company and other New England claimants would address to the president and Congress over the next sixteen years. The purpose of the memorial was "to give formal notice" of the claimants' title to the lands "contemplated to be ceded" to the United States. In defending their title, the memorialists gave relatively little attention to Georgia's rescinding act, contending that it was of no effect and that their right remained "*where it was*" before that act was adopted. Far more troubling and surprising was the claim recently put forward by the United States, to which they professed to be "totally ignorant," noting that they had purchased the Georgia lands on the faith that the United States by certain public acts had in fact acknowledged Georgia's title. Had they been aware of any U.S. claim to the territory, said the memorialists, they would not have entered into the purchase in the first place and thus embroiled themselves in a conflict with the government of their country.

Much of the memorial was accordingly taken up with restating the purchasers' title, premised on Georgia's having the "*undisputed possession* at the time of the sale." It dismissed the novel interpretation of the Proclamation of 1763 as having placed the western lands in possession of the British Crown, which passed them to the United

States in the 1783 treaty. This "new and forced construction," the memorialists protested, ran directly counter to the postwar cessions, which proceeded on the clear understanding that the western lands belonged to individual states. The memorial also disputed the "much more limited claim" that the United States acquired the southern third of the Mississippi territory based on the enlargement of the West Florida boundary. Even admitting a U.S. claim to this tract, the memorial appealed to the established principles of equity that the claimants under Georgia, having purchased on the faith of U.S. recognition of Georgia's title, should be "quieted," that is, their title should be freed of interfering claims by the United States.

As of 1798 the N.E.M. Land Co. had not abandoned plans to colonize the Mississippi territory, acting on the belief that the company's "private interest" was compatible with the nation's interest in "strengthening one of the weakest and most exposed frontiers of the Union." The company, the memorial stated, had hoped for the cooperation and support of the U.S. government in this "salutary" endeavor and expressed dismay at the actions of Governor Sargent in rebuffing the company's agents, who since the governor's proclamation of October 4 had "ceased to act" in the territory. This prohibition against surveys and settlement in the territory was "more fatal" to the claimants "than any act of the State of Georgia," the memorial complained, because it "completely deprived" them of exercising their property rights. Many faced impending financial ruin because holders of their notes were exacting payment and obtaining law judgments based on "a conviction that the *title* and *right of possession* is in the claimants." The memorial concluded with a plea to the president "to interpose his executive authority" to override the territorial governor's ban on settlement and appoint commissioners to decide "definitively" the title question between the United States and the claimants under Georgia.

This memorial eventually came before the U.S. commissioners, who by a supplemental act of May 1800 were empowered not only to negotiate with Georgia for a cession but also to inquire into private claims of individuals and to receive compromise proposals from such claimants. By then the New England claimants had reluctantly concluded that the federal government would not allow private companies to undertake the surveying, selling, and settlement of the Mississippi territory. The danger was too great of provoking hostilities with the Indian tribes who occupied the country. They accordingly focused their efforts on obtaining the best terms they could in compromising with the government. They sent agents to the seat of government and expressed their readiness to compromise. The U.S. commissioners, however, would not consider private claims until they reached a cession agreement with Georgia.

As consideration for ceding its lands west of the Chattahoochee, Georgia sought payment of $1.5 million and—perhaps more important than monetary compensation—a promise that the federal government would extinguish in a timely manner all Indian claims within the state's remaining limits. The state also expected the United States to honor and give full effect to its 1796 act rescinding the Yazoo sale—which entailed not recognizing any claims derived from the "usurped" 1795 act. During the remainder of the Adams administration, negotiations between the two governments moved slowly and from Georgia's standpoint not satisfactorily. Negotiations commenced anew under the administration of President Jefferson, who in January 1802 nominated Secretary of State James Madison, Secretary of the Treasury Albert Gallatin, and Attorney General Levi Lincoln as U.S. commissioners.

These commissioners and their Georgia counterparts—James Jackson, Abraham Baldwin, and John Milledge (all members of the state's congressional delegation)—were able to reach agreement in a few months. By "articles of agreement and cession" signed on April 24, 1802, the United States agreed to pay Georgia $1.25 million for the state's cession of its western lands. It further agreed "as early as the same can be peaceably obtained" to extinguish Indian titles to lands within the remaining limits of the state—a promise that would have fateful consequences for the Creek and Cherokee tribes who lived there. With respect to individual claims, the pact provided that persons who before October 27, 1795—the date of the treaty with Spain—were actual settlers should be confirmed in all grants under the governments of Great Britain and Spain. Claims under Georgia's act of 1785—the so-called Bourbon act—were also recognized. Georgia had always accepted the validity of these private claims.

Except by allusion, the compact said nothing about claims under Georgia's act of January 1795. It stipulated that the United States might within one year set aside up to 5 million acres of the ceded lands to satisfy or compensate claims not previously recognized. If Congress did not pass an act for this purpose within one year, then the United States could not thereafter compensate such claims. The Georgia commissioners would have preferred and no doubt tried to get an explicit rejection of claims under the "usurped" act. In reluctantly acceding to this provision, they perhaps reasoned that the short time limit would discourage Yazoo purchasers from applying to the U.S. government and that in any case Congress with a comfortable Republican majority was not likely in the next year to pass an act. Perhaps, too, the Georgians concluded that this clause was principally intended to embrace other less objectionable classes of claims, including holders of British grants who were not resident in the territory on October 27, 1795, those claiming under incomplete British and Spanish grants, and settlers without any evidence of title.

Following Georgia's ratification of the compact of 1802, the U.S. commissioners proceeded to hear applications from private claimants as provided in the supplemental act of 1800. Under this act the commissioners were authorized to make a full statement of the claims and compromise propositions together with their recommendations and present it to Congress for a final decision. The New England claimants interpreted this act and the 1802 compact with Georgia in the most favorable light and acted promptly to present their case. In June 1802 agents representing "a large proportion of the purchasers in New-England" inserted a notice in a Boston newspaper urging interested persons to "deposit immediately" with their clerk all deeds and other papers necessary to establish their titles. When Congress convened in December 1802, the agents along with a few individual claimants went to Washington to meet with the U.S. commissioners. There the New Englanders, nearly all of whom claimed under the Georgia Company or the Georgia Mississippi Company, joined with purchasers under the Tennessee Company and the Upper Mississippi Company in a proposal submitted to the commissioners on January 19, 1803. Among the thirteen agents and individuals who subscribed to this proposition was John Peck, "for myself as represented in my claim."

The Yazoo claimants clearly expected that the 5 million acres reserved under the Georgia cession of 1802 would go toward compensating them. They agreed to release their claims provided that Congress during the present session made an appropriation of the 5 million acres at not less than $2 per acre. Estimating the proceeds of the sale "at the *minimum* sum" of $10 million, they proposed apportioning all but a small fraction of this sum to compensating those claiming under the four purchasing companies, with $8 million going to holders under the Georgia Company and the Georgia Mississippi Company. In essence, they asked compensation at the rate of 25 cents per acre for the nominal quantity of lands they claimed.

A month later, on February 16, 1803, the commissioners presented their report to Congress, a seminal document with voluminous attachments (including full texts of Georgia's acts of 1795 and 1796) that was frequently cited and quoted by both sides in the Yazoo debate during the next decade. Opponents of compensation for claimants under Georgia's 1795 act seized upon the commissioners' statement that they felt "no hesitation in declaring it as their opinion, that, under all the circumstances which may affect the case, as they have come within their knowledge, and as herein stated, the title of the claimants cannot be supported." For supporters of accommodation, the very next sentence was the commissioners' key conclusion: "But they, nevertheless, believe that the interest of the United States, the tranquility of those who may hereafter inhabit that territory, and various equitable considerations which may be urged in favor of most of the present claimants, render it expedient to enter into a compromise on reasonable terms." These two sentences—seemingly inconsistent if not contradictory—neatly encapsulated the report's delicate balancing act, acknowledging on the one hand the obligation to adhere to the terms of the compact with Georgia while on the other recognizing the responsibility of the United States to provide some measure of restitution to a numerous class of purchasers who relied on the faith of a legislative act as giving a good title.

To the New England claimants the commissioners' report was a keen disappointment, notwithstanding its endorsement of a compromise. They saw it as decidedly tilted in favor of Georgia's view of the Yazoo sale as expressed in the rescinding act and accompanying affidavits and testimony alleging corruption. The commissioners gave no consideration to arguments upholding the title or opposing the rescinding act. Of the latter, they said only that they did not pretend "to affirm that the Legislature of the state of Georgia was competent" to revoke the sale. Although asserting that the claimants' title "cannot be supported," the commissioners nevertheless implicitly conceded its legal validity. The purpose of compromising with the claimants was to ensure that the United States would have a free and clear title to the Mississippi territory and give "tranquility" to potential purchasers of U.S. patents to those lands. Without an accommodation, settlement of the territory would be impeded by lawsuits challenging the U.S. title.

In slighting their title while at the same time seeming to acknowledge its legal force, the commissioners' report further disappointed the New England claimants with its proposed compromise. Rejecting the New Englanders' proposal as "inadmissible," the commissioners gave them the option of taking lands from the allotment of 5 million acres or of receiving interest-bearing certificates to the amount of $2.5 million or of $5 million without interest, to be paid out of the proceeds of the sale of the 5 million acres. These sums were to be apportioned among the four purchasing companies according to the amount of their contributions to the total purchase price paid for the Yazoo lands. This was considerably less than the $8 million they were seeking as purchasers under the Georgia Company and the Georgia Mississippi Company. The commissioners acknowledged that their proposal did "not give a full indemnity to every claimant" but believed that it provided "in the aggregate" about what they had paid for their lands. The New Englanders complained that this fell "far short of an average indemnity" when taking into account the lapse of time since paying the purchase money and the "great expenses" they had incurred in the meantime.

Soon after receiving the commissioners' report, Congress took up a bill "for settling sundry claims to public lands of the United States, south of the State of Tennessee," which embodied the compromise proposed for settling with the claimants under the Georgia act of 1795. A Georgia member, however, succeeded in drastically altering the bill, striking much of it out, including all references to the four purchasing companies. A new section was added directing the commissioners to receive proposals from the claimants and make a report at the next session of Congress. The act as adopted on March 2, 1803, stripped the Yazoo claims of any separate identity, placing them in a subordinate category of claims not otherwise recognized or provided for and "derived from any act or pretended act of the State of Georgia, which Congress may hereafter think fit to provide for." Such claims if approved were to be satisfied by the "residue" of the 5 million acres after satisfying other claims.

The act of March 1803 in effect postponed consideration of the Yazoo claims to the next session and in the meantime allowed the claimants to lay before the commissioners their proposals for compromise and settlement. The New England purchasers were inclined to put the most favorable construction on this act as signifying Congress's willingness to provide compensation for their Yazoo investments. They may have been pleased that Congress did not enact the commissioners' compromise into law, for now they had an opportunity to obtain better terms. Believing earnestly in the justice of their cause, they remained optimistic about the prospects for a prompt and satisfactory settlement.

CHAPTER FOUR

Fletcher Sues Peck; Congress
Debates Yazoo

The case of *Fletcher v. Peck* commenced with a writ dated May 18, 1803, commanding John Peck of Newton, Massachusetts, to appear at the ensuing June term of the U.S. circuit court at Boston to answer a plea of "covenant broken" brought by Robert Fletcher of Amherst, New Hampshire. The decision to go to court at this time between these two parties resulted from a carefully worked out plan by New England purchasers of Mississippi lands holding titles under the Georgia sale act of January 1795. The largest group of these purchasers was the N.E.M. Land Co., which had acquired the Georgia Mississippi Company's grant in 1796. Other groups and individuals held their titles under the Georgia Company grant. Peck was a Yazoo purchaser in his own right under the Georgia Company and also as a member of the N.E.M. Land Co., for which he had served as a director since 1797. The case for his title was the same as that of all the New England purchasers.

Lawyers for the claimants no doubt considered various ways in which their clients might pursue their rights at law. But there were few options, and virtually none that would put the claimants in actual possession of their lands. While Georgia still retained its western lands, a suit against that state in its courts was precluded by the 1796 rescinding act. In 1798 redress in the federal court was foreclosed by the Eleventh Amendment, which prohibited the extension of federal judicial power to suits against states brought by citizens of another state. Just such a case, *Moultrie v. Georgia*, had been brought by the South Carolina Yazoo Company in a dispute over payments under Georgia's 1789 Yazoo sale. It was discontinued after the amendment was adopted.

In 1802 Georgia ceded its Mississippi lands to the United States.

American citizens did not have recourse to the English remedy by "petition of right" to the Court of Chancery, whereby lands in the Crown's possession could be restored to subjects. New England claimants could have contested their titles against that of the United States by suing holders of U.S. patents for Mississippi lands. Such suits would be brought in the territorial court of Mississippi as actions of "ejectment," the principal common law means of trying title to land. The prohibitive obstacle in 1803 to this legal remedy was that there was no one to sue. The first land office in the Mississippi Territory did not open until 1805, and the earliest land grants were to citizens holding originally under patents from France, Great Britain, and Spain. In 1807 Congress passed an act preventing those whose claims had not been recognized or confirmed by the United States (that is, the New England claimants) from entering upon lands ceded to the United States. As they complained in a memorial of 1804, the claimants could recover possession "only lot by lot as the government might see fit to dispose of them." The result would be "a multiplicity of law suits for time immemorial, the expenses and delay of which would probably be more ruinous to them than the loss of their property in the first instance."

With no possibility of trying their claims at law in the territorial court of Mississippi, the claimants' lawyers were compelled to seek other means of obtaining a judicial vindication of the Yazoo title, eventually settling upon the plan of a lawsuit in the federal court between two residents of New England. From the outset the sole purpose for bringing the case was to obtain the Supreme Court's opinion on the merits of that title. It was understood that a favorable decision would not put the claimants in actual possession of their Mississippi lands but could serve as an authoritative influence upon Congress to enact legislation compensating the claimants as provided by the act of March 1803. *Fletcher v. Peck* was not an alternative or independent action for redress but part of a broader campaign by the New England claimants to secure an indemnity on favorable terms from Congress.

Even as *Fletcher* was proceeding in the U.S. circuit court in Boston, the New England claimants repeatedly requested Congress to pass an act referring the title question directly to the Supreme Court for "decision and final determination." In the unlikely event that Congress enacted such legislation, the Court might refuse to act on the ground that it was being asked to give an advisory opinion. In 1793 Chief Justice John Jay refused President Washington's request for answers to a detailed list of questions arising from the administration's neutrality policy. He cited the separation of powers and the fact that Supreme Court justices were "Judges of a Court in the last Resort" as arguing strongly "against the Propriety" of deciding such questions "extrajudicially." Although early national history affords numerous instances of individual justices giving formal and informal advice, the Supreme Court as an institution has adhered to this 1793 precedent by interpreting Article III of the Constitution as restricting it to deciding "cases" or "controversies" and prohibiting it from issuing advisory opinions.

In 1803 it was not settled what the Supreme Court would do when confronted with a case that was presented in all the forms of a regular lawsuit but whose real purpose was not to award or deny relief to a party but to obtain what in effect was an advisory opinion by the Court on an important legal question. In the long history of the common law, resourceful lawyers had learned how to make up cases to achieve desired legal results and courts had readily cooperated. The records and reports of cases were full of fictitious parties and feigned issues or pleadings. Perhaps the most famous legal fictions of the common law occurred in the action of ejectment, in which imaginary parties with colorful names such as "Plunderer" and "Goodtitle" sued on the basis of a fabricated lease. Courts of equity frequently directed some contested factual matter to be tried by a jury, for which purpose a feigned action was brought by a pretended plaintiff against the defendant. Of course these legal fictions were mainly used as shortcuts through what otherwise could be a daunting procedural maze that consumed much time and expense. They expedited the legal process, enabling litigants to evade requirements that seemed archaic or arbitrary.

As practitioners of the common law, American lawyers were familiar with the use of legal fictions and feigned cases. They proved adept at applying this knowledge to the novel problems arising in a legal system whose organization and jurisdiction were creatures of the Constitution and statutes. For instance, they quickly recognized the expediency of getting a definitive ruling on contested legal questions from the highest court in the land. One such case was *Hylton v. United States* (1796), which tested the constitutionality of a tax on carriages. Daniel Hylton of Richmond owned one carriage, on which the tax and penalty for not paying amounted to $16, far below the $2,000 minimum for an appeal to the Supreme Court. Counsel on both sides devised a strategy to circumvent this statutory jurisdictional requirement. Because he protested the tax and wanted a decision on its constitutionality, Hylton agreed to the fiction that he owned 125 "chariots" on which he had not paid tax. The amount in dispute in his case was now $2,000. The Court upheld the constitutionality of the carriage tax, but it had been stipulated at trial that if Hylton lost he would have to pay only $16.

In April 1803 (a month before *Fletcher* was filed in Boston), *Coxe v. Pennington* was brought in the U.S. Circuit Court for Pennsylvania. The case on the record was stated to be "a feigned action" concerning a duty on sugar imposed by a 1794 revenue law. The question for the court was whether the duty on sugar refined before the expiration of the law (which had been repealed in 1802) but not yet sent out was due and payable to the United States. Adopting a stratagem frequently used in common law practice, the U.S. commissioner of the revenue and a sugar refiner brought a case on a fictional wager of $2,500 that the United States was entitled to the duty. The wager amount of course met the jurisdictional amount for an appeal to the Supreme Court. The lawyers also made sure that the parties were citizens of different states in order to meet the constitutional and statutory requirement for federal jurisdiction. The revenue commissioner, a resident of Philadelphia, accordingly sued a New York sugar refiner. The circuit court upheld the duty, but in *Pennington v. Coxe* (1804) Chief Justice Marshall for the Supreme Court overruled the lower court, holding that the United States could not collect the duty on refined sugar that had not been sent out.

Although different from *Hylton* and *Pennington* in its facts and circumstances, *Fletcher v. Peck* was also an arranged case between friendly parties, brought originally in the U.S. circuit court for the purpose of an appeal to the Supreme Court for ultimate decision.

The Court raised no objections to hearing and deciding the earlier cases despite the artifice employed to obtain jurisdiction. By 1809, however, when the Court first heard *Fletcher*, some justices expressed reservations about deciding a case so obviously made up for getting the Court's opinion. These doubts gave credence to charges voiced at the time and reiterated by modern commentators that *Fletcher* was a sham case with parties having no genuine adversarial interests and therefore presenting no real legal dispute for judicial resolution.

To some degree, modern criticism of *Fletcher* as "a mere feigned case" reflects the hardening of the Court's stance against collusive suits that began in the mid-nineteenth century. Yet the lawyers who contrived the suit between Fletcher and Peck in 1803 could reasonably believe that such a case fell within the acceptable boundaries of legal practice and that in pursuing this means of vindicating their clients' rights they were doing their professional duty.

Although there was much art in the way they fabricated this dispute, they did not attempt to disguise what they were doing. No one acquainted with the case, least of all the Supreme Court justices, could have mistaken *Fletcher* for anything but a made-up suit to get the Supreme Court's advisory opinion on the validity of the titles of New England purchasers of Mississippi lands. Everything about the case—the venue, the parties, the type of action, and the pleadings—bespoke this end. The lawyers left nothing to chance, even seemingly minor details such as who would be plaintiff and who defendant.

The collusive nature of the case was apparent at the outset in the writ of attachment. It was delivered to Peck on May 18, 1803, just four days after he sold 15,000 acres of his Yazoo lands to Fletcher for $3,000. Fletcher cooperated in this scenario even though it made him appear to have questionable judgment as a dealer in land. If he bought only to sue immediately to recover the money paid, why did he purchase in the first place? The writ commanded the U.S. marshal to attach Peck's property to the value of $2,000, making the amount in controversy equal to that needed for an appeal to the Supreme Court. This figure was later corrected to $3,000 to conform to the sum Fletcher was stated to have paid Peck. On the return the marshal noted that he had "attached a Button the Property of John Peck" on delivering the writ.

Fletcher brought his suit in the U.S. circuit court at Boston in accordance with the federal court system established by the Judiciary Act of 1789. The circuit courts were not separate courts but were composed of a Supreme Court justice and the U.S. district judge of the district where the court was held. They had original jurisdiction to try suits at common law or in equity and to try crimes cognizable under federal law. The U.S. Circuit Court for Massachusetts, sitting in Boston at the center of the Yazoo speculation, was part of the first circuit (there were then six circuits), which also included Rhode Island and New Hampshire. The Supreme Court justice who rode the first circuit was William Cushing, one of President Washington's original appointees to the Court in 1789. When Fletcher's suit began, Cushing was over seventy, nearing the end of his long career as a state and federal judge. His colleague in Boston was U.S. district court judge John Davis, who was forty when President Adams appointed him in 1801 and who would hold this office for the next forty years. The judges, no doubt by prearrangement, cooperated in the plan to get the case to the Supreme Court as expeditiously as possible. Other than render a pro forma judgment on written pleadings and allow a writ of error for an appeal, Cushing and Davis had nothing to do in *Fletcher v. Peck*. They did not preside at a trial, hear arguments, or deliver an opinion.

The choice of litigants from New Hampshire and Massachusetts accorded with Article III of the Constitution, which extended federal judicial power to cases between citizens of different states, and the 1789 Judiciary Act, which gave the circuit courts original cognizance of civil suits between a citizen of a state where the suit was brought and a citizen of another state. The "diversity" of jurisdiction requirement apparently explains why Peck rather than the N.E.M. Land Co. was the defendant of record. The company's shareholders, though concentrated in Massachusetts, resided throughout New England, including New Hampshire. If the company was a party, the case might not meet the diversity test; indeed, in 1806 the Supreme Court held that no party on one side could be a citizen of the same state as a party on the other side. Designating an individual citizen of Massachusetts as the defendant avoided a potential problem.

That Peck was defendant rather than plaintiff, even though he was the party seeking to validate the Yazoo title, was also indicative of a calculated legal strategy. The case arose from a deed of sale whereby Peck sold Fletcher 15,000 acres of Yazoo land for $3,000. Fletcher ostensibly sued to recover the money he paid Peck on the ground that the title was defective. However, the case could have been framed so that Peck was plaintiff and Fletcher defendant. If by mutual agreement Fletcher had withheld the purchase money, Peck could have sued for recovery. Presumably the pleadings in such a case would get all the title issues on the record in much the same way as in the case that actually occurred. Yet if Peck sued Fletcher and won in the circuit court there would be no ground for an appeal to the Supreme Court, defeating the whole purpose for bringing the case. Alternatively, the parties and the judges might agree to have judgment rendered against Peck so he could take an appeal. Still, even as a mere a matter of form, a judgment against Peck and the Yazoo title in a federal court would not look good. The more prudent course then was for Fletcher to sue Peck.

How Robert Fletcher was enlisted in this cause is a matter of conjecture. He and Peck might have crossed paths while pursuing their various business enterprises. Or perhaps a lawyer connected with the Yazoo claimants suggested Fletcher as a suitable party to oppose Peck in the federal court. Born in 1762, Fletcher at the time the case began was a real estate broker who sold farm properties in southern New Hampshire and in neighboring Massachusetts as well. With a large family to support, he had difficulty achieving prosperity. Fletcher was forced to sell his Amherst homestead in 1806, evidently to satisfy creditors. The same year he moved to Boston, setting up as a broker and building a house on Beacon Street. He sold it soon afterward, however, evidently again as the result of business failure. An investment in Canadian timberland and establishment of a lumber manufactory also proved unfortunate. Unlike Peck, who was closely involved in the case, Fletcher seems never to have been more than a passive spectator. He ended his life by shooting himself in Montreal in October 1809, five months before the Supreme Court's decision of his case.

Fletcher v. Peck was truly a lawyer's case, replete with the trappings of professional art: exquisitely crafted pleadings, demurrers, and a special verdict that fill thirty-eight closely printed pages. The records of the U.S. circuit court identify five lawyers who represented the plaintiff and defendant. Joseph Hall and Rufus G. Amory acted on Fletcher's behalf. William Sullivan, Perez Morton, and Samuel Dexter served as Peck's counsel. All five were Harvard graduates and prominent practitioners in Boston. Together, these gentlemen of the bar framed the pleadings and special verdict that gave legal form to the contrived dispute between these two parties.

Amory was Fletcher's principal lawyer and attorney of record from the clerk's first entry of the case in June 1803 through final judgment in October 1807. He had been counsel for William Payne in a 1797 case arising from a large purchase of Yazoo lands. In early 1803 he himself bought 160,000 acres and held a part interest in nearly half a million acres as security for Andrew Craigie, a heavy speculator in Yazoo lands. Shortly after representing Fletcher in the U.S. circuit court, Amory purchased his client's Beacon Street house.

William Sullivan was well versed in the affairs of Yazoo claimants before joining Peck's legal team. In 1802 he was clerk to the agents of the N.E.M. Land Co. and of other companies seeking compensation from the U.S. government. Unlike his father, James Sullivan, who was also a lawyer and later Republican governor of Massachusetts, William Sullivan was Federalist in his politics. Both father (80,000 acres) and son (20,000 acres) were Yazoo claimants and were subsequently reimbursed under the act for compensating those claims. While William Sullivan was engaged for Peck in the U.S. circuit court, the elder Sullivan in both his private and official capacities lobbied hard for the Yazoo interests in Congress.

Perez Morton enjoyed a formidable reputation as an orator and advocate who survived personal scandal and made a career in state politics. A leader of the Republican Party in his state, he was twice speaker of the Massachusetts House of Representatives and served two decades as attorney general. Morton actively pursued material wealth through various business enterprises, perhaps most notably the N.E.M. Land Co., for which he served many years as agent and chief lobbyist in Washington. As of January 1, 1802, he held company scrip for 100,000 acres of Mississippi lands in his own name and scrip for nearly 300,000 acres in the names of four other investors, including John Peck. Beginning as early as 1802, Morton was a perennial visitor to the national capital to promote the interests of the N.E.M. Land Co. He was the author of the company's memorial, first presented to Congress in 1804, and inscribed a copy he gave to retired president John Adams.

Sullivan was Peck's attorney of record from 1803 to 1806. When the case was renewed in 1807, Samuel Dexter was listed for the defendant. Dexter served a term in the U.S. House of Representatives and briefly in the Senate before joining President Adams's cabinet, first as secretary of war, then as secretary of the treasury. He resumed law practice after returning to Boston in 1805. Like Morton, his business associate and relation by marriage, Dexter eagerly embraced the pursuit of wealth and the speculative spirit in Georgia lands that swept through New England in the 1790s. He was one of the investors who formed the N.E.M. Land Co. and purchased the Georgia Mississippi Company's tract early in 1796. From that time until his death twenty years later Dexter acted as agent for the company and other purchasers of Yazoo lands.

Fletcher filed his legal complaint, or "declaration," at the June 1803 term. It set forth a case of "covenant broken," the appropriate common law action to recover damages for breach of a sealed "covenant," a written contract or agreement between two individuals. The covenant in this case was the deed of sale of May 1803 by which Peck conveyed 15,000 acres to Fletcher. Fletcher asked for "damages" of $3,000, that is, he sought the return of the money he had paid for the land. Boiled down to its essence, his complaint charged that Peck's deed was defective, that it did not provide a good title as promised by the seller. The complaint alleged four "breaches" in the deed of sale: (1) that Georgia had no power to sell the land in question; (2) that the original conveyance under the act of 1795 was illegal because of the bribery of the assemblymen; (3) that Peck's title was constitutionally and legally impaired by the rescinding law of 1796; (4) that at the time of the 1795 act, the United States, not Georgia, had "fee-simple" possession—that is, absolute or unconditional ownership—of the lands in question. Each count repeated at great length the description of the tract, the chain of title, and the various covenants before assigning the specific breach. The third count included the entire text of the 1796 rescinding law.

After the filing of the declaration at the June 1803 term, the case was continued "by consent" from term to term during the next three years. This lull evidently reflected a decision by the New England claimants to suspend proceedings in the case while waiting to see what Congress would do. In 1803 they were optimistic that Congress would act expeditiously to provide compensation. Frustration with Congress's inaction apparently prompted the resumption of *Fletcher v. Peck* at the October 1806 term of the U.S. circuit court. Peck at this term submitted his responses or "pleas" to Fletcher's declaration. Just as the declaration swelled to great length in reproducing verbatim the various deeds and legislative acts pertinent to proving the counts for breaking the covenant, so Peck's pleas were equally voluminous in inserting texts of official acts—including the Georgia constitution of 1789 and the act of 1795 conveying the Yazoo lands—that went to disprove those counts.

The lawyers took special care to frame Fletcher's declaration and Peck's pleas so that they raised only issues of law for decision by the court, not issues of fact to be decided by a jury. The first three counts and pleas, for example, made use of a pleading device called a "demurrer," by which Fletcher admitted the truth of the facts stated in Peck's pleas but denied that these facts were sufficient in law to give judgment to Peck. Following the agreed-upon script, Peck then formally "joined in demurrer," affirming that his plea was sufficient to preclude Fletcher from having judgment on his counts. The whole point of the demurrer and joinder was to turn the factual statements in the counts and pleas into issues of law to be decided by the court.

To Fletcher's fourth count—that the United States, not Georgia, owned the lands at the time of the sale—Peck made a direct denial. This denial raised an issue of fact to be referred to a jury. No jury actually deliberated on this point, however. Instead, the lawyers prepared a document known as a "special verdict," which stated all the facts necessary to decide the case but left to the court the application of the law to those facts. It was the usual means by which juries in complicated cases relinquished their law-finding power to the court. In form, a special verdict appeared to come from the jury, but the statement of facts was actually drawn up by counsel under the court's supervision. The special verdict on the fourth count, also filed at the

October 1806 term along with Peck's pleas, took up nearly as much space in the record as did the declaration and pleas together. It contained a numbing recital of the various charters, treaties, and other acts relating to the boundaries of Georgia, ending with the jury's admission that on the question of Georgia's ownership of the Yazoo lands they were "ignorant and pray the advisement of the Court thereon."

At the same term the whole case came before Judge Cushing, who sitting alone gave judgment for Peck. Fletcher's lawyer then applied for a writ of error, which Cushing duly approved and issued on November 11, 1806. No appeal to the Supreme Court was prosecuted under this writ, however, apparently because the New England claimants still confidently expected to make their case to Congress without the Supreme Court's aid. Thus far that body had been unable to act on the matter of the Yazoo lands because of implacable opposition to compromise led by Representative John Randolph of Virginia.

As matters stood in March 1803 public law provided for setting aside 5 million acres to satisfy land claims in the Mississippi Territory. It remained for Congress to make specific provision for claimants under the Georgia act of 1795. Late in 1803 Randolph launched his campaign to exclude these claimants, initiating a protracted battle for the soul of the Republican Party. No political issue of the Early Republic matched Yazoo in the intensity of the passions it aroused and in the vitriolic attacks employed by the antagonists, none with more biting sarcasm than Randolph himself. It was testament to his political infighting skills and sheer doggedness that he was able to delay for a decade resolution of the Yazoo question, even when a congressional majority seemed favorably disposed to a compromise settlement.

Elected to Congress in 1799, Randolph was a Virginia patrician, offspring of one of the state's first families. He was well educated and possessed a gift for oratory in an age that prized skill in oral communication and debate. He rose to political prominence despite physical peculiarities that made him an object of scorn and ridicule. Apparently because of a chromosome imbalance, Randolph's physical development was arrested, leaving him permanently with childlike features—a high-pitched voice, lack of facial hair, and presumed sexual incapacity. Contemporaries were struck by his appearance, which a hostile Federalist congressman described as "contemptible," having the beardless face and voice of a "boy of 10 years old." Another Federalist critic described Randolph as "a pale, meager, ghostly man," while acknowledging that he had "more popular and effective talents than any other member of the party." In time he would achieve renown as the eccentric Randolph "of Roanoke," resolutely attached to "Old Republican" values of states' rights and agrarianism, the conservative defender of the patriarchal, slave-owning plantation society of the South.

Although affecting the manners of an English aristocrat, Randolph embraced an idealistic republicanism that rejected hierarchy and privilege and found expression in the Jeffersonian Republican Party. At age thirty in 1803 Randolph was at the zenith of his political power, having emerged as an effective spokesman for the Jefferson administration to become de facto leader of the House Republican majority. Simultaneous with his Yazoo crusade he was floor manager of the impeachment proceedings against Supreme Court Justice Samuel Chase. His failure to convict Chase and his unyielding opposition to a Yazoo compromise undermined his status as a party leader, though he remained an influential figure with powerful allies during the remainder of Jefferson's presidency. Until the middle of Jefferson's first term, Randolph was able to harmonize his republican zeal with loyalty to administration policies, but thereafter he was increasingly troubled by the challenge of being a faithful Republican while staying true to his republican principles.

For Randolph and like-minded Republicans, unbending resistance to the claims of the Yazoo purchasers was a test of true republicanism. Anti-Yazooism had been thoroughly implanted in Randolph's breast during a visit to Georgia in 1796. He fully embraced the outrage that animated James Jackson and his fellow Georgia legislators to pass the rescinding act. He believed the sovereign people of Georgia had every right to pronounce the sale act of 1795 to be nonexistent, to annihilate all its traces, and thereby restore the state's republican well-being. In this light, to compromise with the claimants, to allow even the smallest claim under the despised sale, was to insult a state's honor, to bring back to life what a state had solemnly declared not to exist. Randolph and his Republican followers rejected with alarm and contempt the argument that compromise was "expedient." In truth, they warned, an indemnity act would reward speculation and corruption, the very antithesis of republican virtue. It would be the fatal opening for corruption to penetrate Congress and the administration, sinking them to the level of the Federalists, who a generation earlier had sanctioned the "public plunder" of speculation in government securities.

Disposition of the Yazoo claims was high on the agenda of the first session of the Eighth Congress, which convened in October 1803. By mid-February 1804 the House was considering a bill authorizing U.S. commissioners Madison, Gallatin, and Lincoln to receive compromise proposals from claimants and "to compound and settle" them in a manner "advantageous to the interests of the United States." The bill implicitly endorsed the idea that Yazoo claimants could seek compensation from the federal government out of the 5 million acres stipulated in the 1802 cession and set aside in the March 1803 act. Randolph responded with a series of declaratory resolves restating the political and constitutional theory embodied in the 1796 rescinding act and concluding that no part of the 5 million acres should be appropriated to settle Yazoo claims.

The bill and resolutions came up for consideration in March, a few weeks before the close of the first session. Randolph's early opposition appeared to be unavailing, however, as the House seemed poised to act favorably on a compensation bill. As politically astute as he was adamant, Randolph enlisted support from fellow Republicans who were equally passionate in their hostility to Yazoo. These allies included Speaker Nathaniel Macon of North Carolina, Caesar A. Rodney of Delaware, and Thomas M. Randolph of Virginia, son-in-law of President Jefferson. Together, these Republicans resisted efforts by other party members to report the bill and adjourn without taking up Randolph's resolutions. Republicans who supported compromise with the Yazoo claimants included Samuel L. Mitchill of New York, William Eustis of Massachusetts, John Smilie of Pennsylvania, Matthew Lyon of Kentucky, formerly of Vermont, and James Elliot of Vermont. In the end, the House postponed consideration of both the bill and the resolutions until the next session—a tactical victory for Randolph and the anti-Yazoo Republicans.

This brief debate, almost exclusively among Republicans, exposed a fault line in the party ranks that generally corresponded with a geographical line dividing southern and northern members. The split was markedly acrimonious because it sprang from clashing dispositions and views of what constituted Republicanism. On the one side were Randolph and his followers, dogmatic in their insistence that they were the keepers of the true party faith. On the other side were moderates, less rigid in accommodating principle to expediency and resentful of insinuations that they were party apostates for supporting compromise. Randolph gave classic expression to the former cast of mind in declaring he would exert all his faculties of mind and body "in refuting so nefarious a project." He could not comprehend "expediency" that countenances "fraud" or "policy" that fosters "corruption." He could only act as his "conscience and principles impelled" him. The opposing viewpoint was well represented by Eustis, who privately agreed that Yazoo reeked of fraud and corruption but nevertheless supported the compromise "as founded in justice and in sound policy." He spoke for many who wanted to settle this distasteful business quickly and quietly, "to close this offensive wound; to bury it in eternal oblivion." Other Republicans, such as Lyon, went so far as to express the belief that the Yazoo land titles were good despite the allegations of bribery and that compromise would be a great boon for the United States. The fiery Irish-born Lyon, who had been jailed under the Sedition Act and had famously spat on a Federalist congressman in 1798, spoke as a "democrat" who was "free to declare" that Randolph's republican creed was not his own.

At the second session of the Eighth Congress, which convened in November 1804, the Yazoo debate entered a more acrimonious phase. Early in the session Congress received a memorial from Perez Morton and Gideon Granger, the agents of the N.E.M. Land Co. The company had recently hired Granger, U.S. postmaster general, with a view to having influential representation at the seat of government. The memorial set forth the company's efforts during the preceding six years to obtain compensation for its Yazoo investment and declared its readiness to negotiate a compromise of its claims.

The company preferred this mode of compensating its losses and "extinguishing" its claims as being consonant with the federal government's intentions as manifested in the various acts setting aside 5 million acres for this purpose. Indeed, the company relied on these acts as a "pledge of the *public faith and honor*" and "a certain resource of indemnity."

Accompanying the memorial was "A Vindication of the Rights of the New England Mississippi Land Company," a brief exceeding 100 printed pages, a copy of which was to be presented to each member of Congress. This expedient was adopted, the agents explained, because the Yazoo title had been called into question during the congressional debates and by the U.S. commissioners in their report recommending a compromise. The "Vindication" accordingly exhaustively reviewed and answered every argument raised against the title derived from the sale under the Georgia act of 1795. More than a strict legal defense of title suitable for presentation in a court of law, the "Vindication" was aimed at Congress, to reinforce that body's previously expressed disposition to compromise. If it could be shown that purchasers under the Georgia act of 1795 had a credible claim to the entire 35 million acres of Yazoo lands, then surely it was in the best interests of the United States to set aside 5 million to reimburse the New England claimants while removing the cloud over title to the remainder.

The memorial and its accompanying "Vindication" were principally an appeal to expediency, designed to persuade Congress that compromise was sound policy that would confer immeasurable public benefits by clearing the way for the sale and settlement of the Mississippi Territory. It was also an appeal to Congress to uphold "the *public faith and honor.*" By incurring the expense of printing copies for each member of Congress, the N.E.M. Land Co. was counting on the "Vindication" to have its intended effect. During the ensuing debate, friends of the Yazoo claimants and supporters of compromise drew liberally from its fund of arguments.

The memorial and a "representation" from Massachusetts citizens stating a claim to Yazoo lands were referred to the House's standing committee on claims, which henceforth had charge of all matters concerning the Yazoo claims. Although four of the seven members of the committee were Republicans, the chairman was Samuel Dana, a Connecticut Federalist. His report, submitted to Congress in January 1805, concluded with a resolution authorizing three commissioners "to receive propositions of compromise and settlement" from the various claimants of Mississippi lands. This resolution prompted an amendment from a Randolph ally that no part of the 5 million acres could be used to compensate claimants under the Georgia act of 1795. The resolution and proposed amendment set in motion a debate that continued five consecutive days in late January and early February.

Randolph opened the debate on January 29 by accusing an "inflexible majority" of pressing Congress to sanction "public plunder" without public scrutiny. Drawing attention to the N.E.M. Land Co. memorial, he derided the notion that the Yazoo investors were "innocent purchasers." Georgia's 1795 sale, an "act of stupendous villainy," was such a "matter of public notoriety," he insisted, that the purchasers could not claim to have had no notice of the fraud. He also scoffed at the memorial's "barefaced effrontery" in asserting that the Yazoo claimants were specifically included in the appropriation of the 5 million acres. Randolph then abruptly shifted from countering the memorial to a merciless attack on Granger, one of its authors: "His gigantic grasp embraces with one hand the shores of Lake Erie, and stretches with the other to the Bay of Mobile." He classed the postmaster general with speculators who "buy only to sell, and sell only to buy. The retail trade of fraud and imposture yields too small and slow a profit to gratify their cupidity. They buy and sell corruption in the gross, and a few millions, more or less, is hardly felt in the account." The Virginia Republican expressed "apprehension and alarm" that the N.E.M. Land Co. agent was the head of an executive department holding "many snug appointments and fat contracts." Was his "influence and patronage" now to be used to "extort" a compromise? To this party purist, compromise would sanction an "atrocious public robbery," a crime much more to be deplored than the "petty larcenies" of the preceding Federalist administration.

Randolph's intemperate speech provoked supporters of compromise to rise in response the next day, January 30. Elliot of Vermont spoke forcefully for those Republicans who believed a reasonable settlement with the Yazoo claimants was consistent not only with justice and sound policy but also with the principles and interests of their party. He invoked the now-familiar arguments that the state of Georgia possessed title to the Yazoo lands in 1795 and that the Georgia legislature was constitutionally vested with the power to sell the lands. He also contended that the legislature of 1796 could not constitutionally rescind an act of its predecessor that was in its nature a contract, though this was a question Congress was incompetent to decide. While endorsing the doctrine of judicial review, Elliot denied the judiciary's authority to void an act on the ground of corruption. The Vermont representative urged compromise principally on the equity of the Yazoo claims arising from the purchasers' "strong color of title." Without accepting the N.E.M. Land Co.'s contention that the reservation of 5 million acres in the cession of 1802 and act of 1803 particularly contemplated the Yazoo claims, he conceded that such claims were recognized by "strong implication." Elliot chastised Randolph's speech as "destitute of argument" and took particular offense at the insinuation that Republicans like him were "guilty of political apostasy" and outdoing the Federalists in plundering the public. He was "a republican—a democratic republican," who believed compromise was an "act of equity, good faith, and good policy."

On January 31, John G. Jackson, representing a western Virginia district, presented the most comprehensive statement of the case for settling with the Yazoo claimants. Because of his connection by marriage to Secretary of State Madison, Jackson plausibly spoke for the Jefferson administration. The president tried to distance himself from Yazoo and avoid its toxic fallout, which threatened not only to tarnish his reputation as a pure republican but also to split his party asunder. Distasteful as it was, Jefferson agreed with Madison that a settlement was necessary, and the two were undoubtedly embarrassed and frustrated by Randolph's obstinate refusal to allow it to go through quickly and quietly. In denouncing Granger and the Yazoo claimants, Randolph did not attack Jefferson directly. Publicly, he continued to revere the president, whose two sons-in-law in the House were staunch allies of Randolph, and absolved him of any taint of Yazoo. His real target was Madison, whom he regarded as the principal champion of compromise and the government officer and organizer of the campaign of "influence" designed to seduce members of Congress into approving an act of public iniquity.

Jackson's reply to Randolph aimed to persuade the House that settling with the claimants was not merely expedient but a moral obligation of the government to do justice and uphold the public faith. At the outset he denied Randolph's contention that President Washington's February 1795 message to Congress communicating a copy of Georgia's Yazoo sale act constituted notice of fraud, thus proving that the claimants were not innocent purchasers. Jackson read the message and related legislative proceedings to show that they evinced no knowledge of fraud but rather expressed fear that settlement of these lands would spark an Indian war. Jackson also disputed Randolph's accusation that the N.E.M. Land Co. memorial falsely asserted that Congress specifically intended the company's claims to be part of a compromise settlement. He contended (going beyond Elliot) that the public record—the cession of 1802, the commissioners' report, and the act of March 1803—made "explicit reference" to those claims.

In contrast to Randolph's lurid portrait of the claimants as rapacious speculators, Jackson depicted them as honest supplicants, even unfortunate victims, seeking a modest recompense from their government. Their willingness to accept a fraction of the acreage claimed under their title was not an admission of its fraudulent nature, insisted Jackson, but recognition that compromise was their only hope of recovering anything. He further pointed out that the claimants were precluded from asserting their legal title so long as the government refrained from issuing patents to these disputed lands. In any event, he added, a multitude of lawsuits would prove financially ruinous to the claimants and impede the government's policy of selling and settling the Mississippi lands. The Yazoo claimants' offer of compromise, Jackson urged, showed their willingness to cooperate with the government and "affords a great proof of their magnanimity and patriotism." Jackson conceded nothing to his opponents and took particular care to repel arguments that the claimants had notice, the issue on which their claim to be innocent purchasers hinged. But for him the case for compromise was compelling solely on the ground of policy, even as he made clear his belief that a settlement accorded with the dictates of justice.

Perhaps sensing that momentum for compromise was building after two more speakers followed Jackson in supporting the measure, Randolph put aside "extreme indisposition and excessive hoarseness" so he could have the last word on January 31. In his second major speech of this session on the Yazoo question, the Virginian remained as intransigent as ever while raising his level of invective. Believing with all his being that the Georgia sale of 1795 was a measure of the deepest iniquity, Randolph was impervious to appeals from any person or group linked to that wicked transaction. No arguments based on law, equity, or policy that in any degree sanctioned—or appeared to sanction—the original fraud could move him. Claims derived from a sinful bargain could not be innocent.

Randolph relentlessly challenged the notion of "innocent purchasers," including persons of wealth and prominence who were recruited to draw in other investors without having to pay a cent themselves. "These were the decoy-birds to bring the ducks and geese into the net of speculation," or, as he less charitably called them, "the vile panders of speculation." Warming to his theme, he portrayed Yazoo as a vast conspiracy of sellers and buyers, knowing partners in the crime of fraudulent speculation. The plan of selling Georgia's western territory did not originate there but was "hatched" by the "moneyed capitalists" in Philadelphia, New York, and perhaps Boston. Was there not a "strong probability" that those now appearing as purchasers from the original grantees under the 1795 act were "in fact partners, perhaps instigators and prime movers of a transaction in which their names do not appear?" As for secondary purchasers and small investors, they were unlucky "dupes," no different from "the losers in any other gambling or usurious transaction" and no more deserving of indemnification from the public.

In response to those who decried his earlier attack on Granger as a peddler of official influence and outright bribery in awarding mail contracts, Randolph denounced the postmaster general in the bitterest and most unforgiving language uttered in public debate. Relating a story in which Granger's intermediary allegedly offered a profitable mail contract to a member of the House, he accused that officer of maintaining "a jackal, fed, not (as you would suppose) upon the offal of contract, but with the fairest pieces in the shambles; and, at night, when honest men are in bed, does this obscene animal prowl through the streets of this vast and desolate city, seeking whom he may tamper with."

Randolph closed more in sorrow than in anger, bewailing the impending "death-blow" to republicanism from Yazoo, whose corruption had not only seduced his party's majority to abandon their principles but also extended its malignant hand to the executive department. He cast himself as the resolute upholder of republican virtue, who would "not connive at public robbery." He was proud to be in a minority that met the test of "rigorous principle" and resisted the "obnoxious measures" of an unyielding and dishonest majority. He even defended his intemperate language as proceeding from his "heart," adding that a "position in itself just, can lose no part of its truth from the manner in which it is uttered."

Randolph's attack on Granger brought forth a response from Representative Lyon that matched the Virginian's talent for merciless verbal abuse. As one of those members holding mail contracts, Lyon angrily disputed the charges of bribery as "fabricated" in Randolph's "disordered imagination." He portrayed his accuser as a haughty aristocrat who turned up his nose at "the very sight of my plebeian face." Randolph, he continued, was "nursed in the bosom of opulence," a wealthy and leisured heir to numerous slaves and lands, who possessed a superior book education but lacked worldly experience, knowledge of men and affairs. The Virginia planter's "insulated situation, unconversant with the world," made him suspicious of merchants and men of business, believing no one could "be honest or independent unless he has inherited lands and negroes." But Lyon's otherwise incisive rebuke of an adversary was undercut by a demeaning taunt: "I thank my Creator that he gave me the face of a man, not that of an ape or a monkey, and that he gave me the heart of a man also."

After Lyon's rancorous reply to Randolph, the remainder of the debate was largely anticlimax. At the end of the day on February 2, a vote was finally taken on Dana's resolution authorizing commissioners to settle the Yazoo claims. Although the resolution passed sixty-three to fifty-eight, as did a subsequent motion to refer the resolution to a committee to report a bill, Randolph was far from discouraged and remained defiant as ever: "In whatever shape the subject may be again brought before the House, it will be my duty, and that of my friends, to manifest the same firm spirit of resistance, and to suffer no opportunity to pass of defeating a measure so fraught with mischief." Dana presented a bill on February 5, which passed two readings and was referred to the committee of the whole for February 8. No action took place on the appointed day, however. By this time the committee was suspending much of its business to attend the trial of Justice Chase in the Senate. The bill did not come up for consideration during the remainder of the Eighth Congress, which adjourned on March 3.

This was the closest the House came to passing a bill to compensate the Yazoo claimants while John Randolph continued to sit as a member. When the Ninth Congress assembled in December 1805, anti-Yazoo Republicans in the House were adamant as ever and increasing in numbers. The friends of compromise on the other hand were less inclined to bring the subject up as producing division at a time when unity was needed to support the Jefferson administration's foreign policy. Negotiations with Spain over contested territory on the United States' southern border and measures to combat British aggression against American shipping on the high seas commanded Congress's primary attention.

Yazoo continued to simmer, however, as the N.E.M. Land Co. and other claimants under the Georgia title renewed their efforts to obtain compensation. In a change of tactics, they decided to approach the Senate first, apparently hoping that this smaller and more temperate chamber would pass a bill that the House would be forced to vote upon. Petitions from New England claimants were communicated to the Senate in January 1806 by Senator John Quincy Adams. He dutifully performed this office at the request of the petitioners' agent, feeling "very reluctant at being thus engaged in an affair which has already occasioned so many unpleasant altercations." He had no personal stake in the Yazoo speculation, though he would later represent John Peck in the Supreme Court.

The petitions provoked "violent invective" from James Jackson of

Georgia, who ten years earlier had led the campaign to revoke the Yazoo land sale. Until then Jackson, ailing with only two months to live, had not participated in the debate, which had taken place exclusively in the House. The Georgian could not have been more gratified that leadership of the anti-Yazoo forces in the lower chamber was in the capable hands of Randolph, who yielded nothing to Jackson in the ferocity of his opposition to the great Georgia land speculation as a mortal threat to republicanism. Before his death, Jackson delivered a final blow of his own on behalf of the cause in the form of a pamphlet, *Facts, in Reply to the Agents of the New England Land Company* (1805). Reprising arguments he had made as Sicilius and borrowing from Abraham Bishop's *Georgia Speculation Unveiled,* Jackson reaffirmed his conviction that the "usurped act" of 1795 was from its enactment "legally void, and a nullity in itself"; that all grants and purchases under that act were also void; and that "if any claim can be made by the New England Mississippi Land Company, it must be to the compassion, not the justice, of the Legislature of the Union."

Adams's motion to refer the petitions to a committee produced an evenly divided Senate but carried on Vice-President Clinton's casting vote. Adams was the only Federalist on the committee of five appointed to consider the petitions. This committee met regularly during the next month, hearing directly from the petitioners' agents, who indicated that the claimants would acquiesce to the compromise plan proposed by the U.S. commissioners in February 1803. The committee's deliberations eventually resulted in a bill drawn by Adams, though the Massachusetts senator had to contend with outright opposition from Chairman Abraham Baldwin of Georgia and the delaying tactics of other members who preferred that the Senate do nothing until the House acted.

Adams's bill as amended was approved by the committee on March 7. It provided that if claimants under the Georgia act of January 1795 lodged sufficient legal releases of their claims to the United States by January 1, 1807, then Congress would provide by law for their indemnification according to the principles proposed by the U.S. commissioners in February 1803. Chairman Baldwin presented the bill to the Senate on the same day, and it eventually passed to a third reading, "without debate, though not without difficulty," according to

Adams. When Baldwin spoke against the bill after the third reading on March 21, a fellow committee member pressed Adams to speak in support. In an ill humor after hearing the person who reported the committee's bill publicly oppose it, Adams replied "with too much warmth, that I cared nothing for the bill, and was not obliged to take its defence: it was not my bill, and its proper fathers must take charge of it."

When the bill came up again on March 28, a more composed Adams opened in support, joined by three Republicans and two other Federalists. The debate of three and half hours was "perfectly cool and temperate," said Adams. The Senate passed the bill by a vote of nineteen to eleven. The only New Englander and only Federalist (of seven in the Senate) to vote nay was William Plumer of New Hampshire. Sounding like an anti-Yazoo Republican (he would in fact soon switch his allegiance to the Republicans), Plumer denounced the Georgia land sale as "conceived in iniquity—bro't forth & supported in every stage of it in fraud of the deepest dye." Thirteen Republicans voted for the compromise bill, nine of whom represented northern and middle states.

The bill came before the House on March 29, provoking an anti-Yazoo member to move its immediate rejection as a "stain on the statute book, and a disgrace to the nation." A debate of three hours ensued, which Randolph dominated. Seizing the opportunity to slay the Yazoo dragon once and for all, the Virginia Republican urged the House to act without delay lest more members fall prey to the insidious influence of the executive. "The whole weight of the Executive Government presses it on," he exclaimed. "We cannot bear up against it." Unless the House acted swiftly and decisively, he warned, land-jobbers would control the country. Yield ever so little on Yazoo, and the "whole of the public lands" would become a source of speculation and corruption. "With all our virtue," he lamented, "there is land enough in the United States to buy us." Indeed, the fund used by the British ministry to corrupt Parliament would "dwindle into insignificance" compared to the one that would come into play if the Yazoo compromise was enacted.

As portrayed by Randolph, Yazoo was a question of great "magnitude," as important as any yet faced by the new nation, whose future hinged on its decision. If Congress approved the compromise, the republic, already on the slippery slope, would plunge over the precipice into a mire of speculation and corruption from which it could never extricate itself. This exhortation carried the day by a vote of sixty-two to fifty-four. Exulting in victory as he moved for adjournment, Randolph recalled the recent adjournment on the death of Senator Jackson of Georgia. He hoped the House would now adjourn on the Georgian's "resurrection," for Jackson "had told him, that if he could give a death-blow to the Yazoo business, he should die in peace."

Yazoo was indeed dead, at least for the remainder of the Ninth Congress. Still, the claimants persisted, submitting yet another petition from New England purchasers at the next session. All along these petitions had requested Congress to refer the Yazoo title to the decision of the Supreme Court if no compromise settlement could be reached. Now, with little prospect for compromise, the claimants pushed the judicial alternative. But there was little chance Congress would pass an act for this purpose. In January 1807 the House of Representatives by large majorities rejected motions to refer the latest Yazoo petition either to a committee of the whole or to a special committee.

Congress evinced further hostility to the Yazoo claimants at this session by passing an act "to prevent settlements being made on lands ceded to the United States, until authorized by law." The first section of this law provided for the forfeiture of the titles of "intruders," that is, those who took or attempted to take possession of public lands without the consent of the United States. It also authorized the president to remove such intruders by force. Though expressed in general language, the law's "main object," a supporter frankly stated, was "to drive off from the Yazoo land by military force, intruders, who might settle under the Yazoo claim." This measure originated in the Senate, which passed it seventeen to fifteen "after an animated debate." Senator Adams in vain objected to the bill on constitutional grounds, noting that it provided for forfeiture of land titles "for acts less than treason, the Constitution having expressly provided against such forfeiture for treason itself." The House approved the bill fifty-seven to forty-four on March 2 and easily defeated a motion by Federalist Josiah Quincy of Massachusetts to strike out the forfeiture provision.

By an even larger margin it rejected Quincy's amendment allowing persons claiming title "by virtue of an act or grant of any State" to enter "peaceably thereon" in order to obtain a judicial decision on the validity of their titles. The House, like the Senate, was unmoved by arguments that the bill trampled upon the constitutional rights of persons to assert a claim to property.

When Congress adjourned on March 3, 1807, Randolph and his followers could take great satisfaction that the federal legislature had stood firm on Yazoo despite pressure from the administration to reach a settlement with the purchasers of Mississippi lands under Georgia's act of 1795. As for the claimants, they were disappointed and increasingly frustrated by Congress's failure to act on what they regarded as their just and reasonable requests. As the prospects for a satisfactory resolution seemed ever more remote, the N.E.M. Land Co. and other groups of purchasers doggedly pursued their lobbying campaign.

The New Englanders tried yet another tactic with the Tenth Congress, which met from October 1807 to April 1808. The preceding summer they obtained a resolution from the Massachusetts legislature authorizing Governor James Sullivan to petition Congress for the relief of the Yazoo investors. Sullivan, father of William Sullivan, Peck's counsel in the U.S. circuit court, was elected governor as a Republican in May 1807. Before his election, Sullivan in his capacity as agent for Massachusetts purchasers of Georgia land had signed a memorial presented to the Senate in January 1806.

Governor Sullivan's memorial repeated the requests contained in previous applications that Congress either submit the purchasers' "claims of right to an impartial tribunal" or settle their claims "on the principle of an indemnity." Its language was direct and insistent, not asking "for *favor,* but for *right.*" The governor acted on "*the unanimous request*" of his state's legislature "to urge the *imperious* dictates of justice" on behalf of those Massachusetts citizens. The denial of an impartial investigation or of some equitable compromise, the memorial concluded, appeared "to be a violation of fundamental axioms and *tending to a dissolution of the social compact.*"

When presented to Congress on January 4, 1808, the memorial

touched off an angry debate on a motion to refer it to a committee. The House ultimately agreed by a large majority to refer the memorial to a committee of the whole. Many members otherwise opposed to the Yazoo claim believed Congress should accord a hearing to a petition or memorial, particularly one from a state governor. Intransigent opponents urged immediate rejection or even throwing "it under the table," expressing contempt for what was clearly an attempt to promote a private claim—"evidently founded in fraud and corruption"—under the form of an official request from a sovereign state. The debate was notable for the appearance of a new voice sounding the alarm against the "foul monster, Yazoo." George M. Troup of Georgia conceded nothing to Randolph in the acerbity of his speech and had a particular talent for irritating the sensibilities of New England Yankees.

Consideration of Governor Sullivan's memorial subsequently merged with an even more contentious debate a month later on a motion to admit Joseph Story, counsel for the N.E.M. Land Co., to the bar of the House to speak on behalf of the company's claims. Troup immediately objected to giving the House floor to "speculators or their agents," likening them to "cormorants which perch upon the treasuries of all nations." He later used the occasion to denounce the Massachusetts legislature for arraying itself "against Georgia, and on the side of corruption," prostituting "her power and sovereignty to the basest of and vilest of purposes." He added that if the governor would "prostitute the dignity of his high office to the most ignoble purposes, he ought to be tumbled from his seat," trusting that there was "virtue enough in Massachusetts to put him down."

The House by a large majority rejected the motion to give Story a hearing. This time the most zealous anti-Yazoo members were joined by others who were indifferent or even favorably disposed toward the claimants but who objected to allowing private persons to speak on the House floor. Story, reportedly "much hurt" by the House's refusal, would soon enter Congress as a member of the Massachusetts delegation, and two years later he would have his opportunity to state the case of the Yazoo claimants in the Supreme Court. Not long afterward, President Madison nominated him to the Supreme Court.

No more was heard of Yazoo at this session, though the subject came up indirectly in late April, just before the House adjourned. During a debate on a bill that provided for an appeal from a territorial court in Orleans to the Supreme Court in cases touching the right of New Orleans to the "batture" (the alluvial land near the Mississippi River), a Georgia member expressed concern that it would "establish a principle by which the Yazoo claimants" might bring their case to the Supreme Court. He added that if their case did get to the high court, "it was not difficult to foresee how it would be decided." Randolph also saw "a squinting towards Yazooism" in the bill, that it might be a precedent for giving the Supreme Court an appeal from a decision of a Mississippi territorial court. His own opinion was that "cases of empires," involving immense tracts of land, "were not subjects of judicial decision." A North Carolina Republican replied that he had not expected to hear on the floor of the House that the Supreme Court was "not to be trusted" in cases of property of great value. He considered his colleague's statement that the court would decide in favor of the Yazoo claimants as "clear evidence that it ought to be so decided."

The Supreme Court would indeed soon hear the case of the Yazoo claimants. Six months earlier, in June 1807, *Fletcher v. Peck* had commenced anew, as if the October 1806 judgment for Peck had never occurred. Apparently because the writ of error that issued in November 1806 was not prosecuted, it was necessary to start over in order to obtain a new writ of error. In any event, Fletcher filed his declaration again at the June 1807 term. The case was continued to the October term, when Peck's pleas and the special verdict were filed a second time. Judge Cushing again sitting alone gave judgment for Peck, and a second writ of error issued. Under this writ of error, dated November 30, 1807, a summons was served on Peck, and a certified record of the case was filed with the Supreme Court in February 1808. This filing put the case on the docket for argument at the February 1809 term. The decision to proceed with the appeal at this time was no doubt made in the belief that Congress would not of itself enact a compromise to indemnify the claimants. The time had come to seek vindication of the Yazoo title in the Supreme Court in the hope that a favorable decision would ultimately persuade Congress to act. The claimants had for some time urged Congress, without success, to adopt legislation to refer their case to the Supreme Court, preferring this means of obtaining a judicial decision in the highest court. With that option foreclosed, the only avenue to the Supreme Court was the appeal of *Fletcher v. Peck.*

CHAPTER FIVE

The Contract Clause, Vested Rights, and First Argument, 1809

The Supreme Court on the Eve
of *Fletcher v. Peck*

Contrary to conventional textbook accounts, the history of the Supreme Court did not begin with the appointment of John Marshall, the "great chief justice," in 1801. In fact, Marshall built on foundations laid during the Court's first decade. That it took time for the Court to acquire an institutional identity is not surprising. Article III of the Constitution—the judiciary article—provided only a brief outline for the judicial department, naming just one court, the Supreme Court. It left to Congress's discretion the establishment of inferior federal courts and conferred lifetime appointments on the judges of both the supreme and inferior courts. It prescribed the federal judiciary's jurisdiction as extending to "all cases, in Law and Equity, arising under" the Constitution, laws, and treaties of the United States; to cases affecting ambassadors and other diplomatic officers; to admiralty and maritime cases; and to controversies between specified parties—between two or more states, between a state and citizens of another state, between citizens of different states, and between a state or its citizens and foreign states or citizens. It assigned limited original jurisdiction to the Supreme Court—cases involving diplomats and those in which a state was party—and gave appellate jurisdiction in all other cases "with such Exceptions, and under such Regulations as the Congress shall make."

These provisions were fleshed out in an organic law adopted by the First Congress in 1789. The Judiciary Act provided for a Supreme Court composed of the chief justice and five associate justices. It divided the nation into judicial districts corresponding to the states, in each of which there was to be a U.S. district court composed of a U.S. district judge. The districts, in turn, were divided into three circuits, in each of which there was to be a U.S. circuit court composed of any two Supreme Court justices and the district judge of the district where the court was held. In general, the district courts were to serve as original courts for trying admiralty and maritime causes, including seizures made under the impost, navigation, and trade laws of the United States, and suits for penalties and forfeitures incurred under federal laws. The circuit courts were primarily to be original tribunals for trying civil suits at common law or in equity and for trying crimes cognizable under federal law. A provision of immense importance was section 25, providing for appeals to the U.S. Supreme Court from the highest state courts. Such appeals were restricted to cases involving a "federal" question, as for example when a losing party in a state court claimed a right set up under the federal Constitution, laws, or treaties.

As principally an appellate tribunal, the Supreme Court heard relatively few cases during the 1790s and still fewer important ones. The justices spent the greater portion of their time as trial judges of the U.S. circuit courts. To the extent that Americans came in contact with the Supreme Court, it was in the twice-yearly visits of the justices to the towns and cities where the federal circuit courts sat. A justice formally opened court by delivering a charge to the grand jury. Federal grand jury charges were civic events of much local importance, in which the justices typically used the occasion not merely to invoke the duty to enforce federal criminal law but also to deliver broadly political lectures exhorting citizens to obey the government and support the Constitution.

During the Supreme Court's first decade the federal judiciary became an operative branch of the national government, no mean achievement given the novel and experimental nature of the compound system of government brought into being by the Constitution. As the first chief justice, John Jay brought to the office the prestige of a statesman of broad experience and sound judgment. Oliver Ellsworth, his successor, had equal stature and was the chief architect of the federal Judiciary Act. But neither Jay nor Ellsworth served long enough to leave a significant imprint on the Supreme Court or to develop an institutional esprit de corps among the justices. This would have been difficult in any case because the early Court had so little business that the justices sat together infrequently and for short sessions. Apart from circuit riding, which was onerous and time-consuming, Supreme Court justices had light duties. Chief Justices Jay and Ellsworth spent months in office serving abroad on diplomatic missions.

Among several cases of constitutional significance heard by the early Supreme Court, *Chisholm v. Georgia* (1793) held that the Constitution's extension of federal jurisdiction to controversies between "a State and Citizens of another State" overrode Georgia's claim of sovereign immunity in a suit brought against the state by citizens of South Carolina. This decision was soon overruled by the adoption of the Eleventh Amendment, which took away jurisdiction in suits commenced against a state by citizens of another state or a foreign state. The Court made a more successful assertion of nationalism in *Ware v. Hylton* (1796), which set forth a sweeping interpretation of the supremacy clause as operating retrospectively to abrogate state laws in conflict with national treaties. In *Hylton v. United States* (1796) the Court greatly facilitated the government's power to raise revenue by ruling that a tax on carriages was not a direct tax. This case was also notable for its implicit endorsement of the doctrine of judicial review.

The first Supreme Court justices believed it was their duty to inculcate respect for the federal government and obedience to its laws and to cooperate fully with the political branches in supporting the government's domestic and foreign policies. In adopting this posture, they viewed themselves not as partisans of the Federalist administrations of Washington and Adams but as disinterested upholders of public order. With the advent of political opposition, however, the federal judiciary was inevitably drawn into partisan politics. By the end of the decade, in the wake of prosecutions under the notorious Alien and Sedition Acts, Federalist judges were subjected to scathing censure by the Republicans. These attacks seriously undermined the federal judiciary's prestige and authority, leaving it institutionally vulnerable when President Jefferson took office in 1801.

When Ellsworth resigned in October 1800, President Adams first tried to fill the vacancy by nominating former Chief Justice Jay, who declined. Under pressure to act quickly because of the impending accession of a new Republican administration, he turned to Marshall, his secretary of state. The Senate confirmed Marshall's nomination in late January 1801. The new chief justice took the oath of office on February 4, when a quorum of justices assembled in a "half-finished Committee room" on the first floor of the Capitol for the first Supreme Court session held in the city of Washington. Having little business to transact, the Court adjourned on February 10. For the remaining three weeks of the Adams administration, Marshall continued to serve as secretary of state and stayed on as acting secretary through March 4, Thomas Jefferson's first day in office as president.

The man who was now to preside over the Supreme Court brought a sterling résumé acquired as a soldier, state legislator, lawyer, diplomat, member of Congress, and secretary of state. Indeed, his life and career prior to 1801 seemed specially designed to prepare him for the office of chief justice of the United States. Along with a wealth of experience Marshall possessed attributes of intellect, learning, and personality that were ideally suited to leading a small assemblage of individual justices and molding them into a collective entity that spoke with a single authoritative voice. He had a first-class mind, with keen powers of logic, analysis, and generalization that enabled him to master complex legal issues with quick and discerning comprehension. On first encountering the chief justice in 1808, Joseph Story observed a "vigorous and powerful" intelligence that "examines the intricacies of a subject with calm and persevering circumspection, and unravels the mysteries with irresistible acuteness." Two decades spent in close company as the chief justice's associate only confirmed this first impression. "In strength, and depth, and comprehensiveness of mind," Story wrote in his eulogy, "it would be difficult to name his superior."

The prospects for the federal judiciary were scarcely auspicious in 1801. In the high political excitement accompanying the Republicans' transition to power following the electoral defeat of the Federalists, the judiciary became the focal point of the victorious party's resentment and mistrust. Memories were fresh of the federal courts' vigorous enforcement of the Adams administration's efforts to suppress internal dissent during the war crisis of 1798 and 1799, most conspicuously in prosecuting, fining, and jailing Republican newspaper editors on indictments brought under the notorious Sedition Act. Federal judges also rendered themselves obnoxious by delivering grand jury charges that intemperately denounced opposition to government and exhorted the citizenry to support the administration's policies. In the eyes of Republicans, the judiciary had relinquished any semblance of independence and impartiality and become a tool of the executive and an instrument of party politics.

Marshall's immediate goal in 1801 was to repair the federal judiciary's damaged reputation by making a strategic retreat from the aggressive, partisan posture it had lately exhibited. The change of administration made such a retreat advisable, and happily for this purpose the new chief justice was a man of prudence and moderate political temperament. However, things got worse before they got better. At the very moment Marshall was confirmed as chief justice, the lame-duck Federalist Congress passed a judiciary act creating a host of new federal circuit court judgeships, which were promptly filled by Adams's appointees. Republicans cried foul at what appeared to be a brazen attempt by the defeated party to perpetuate its control of government through the judiciary. Shortly thereafter, a Federalist-appointed justice of the peace for the District of Columbia sued in the Supreme Court for a writ of "mandamus," commanding the secretary of state to deliver his commission, which had been withheld by the Jefferson administration. Taken together, these events brought the judiciary to the brink of crisis, creating a severe test for the new chief justice.

In December 1801 the Supreme Court agreed to hear the mandamus action brought by William Marbury and assigned the case to be argued at the next term. Irritated by what it perceived to be an unwarranted judicial intrusion into executive matters, the Republican majority in Congress in March 1802 secured the repeal of the judiciary act enacted the previous year. The repeal and a subsequent judiciary act adopted in April 1802 restored the former system by which circuit courts were composed of Supreme Court justices and judges of the U.S. district courts. This legislation also provided for an annual term of the Supreme Court, commencing the first Monday in February, which meant that the Court would not meet again until February 1803, when Marbury's case was to be argued.

Before that case could be heard, the Supreme Court justices in the spring of 1802 faced a dilemma. Should they hold the circuit courts established by the recent legislation? By attending their circuits, they would signify their acquiescence in Congress's authority to reinstate circuit riding by Supreme Court justices. Chief Justice Marshall himself doubted the constitutionality of the measure, believing that Supreme Court justices could not perform circuit duty without separate and distinct commissions as circuit judges. Unable to consult personally with his brethren because of the postponement of the Court's next term, Marshall initiated a correspondence with Justices William Paterson, William Cushing, Bushrod Washington, and Samuel Chase. In these letters, Marshall set forth his doubts, while adding that it was "my duty & my inclination in this as in all other cases to be bound by the opinion of the majority of the Judges." On learning that a majority of the justices considered this question as fully settled by the practice of riding circuit from 1789 to 1801, the chief justice readily assented, remarking that "policy dictates this decision to us all."

The justices averted a showdown by attending their circuits in the fall of 1802. They further demonstrated their intention not to become instruments of party politics by steadfastly resisting attempts by Federalist lawyers to deny the authority of the courts to hear cases continued from the former circuit courts established under the repealed 1801 act. One such attempt occurred in Marshall's own circuit in Richmond in December 1802, when a defendant pleaded that the Judiciary Act of 1802 was unconstitutional and void. The chief justice rejected the sufficiency of this plea in the case of *Stuart v. Laird*, which was appealed to the Supreme Court at the February 1803 term. In a brief opinion, Justice Paterson for the Court reaffirmed the decision the justices had reached the preceding spring.

This episode provided a revealing preview of Marshall's collegial style of leadership of the Supreme Court. The repeal crisis also brought forth Marshall's essential moderation, his pragmatic recognition that "good policy" at times should supersede doctrinaire adherence to strict law. Marshall was instinctively cautious, acutely aware of the judiciary's weakness and vulnerability. His overriding concern during his first years as chief justice was to ensure the judiciary's survival by directing a prudent retreat away from "politics" and into the comfort zone of "law." Only in the safety of that refuge, Marshall recognized early on, could the judiciary hope not only to weather the immediate storm but also in the longer run to build up its institutional strength and elevate its status and authority.

The separation of law and politics was also the larger meaning of *Marbury v. Madison*, even though in the short run that case further implicated the Supreme Court in the partisan warfare of the day. In announcing the Court's opinion in February 1803, Chief Justice Marshall affirmed that Marbury had a legal right to his commission but ultimately denied relief on the ground that the Court lacked jurisdiction to issue a writ of mandamus to government officers. Although a provision of an act of Congress authorized such actions, the chief justice pronounced that provision unconstitutional as purporting to enlarge the Supreme Court's original jurisdiction beyond that prescribed by Article III of the Constitution.

The refusal to issue a mandamus was thus a victory for the Jefferson administration, but at the time the opinion only exacerbated Republican opposition to the judiciary. Their anger was directed at the Court's presumption in deciding the merits of the case, gratuitously charging the administration with acting unlawfully, before ultimately denying jurisdiction to hear the case. They were not mollified by Marshall's assurances that the Court's province was solely to decide on individual rights and not to inquire into executive conduct where the executive had discretion to act. However, by denying jurisdiction, Marshall managed to uphold the claims of judicial power without having to issue an order commanding the executive to deliver the commission.

By contrast, the Court's assumption of authority to declare a law of Congress unconstitutional provoked scarcely a murmur at the time. Here again Marshall acted opportunely to assert the judiciary's "duty" to regard the Constitution as a law and to disallow legislative acts deemed to be repugnant to it. A broad spectrum of American opinion in 1803 did not dispute this proposition, and Marshall appealed to this consensus in making the case for what came to be known as "judicial review." It helped enormously that *Marbury* was a case of judicial self-denial, of refusing jurisdiction that Congress had given, so that the Court could present itself as a high-minded, impartial tribunal concerned solely with expounding law. Considered together, *Marbury v. Madison* and *Stuart v. Laird* amounted to a declaration of independence by the Supreme Court, an announcement of withdrawal from the political realm. On the one hand, it refused to capitulate to the Republican administration's contention that executive conduct was completely exempt from judicial oversight; on the other, in pointedly refusing to reconsider the constitutionality of circuit riding by Supreme Court justices, it resisted pressure to carry out Federalist party goals.

Still, in the wake of *Marbury*, Republican rancor toward the judiciary had not exhausted itself, as signified by impeachment proceedings against federal judges. In February 1803, while *Marbury* was pending, the House impeached a Federalist district judge from New Hampshire who was notoriously alcoholic and probably insane. Despite misgivings among Republicans about impeaching a judge who was obviously unfit but had not committed a crime, the Senate convicted him in March 1804. This action encouraged radical Republicans who wanted to use the impeachment process to remove judges regarded as politically hostile to the administration. On the day of the New Hampshire judge's conviction, Congressman John Randolph initiated proceedings against Supreme Court Justice Samuel Chase. The irascible, overbearing Chase was a prime target, reviled for his partisan and intemperate conduct of sedition and treason trials during the Adams administration and more recently for a grand jury charge denouncing the Jefferson administration and expressing contempt for democracy. In March 1805 the Senate failed to convict Chase by the necessary two-thirds majority. Apart from establishing a precedent restricting grounds for impeachment to criminal conduct, the acquittal of Chase (the only Supreme Court justice to be impeached) signified a triumph of moderation within the Republican ranks that was further demonstrated by the rejection of proposals to amend the Constitution so as to enable the president to remove federal judges by joint address of the House and Senate.

By 1807 Jefferson had three of his own appointees, William Johnson, Brockholst Livingston, and Thomas Todd, on the Supreme Court, a circumstance that resulted in improved relations between the judiciary and the political branches. This accord was temporarily set back by the treason trial of Aaron Burr, which took place on Chief Justice Marshall's circuit in Richmond in the summer of 1807. In response to Burr's military expedition to the Southwest in the fall of 1806, the government vigorously prosecuted the former vice president and his followers for provoking war against Spain with the traitorous design of detaching the West from the United States. At the close of the trial Marshall delivered an elaborate opinion narrowly defining treason and excluding most of the testimony, which in effect compelled the jury to acquit Burr. Republican papers predictably denounced the chief justice for twisting the law to allow a traitor to go free, and once again there were calls for reforming a partisan judiciary that ignored the people's will with impunity.

But the furor over the Burr trial eventually subsided, and aside from verbal assaults the judiciary emerged relatively unscathed. In the common cause of upholding national authority, the administration and the federal courts needed each other. As it attempted to steer a neutral course in the midst of the Napoleonic Wars, the government depended on the courts to enforce its stringent embargo laws interdicting trade with the belligerent nations—laws that were openly resisted and repeatedly denounced as unconstitutional, particularly in New England. While interpreting these laws strictly to preserve the rights of individuals against abuse by government officers, federal judges never questioned the power of Congress to enact such legislation—indeed, a Federalist judge in New England forcefully upheld the constitutionality of the embargo.

A clear indication of how far accommodation had progressed was the Madison administration's response to a Supreme Court decision of 1809 ordering the state of Pennsylvania to abide by a lower federal court decree. When the state resisted, President Madison reminded the governor that the federal executive was legally bound to carry into effect any federal court decree, "where opposition may be made to it." After eight years under the leadership of Chief Justice Marshall, the Supreme Court had emerged from crisis and confrontation to a state of mutual respect if not harmony in its relations with the other branches of government. It was not yet the "Marshall Court," though the chief justice had begun to shape the institution and define the office in certain characteristic ways.

From the outset Chief Justice Marshall adopted the mode of a single majority opinion in preference to seriatim opinions by each of the justices, consolidating a practice that actually had begun under his predecessor. He recognized the advantages of a single statement in imparting weight and authority to the Court's pronouncements and thereby promoting certainty and stability in the law. The public would come to perceive the Court as a unified and independent institution whose judgments were formed by solemn collective deliberation. The Court would enhance its authority and prestige while the chief justice as its spokesman would become the personal embodiment of its stature and dignity. The single majority opinion had the effect of projecting unity even when the judges were divided. The internal dynamics of this collegial institution encouraged silent acquiescence by justices who dissented from the majority.

In his broader project of promoting institutional unity, Chief Justice Marshall brought his fellow justices together in the same Washington boardinghouse during Supreme Court terms. This is where the justices adjourned after hearing cases between eleven and four and where the all-important Court conference took place. The harmonizing and unifying effects of communal living were well described by Joseph Story soon after he joined the Court in 1812, writing that he lived with his brethren "in the most frank and unaffected intimacy" and being "all united as one, with a mutual esteem which makes even the labors of Jurisprudence light." In the boardinghouse conference, Marshall proved adept at conducting serious business in an atmosphere of conviviality, even mirth. The usually ascetic justices were known on occasion to stretch their rule of drinking wine only in wet weather. Marshall would sometimes ask "Brother Story" to "step to the window and see if it does not look like rain." And if Story informed him that the sun was "shining brightly," the chief justice might reply, "all the better; for our jurisdiction extends over so large a territory that the doctrine of chances makes it certain that it must be raining somewhere."

In order of seniority Chief Justice Marshall's colleagues on the

Supreme Court in 1809 were Cushing, Chase, Washington, Johnson, Livingston, and Todd. The first three were appointed by Presidents Washington and Adams, the last three by President Jefferson. Cushing, the last remaining original justice, gave the pro forma judgments for Peck in the U.S. circuit court in 1806 and 1807. Elderly and infirm, he attended the 1809 term but missed the 1810 term and died later that year. Chase had been a member of the Court since 1796. Along with advancing years, Chase's impeachment ordeal appears to have chastened him into silence. Declining health kept him from attending the 1806, 1809, and 1810 terms. He therefore did not participate in *Fletcher v. Peck*. Washington, nephew of the first president, began his long tenure on the Court in 1799. He and Marshall were close personal friends as well as professional colleagues and shared similar views about the Constitution's protections for property rights and restrictions on state sovereignty. He was an able jurist in his own right despite Justice Johnson's scornful observation in 1822 that the chief justice and Washington were "commonly estimated as one judge."

Johnson, Jefferson's first appointee to the Supreme Court, took his seat in 1804 after serving as a judge of South Carolina's highest court. During his long tenure, Johnson acquired a reputation as the Court's most independent-minded jurist, as reflected in numerous concurring and dissenting opinions. In 1809 he had not established this judicial identity and mostly acquiesced with his brethren in allowing the chief justice to speak for the Court. In *Fletcher* he gave an early hint of judicial independence by delivering a separate concurring opinion. Livingston of New York and Todd of Kentucky, Jefferson's other two appointments, joined the Court in 1807. The former served in the New York legislature as a Republican before his appointment to the state supreme court in 1802. Story in 1808 described Livingston as "luminous, decisive, earnest, and impressive on the bench." Todd took the new seat on the Court created when Congress established the Seventh Circuit, embracing Kentucky, Tennessee, and Ohio. He previously served as chief justice of Kentucky's supreme court. Illness caused him to miss five terms during his nineteen years on the bench, including the 1809 term, when *Fletcher* was first heard. In time, to Jefferson's disappointment, Livingston and Todd would become reliable allies of Chief Justice Marshall in strengthening the constitutional foundations of federal power.

———

John Marshall and the Contract Clause

In February 1809 perhaps few could have predicted that Chief Justice Marshall in deciding *Fletcher v. Peck* would rely principally on a particular clause of Article I, section 10, of the Constitution, which prescribes prohibitions and restrictions on the state legislatures. This section among other things declares that no state shall "emit Bills of Credit; make any Thing but gold and silver Coin a Tender in Payment of Debts; pass any bill of attainder, ex post facto Law, or Law impairing the Obligation of Contracts." It was clear of course that the validity of Georgia's 1796 rescinding act would be one of the points to be determined and that the act had been censured as an "ex post facto Law" and "Law impairing the Obligation of Contracts." Yet these clauses if invoked at all were typically cited to supplement the broader argument that Georgia's revocation of the Yazoo grant was contrary to fundamental principles of law. No one who examined the voluminous record of the case—a copy of which was printed in Boston in December 1808—could be sure that in this action of covenant broken the legality of the rescinding act would be the central issue or that this act if nullified would be held to violate general principles of law or the U.S. Constitution or both.

That *Fletcher* became a landmark case of American constitutional law—the first in a series of notable cases in which the Supreme Court under Chief Justice Marshall expounded and applied the contract clause—invites consideration of how Marshall understood the law of contract and what the framers of the Constitution intended by declaring that no state could impair the obligation of contract. As a lawyer and member of the founding generation, he learned about contract law from Blackstone and English common law and also from treatises on natural law and the law of nations by writers such as Pufendorf and Vattel. In the eighteenth century "contract" had a less restrictive and technical meaning than it subsequently acquired. A succinct definition drawn from the common law and natural law was provided in John J. Powell's *Essay upon the Law of Contracts* (1790), a copy of which Marshall owned: "'A contract is a transaction in which each party comes under an obligation to the other, and each reciprocally, acquires a right to what is promised by the other.'" The author went on to say that this definition embraced "every, gift, lease, loan, pledge, bargain, covenant, agreement, promise, etc."

Marshall drew on a body of legal learning that broadly defined contract to include a grant or conveyance of land ("feoffment"). From Blackstone, he learned that contracts were either "executory," in which a party promises to do or not do something, or "executed," in which the contract has been performed. In *Fletcher*, he quoted the commentator's remark that a contract executed "differs nothing from a grant." Marshall could also find authoritative support for the idea that governments as well as individuals were legally bound by their contracts. Pufendorf, for example, wrote that "upon the whole all contracts made by the prince oblige the commonwealth, unless they are manifestly absurd or unjust." There was broad understanding that a citizen or subject of a state acquired legal rights arising from contracts made with the state. A person who obtained a conveyance of land from the state was regarded as having as strong a legal title as one who received land from an individual.

If there was widespread acceptance of the idea that a grant of land was a contract, so too there was much support in common law and "universal" law (a term often used interchangeably with "natural law" and the "law of nations") that a corporation was a franchise, a grant of private property, and that a corporate charter constituted a contract conferring legal rights. This notion took hold and gained new life in post-independence America, where corporations adapted to republican circumstances proliferated in the decades following the Revolution. The argument that a corporate charter was a compact that could not be revoked or altered by a legislature received early judicial expression. In *Dartmouth College v. Woodward* (1819), Chief Justice Marshall assumed without argument that the college's charter was a contract.

There was nothing particularly controversial in regarding land grants or corporate charters as contracts even well before the Supreme Court decided *Fletcher* and *Dartmouth*. More problematic was whether such grants by public authority were contracts meant to be protected by the Constitution. To what extent were states obligated by their own contracts? For that matter, what was the "obligation of contract" in contracts between private individuals? Marshall, like many of his contemporaries, subscribed to a natural law theory of the obligation of contract. He would spell this out at length in *Ogden v. Saunders* (1827), where he posited that contracts and their attendant obligations existed "anterior to, and independent of society." The right to contract, he wrote, "like many other natural rights," was "brought with man into society." The duty of government, of "human legislation," was to enforce the contractual obligations that were founded in nature. To jurists and statesmen of Marshall's generation, the natural law foundation of contract gave a transcendent moral dimension to contractual relations that positive law was bound to respect. They typically spoke of contracts in reverent terms such as "sacred," "inviolable," and endowed with "sanctity."

Natural law theory acknowledged the state's power by positive legislation to regulate contracts, whether made by individuals or the state. For example, states could pass laws outlawing gambling contracts, enact usury laws that voided contracts for charging excessive interest, and adopt statutes of frauds and limitation. Such laws were regarded as prescribing rules and remedies for enforcing contracts while not modifying or in any way impairing their intrinsic obligation. There was, to be sure, an inescapable tension between the idea of contractual obligation based on natural law and the power of the state to regulate contracts, a tension that would eventually lead to the rejection of natural law theory and its replacement with a "civil" obligation of contract based on positive law.

The founders' natural law conception of contract does not sufficiently explain what they intended with respect to the scope and extent of the prohibition on laws impairing the obligation of contract. The contract clause clearly originated in anxiety about the security of what the founders called "private rights" in the states. This concern was at the heart of a transformation in thinking about republican government that took place during the decade after independence. The republican commonwealths that came into being in 1776 were clothed with vast public power of a kind unknown to their colonial counterparts. This power was concentrated in the popularly elected legislatures, who regarded themselves as the embodiment of the people's sovereign will. Their acts were accordingly seen as expressing and promoting the public good of the whole society that transcended the private interests of individuals and groups within the society.

A few years' experience of republican self-government brought the sobering realization that the state legislative assemblies did not behave as disinterested brokers of the common weal. They enacted legislation on a hitherto unprecedented scale directed at broad public matters such as economic and commercial development. But their proliferating codes contained an increasing number of confusing, contradictory, arbitrary, and even unjust laws. The legislatures, as soon became evident, were not united bodies but unstable compounds of clashing groups, classes, and interests, principally founded on differing degrees and kinds of property. Instead of pursuing a transcendent public interest, legislators merely represented the partial interests of various factions. Public law thus often reflected the selfish views of popular majorities who, given the opportunity, remorselessly trampled on the rights of individuals and minorities. No one more acutely diagnosed this disturbing defect of popular government than James Madison, the acknowledged leader of the movement for comprehensive federal reform in the 1780s. Madison scathingly criticized the "multiplicity," "mutability," and above all the "injustice" of state laws. The unpleasant truth he communicated was that governments in which all power was concentrated in popular assemblies posed as much a danger to liberty, and could act just as despotically, as government by royal governors and aristocratic councilors.

This disparagement of the legislatures as despotic produced a shift in Americans' thinking about their republican constitutional arrangements. Much of this rethinking consisted of defining and drawing boundaries— between legislative, executive, and judicial powers, between "public" and "private," and between "law" and "politics." Although many of the first state constitutions professed adherence to the doctrine of separation of powers, virtually all important governmental powers were placed in the legislative assemblies to forestall the danger of executive aggrandizement. Now, having been alerted to the perils of unchecked legislative government, Americans adopted a revised understanding of separation of powers. They acquired a new appreciation for the role that the executive and judiciary departments could play in preventing or moderating the abuses liable to be committed by the legislatures. In the revised scheme sovereignty was detached from the assemblies and located in the people themselves. The legislatures suffered a corresponding diminution of power and prestige, losing their superior status as the embodiment of the people's will.

The judiciary department, in particular, gained a new lease on life in post-independence America, carving out an essential role for judicial power in a republican polity. In addition to the traditional task of applying English common law and equity, judges took on the task of interpreting the profusion of confusing and contradictory acts of republican legislatures. Americans became accustomed to the idea that their courts were necessary to prevent or ameliorate mischiefs arising from the laws and that their intervention was vital to ensure that statutes conformed to reason and justice. Judges increasingly engaged in defining the judiciary's special province to expound the law, to say what the law is, and stoutly resisted perceived intrusions on its turf by the legislative branch. They were fond of saying that legislatures could only make law, that is, declare what the law shall be. To venture beyond this sphere, say by retrospectively interfering with private rights, was an unwarranted exercise of judicial power. One of the chief complaints about the state assemblies was that their acts amounted to adjudication rather than legislation. According to Madison, "many of the most important acts of legislation" were "so many judicial determinations, not indeed concerning the rights of single persons, but concerning the rights of large bodies of citizens." In its campaign to define its boundaries, to set itself apart from legislative power, the judiciary presented itself as the proper arena for protecting private rights against the abuses of public power. Judges distanced themselves from politics and its clashing passions and interests and took refuge in the "law," a sphere where they were uniquely qualified by professional expertise and disinterestedness to adjudicate disputes involving private rights.

At the Philadelphia Convention of 1787, Madison took the lead in making sure that the cause of federal constitutional reform embraced the internal administration of the states. His solution to the problem of protecting private rights was a national government of extensive electoral districts that would be largely free of factional politics. Composed of enlightened and impartial statesmen, this government would act in a judicial-like way as "a disinterested & dispassionate umpire in disputes between different passions & interests" in the states. He proposed to vest the national legislature with a "negative," or veto, over the acts of the state legislatures. This radical proposal won early approval, but ultimately Madison's fellow deputies rejected the negative, a defeat that left the Virginian dejected and apprehensive that the proposed Constitution would be an ineffectual remedy for the ills of republican government.

In refusing to adopt Madison's negative, the convention denied only a means of implementing a principle, not the principle itself. The negative's essential idea was embodied in the Constitution in the form of the supremacy clause (Article VI), the judiciary article (Article III), and the restrictions and prohibitions on the state legislatures (Article I, section 10). Together, these provisions constituted a judicial substitute for a legislative negative on state laws. Instead of a prior legislative veto, the framers chose subsequent judicial review as a more practical means of protecting individual rights from the injurious acts of the states. The contract clause itself was not introduced until late in the convention and was adopted and ratified without much discussion either at Philadelphia or in the state ratifying conventions. As originally proposed, the text of the contract clause was taken from the recently enacted Northwest Ordinance, which read in part: "And, in the just preservation of rights and property, it is understood and declared, that no law ought ever to be made, or have force in the said territory, that shall, in any manner whatever, interfere with or affect private contracts or engagements, *bona fide*, and without fraud, previously formed."

In its final form the contract clause was reduced to a succinct prohibition to pass laws "impairing the obligation of contracts." The substitution of "impairing the obligation" in place of "interfere with or affect" was likely done to ensure that the prohibition did not include remedial laws such as statutes of limitation. If this change restricted the scope of the prohibition, the omission of "private" and "previously formed" appeared to give room for interpretive discretion. Among the handful who uttered thoughts on the subject at the federal convention and state conventions, the prevailing but by no means universal assumption appears to have been that the contract clause was intended to embrace only private contracts. But the record is so scanty as to be inconclusive. One might as reasonably conclude that the clause's final draft reflected the collective and deliberate intention of the convention to enlarge the scope of the prohibition beyond the terms in which it was originally proposed.

The absence of discussion or controversy surrounding the adoption of the contract clause in 1787 and 1788 does not imply that the framers of the Constitution regarded this provision as trivial or innocuous, having only a restricted applicability to state legislation. The origin of the clause was not its formal introduction late in the convention but can be traced to the broader reaction against the state legislatures in the 1780s and to Madison's efforts to secure private rights by means of a federal veto on state laws. Madison was among those who supported what eventually became the contract clause, though he doubted its effectiveness: "He conceived however that a negative on the State laws could alone secure the effect. Evasions might and would be devised by the ingenuity of the Legislatures." Soon after, writing as "Publius" in *The Federalist*, the Virginian made the best case he could for the contract clause and the other prohibitions on the states, defending their utility in precisely the same terms as he had earlier advocated the legislative veto on state laws. "Bills of attainder, *ex post facto* laws, and laws impairing the obligation of contracts," he wrote, "are contrary to the first principles of the social compact and to every principle of sound legislation. . . . Very properly, therefore, have the convention added this constitutional bulwark in favor of personal security and private rights."

John Marshall served with Madison in the Virginia legislature and followed his lead as "the enlightened advocate of Union and of an efficient federal government." He joined Madison in advocating adoption of the new Constitution at the Virginia ratifying convention in June 1788. According to his later recollection, he attributed his support for federal reform to "the general tendency of state politics," which had convinced him "that no safe and permanent remedy could be found but in a more efficient and better organized general government. The questions too, which were perpetually recurring in the state legislatures, and which brought annually into doubt principles which I thought most sacred, which proved that everything was afloat, and that we had no safe anchorage ground, gave a high value in my estimation to that article in the constitution which imposes restrictions on the states."

As a follower and ally of Madison, Marshall had good reason to believe the framers intended the contract clause to have a comprehensive reach, to embrace, like Madison's negative, not just past and present evils but also to guard against unforeseen cases that might arise in consequence of state legislative ingenuity. In other words, he believed the framers regarded the contract clause as qualitatively different from the other prohibitions on the states, which were directed against specific mischiefs such as bills of attainder, paper money, and tender laws. Rather than aimed against particular laws, the contract clause was designed to embody a general principle of extensive application for protecting the sanctity of contract and the rights of property.

Ultimately, Marshall came to view the contract clause as giving constitutional sanction to the doctrine of "vested rights," rights acquired by individuals under the law, foremost of which was the right to the security and free enjoyment of property. Vested-rights doctrine emerged as part of the process of redefining and limiting legislative power that occurred in reaction to the state legislatures' interferences with private rights during the 1780s. According to an eminent constitutional scholar, this doctrine formed the core of an American constitutional law whose principal function was to set limits on governmental power, especially legislative power. In this respect, it provided vital support for the idea that judges could disallow acts that impaired a person's vested rights.

Justice Paterson gave classic expression to the doctrine in *Vanhorne's Lessee v. Dorrance* (1795) when he stated "the right of acquiring and possessing property and having it protected, is one of the natural inherent and unalienable rights of man." A legislature "had no authority to make an act divesting one citizen of his freehold, and vesting it in another, without a just compensation." Justice Chase in *Calder v. Bull* (1798) offered another standard articulation of the doctrine in 1798: "There are certain vital principles in our free republican governments, which will determine and overrule an apparent and flagrant abuse of legislative power; as to authorize manifest injustice by positive law; or take away that security for personal liberty, or private property, for the protection whereof the government was established. An act of the legislature (for I cannot call it a law) contrary to the great first principles of the social compact cannot be considered a rightful exercise of legislative authority."

Republican as well as Federalist judges espoused vested-rights doctrine. In 1802, Judge Spencer Roane of the Virginia Court of Appeals stood "upon this broad principle, that men, in regulating their contracts, shall have the benefit of existing laws, and not have them overturned or affected by future laws, which they certainly could not foresee, or provide against." Two years later he declared that he would "not be among those, who assert a right in the government, or even in the people, to violate private rights, and perpetuate injustice." Again, in 1809, Roane emphatically denied the principle of legislative omnipotence, which would "lay prostrate, at the footstool of the legislature, all our rights of person and of property, and abandon those great objects, for the protection of which, alone, all free governments have been instituted." Although they were otherwise inveterate judicial antagonists, Roane and Marshall were in fundamental agreement that vested rights should be protected against legislative overreach.

In early instances in which judges and lawyers invoked vested-rights doctrine to challenge the validity of a state legislative act, the contract clause played a distinctly secondary role. If cited at all, the contract clause was employed mainly to supplement arguments founded on natural law, on the established principles and maxims of common law, and on the constitutional principle of the separation of powers. Judges' opinions typically followed a hierarchical pattern that began by invoking natural law and concluded with citing particular provisions of written constitutions, as shown by Paterson in his charge to the jury in *Vanhorne's Lessee v. Dorrance* (1795). A legislature, he wrote, "had no authority to make an act divesting one citizen of his freehold, and vesting it in another, without a just compensation. It is inconsistent with the principles of reason, justice, and moral rectitude; it is incompatible with the comfort, peace, and happiness of mankind; it is contrary to the principles of social alliance in every free government; and lastly, it is contrary both to letter and spirit of the constitution."

Vanhorne's Lessee v. Dorrance, a case between Pennsylvania and Connecticut claimants to lands in Pennsylvania, brought into question the legitimacy of a 1787 Pennsylvania act for quieting and confirming the lands of the Connecticut claimants. As a case arising from land speculation and involving the constitutionality of a state law, *Vanhorne's Lessee* has some parallels with *Fletcher v. Peck*, though the federal contract clause figures only obliquely in the former. In condemning the confirming act, Paterson delivered an impassioned primer on the constitutional limits placed on legislative power and a robust assertion of judicial power to enforce those limits. "Omnipotence in legislation," he wrote, "is despotism." He took "to be a clear position, that if a legislative act oppugns a constitutional principle, the former must give way, and be rejected on the score of repugnance," adding the "equally clear and sound" position "that, in such case, it will be the duty of the court to adhere to the constitution, and to declare the act null and void."

In *Vanhorne's Lessee*, Paterson held the 1787 confirming act to be repugnant to Pennsylvania's constitution. In 1790 the state legislature repealed the confirming act. Contending that the confirming act was a contract, counsel for the Connecticut claimants argued that the 1790 repeal violated the contract clause of the U.S. Constitution. While emphatically denying that the 1787 act ever had "constitutional existence," much less that it was a contract vesting the lands in the Connecticut settlers, Paterson acknowledged that if that act was a contract between the Pennsylvania legislature and the Connecticut settlers, "it must be regulated by the rules and principles, which pervade and govern all cases of contracts." Even according to those rules, said the judge, the Pennsylvania act was "clearly void." Paterson did seem to imply, however, that there might be circumstances in which a state act conveying land could be considered as a contract protected by the Constitution. The confirming act was not such a contract because the state did not own the land in dispute. It purported to divest one claimant of his land and vest it in another without compensation—an act of "despotic authority" that was flagrantly unconstitutional. The case was otherwise, Paterson suggested, when a state legislature exercised its rightful power to dispose of the state's public lands.

Although the facts and circumstances of the Pennsylvania case were different from those arising from Georgia's sale of its western lands, *Vanhorne's Lessee* may well have provided Marshall with an authoritative judicial precedent, particularly inspiring for its powerful affirmation of a judge's "duty" to annul acts that contravened the constitutional limits of legislative power. Also, Paterson's statement that contracts in which a state was a party were to be regulated by the same principles as governed all cases of contract was echoed by Chief Justice Marshall in *Huidekoper's Lessee v. Douglas* (1805), another case between rival claimants to land in Pennsylvania. In his opinion for the Court, the chief justice described a state law as "a contract, and although a state is a party, it ought to be construed according to those well established principles which regulate contracts generally."

With respect to how vested-rights doctrine and the contract clause applied to the particular case of the Yazoo sale and its revocation, sources that likely engaged Marshall's attention were Robert G. Harper's pamphlet, with Alexander Hamilton's appended opinion, and the extensive debates in Congress. Harper, who was counsel for Peck in 1809 and 1810, had defended the legality of Georgia's sale of the Yazoo lands in *The Case of the Georgia Sales on the Mississippi Considered*, published in 1797. Most of this pamphlet was devoted to defending Georgia's title to the Mississippi lands as against that of the United States. In a relatively brief argument against the legal validity of the 1796 rescinding act, Harper ignored the contract clause except for a footnote reference to Hamilton's opinion. Instead, he asserted two grounds for denying the "legal effect" of the 1796 act. First, it was an unwarranted assumption of the judicial power "to declare what the *law is*" and thus violated the "fundamental" constitutional principle of the separation of powers. Second, in revoking the sale contracts the act flouted the "invariable maxim of law and of natural justice, that one of the parties to a contract, cannot by his own act, exempt himself, from its obligation."

No one who argued against the constitutionality of Georgia's rescinding act was content to rest the case solely on the ground that it impaired the obligation of contract and was void under the contract clause of the Constitution. Even Hamilton prefaced his 1796 opinion by pronouncing the rescinding act "a contravention of the first principles of natural justice and social policy." The subordinate role of the contract clause was also evident in the congressional debates on the Yazoo question. Those who contested the legality of the Georgia act put greater emphasis on natural law and vested-rights arguments. These arguments in turn borrowed heavily from the N.E.M. Land Co.'s "Vindication," which had been presented to Congress in 1804. The "Vindication," whose principal author was Perez Morton, provided the most exhaustive statement to date of the case against Georgia's rescinding act, bringing together arguments that had previously been advanced individually.

The "Vindication" contended that the rescinding act was "void in law" no matter whether the Georgia legislature acted as party to the contracts under the 1795 law, as a judicial tribunal, or in its "common capacity as a legislature." In the first capacity, as a party, the legislature violated the well-known maxim that "'no man has a right to be a judge in his own case.'" Harper and others had cited this maxim in slightly different form as stating that a party to a contract could not exempt himself from its obligation. The "Vindication" next denied that the legislature could act as a judicial tribunal, repeating the familiar principle of separation of powers—a principle secured by both the national and state constitutions.

The "Vindication" gave closest attention to considering the Georgia Assembly's "common capacity" as a legislature. Here it recapitulated themes others had invoked against legislative power, particularly in denying that a legislature's power to repeal its own acts was absolute. Legislative acts, it was argued, were essentially of two kinds. One was "public acts for the government of all the citizens," which could be repealed or modified as the legislature saw fit. Other acts were "of a very different nature," such as "contracts, pacts and agreements entered into for certain purposes." Although both kinds of acts were termed "laws," the latter were contracts between two parties, in which rights were "acquired, and vested." These could not, "from the nature of things, be annulled, abrogated or repealed." Other acts belonging to this category were grants of public privileges such as tolls or grants of land or any grant in which individuals were "vested with a particular right." This was classic vested-rights doctrine: to abrogate rights acquired under these laws was to annihilate "every principle of civil liberty."

The "Vindication" then proceeded to divide acts in the nature of contracts into two classes, "executory and executed," a distinction borrowed from Blackstone that Chief Justice Marshall would also employ. In the former the benefit was to vest in the future, while in the latter it had already vested. Executed acts could not be repealed because the rights acquired under the act had vested in another party and "the thing contracted for is actually transferred, and the possession vested in the grantee." On this ground the rescinding act was "void and of no effect" because the act of 1795 had vested rights in certain persons of which they could not be "rightfully deprived" by subsequent legislation without violating "the very fundamental principles on which all our governments rest, and of every principle of national and municipal law." Only after many pages expatiating on vested rights, including extensive quotations from Vattel's *Law of Nations* and Chase's opinion in *Calder v. Bull*, did the "Vindication" finally declare the rescinding act to be "a direct infringement and violation" of the contract clause of the Constitution. That clause expressly prohibited not only the legislature but also the people of Georgia in convention from impairing the obligation of contract. Ultimately, the "Vindication" chose to clinch the case against the rescinding act by invoking "still higher authority than the national constitution." Georgia's claim of power to abrogate the sale contracts was "denied by every principle of NATURAL LAW. Power may vanquish but it cannot destroy right, since that is derived from the nature of things, and, while the passions and feelings of men are governed by the circumstances of the moment, remains founded on a firm and solid basis, which will abide forever."

As he prepared to hear *Fletcher v. Peck* at the 1809 term of the Supreme Court, Chief Justice Marshall was no doubt thoroughly familiar with all the arguments derived from natural law, vested-rights doctrine, and the contract clause in favor of circumscribing the powers of the state legislatures and justifying judicial intervention to enforce those limits. He had himself expounded on vested rights in

Marbury v. Madison, though this was a case of executive rather than legislative deprivation of rights. Withholding Marbury's commission, he wrote, was "an act deemed by the court not warranted by law, but violative of a vested legal right," adding that the "question whether a right has vested or not, is, in its nature, judicial, and must be tried by the judicial authority." More directly relevant to the issues in the Yazoo case was a brief opinion he gave in *Ogden v. Blackledge*, decided in the U.S. Circuit Court for North Carolina in January 1803. To remove doubts whether an act of 1789 had repealed a 1715 act of limitations, the North Carolina legislature in 1799 enacted a statute declaring the 1715 act to be in force. Marshall adjudged the 1799 act void as a violation of the principle of separation of powers, which was explicitly declared to be part of North Carolina's constitution. It was the judiciary's province "to decide upon laws when made, and the extent and operation of them," he wrote, so the question whether the 1789 act repealed the 1715 act was "a judicial matter, and not a legislative one." After invoking separation of powers to protect vested rights and enforce constitutional limits, he then suggested as an afterthought another explicit protection. The 1799 law, he said, seemed "also to be void" as contravening the contract clause of the Constitution. Would not the obligation of contract be impaired, he asked, if a creditor who in 1789 could recover his debt would by the 1799 act "be entirely deprived of his remedy?"

Fletcher v. Peck: First Argument, March 1809

After the U.S. Circuit Court ruled in Peck's favor in October 1807, Fletcher filed his appeal in the Supreme Court in February 1808. The case was scheduled for argument at the February 1809 term. To represent Peck in the appeal, the N.E.M. Land Co. hired John Quincy Adams, who had recently resigned from the U.S. Senate after breaking with the Federalist Party. After resigning, Adams resumed the practice of law in Boston while continuing to serve as the Boylston Professor of Rhetoric and Oratory at Harvard. In 1806 Adams had managed to get the Senate to adopt his Yazoo compromise bill, only to watch the House reject it the same day the bill was received.

Benjamin Joy, a N.E.M. Land Co. director, had approached Adams in October 1808 about going to Washington to argue the case before the high court. The latter was already engaged to be in the capital the next term as counsel for the defense in *Hope Insurance Company v. Boardman.* Two months of negotiation followed in order to reach mutually acceptable terms—presumably regarding Adams's fee. After the company refused his initial proposal, Adams promised to reconsider. Several weeks later he gave his "final answer" to Joy, which was "not to accede to the terms proposed." Finally, in mid-December, Adams announced that Joy and Peck had accepted his terms for undertaking the business.

With characteristic thoroughness, Adams commenced preparing the case by reading the voluminous record and papers. "Let no neglect or indolence deduct from the sum of exertions which I can apply to this case," he confided to his diary. With a view to understand the case against Peck and the Yazoo claimants, he read Abraham Bishop's *Georgia Speculation Unveiled.* He met several times with Peck and Samuel Dexter, who had represented Peck in the U.S. circuit court and was deeply involved in Yazoo as a purchaser and agent. Adams, however, found Dexter only "slightly acquainted with the facts of the cause, and utterly ignorant of some among the most material." As a lawyer, Dexter thought great preparation was "useless," preferring to shape a case "upon the ground taken by the other party." To which Adams replied, "This may answer for him but will not answer my purpose."

After a final meeting with Peck and Dexter in late January 1809, Adams departed for Washington. The weather was cold and the snow deep enough that part of the journey could be taken by sleigh. After New Haven, the carriages had wheels, "though there was snow enough for travelling in sleighs." He was in Philadelphia by January 30 and there called on Joseph Hopkinson to engage him as cocounsel for Peck. Hopkinson, however, informed him that he did not plan to attend the 1809 term. Adams then wrote to Peck for advice about likely assistant counsel. The latter suggested that Adams consult with Gideon Granger on the spot in Washington. Detained by illness at Baltimore for a day, an exhausted Adams reached Washington on February 3. Soon thereafter he obtained the services of Robert G.

Harper, then in Washington for the Supreme Court term, to join him in arguing *Fletcher*. As an early investor in Yazoo and as a legislator and pamphleteer, Harper possessed an unrivaled knowledge of the case.

The Supreme Court opened on February 6, with Chief Justice Marshall and Associate Justices Cushing, Washington, and Livingston present. Johnson arrived a few days later. Because construction of its new quarters in the basement of the Capitol had not yet been completed, the Court met at Long's Hotel on Capitol Hill. A month later, the city's first inaugural ball would be held at Long's, hosted by President Madison and his wife, Dolley. Because Fletcher was the plaintiff in error, the case would open with the argument of his counsel, Luther Martin. A Baltimore lawyer, Martin two years earlier had scored his greatest forensic triumph by securing the acquittal of accused traitor Aaron Burr. This formidable advocate managed to stay in top form professionally over many years despite habitual drunkenness—"Lawyer Brandy Bottle," as he was known—and careless personal appearance. It is not known whether Martin's fondness for the bottle accounts for his being unprepared when the Court first called *Fletcher* for argument on February 16. The case was called a second time on February 24, and again Martin was not present and not ready.

Finally, on March 1, Martin presented his opening argument. In this action for breach of covenant, the defendant Peck had pleaded four pleas. The plaintiff Fletcher had demurred to the first three pleas, admitting the facts recited in those pleas but denying that they were a legally sufficient response to the breaches of covenant alleged by the plaintiff. Although Judge Cushing in the circuit court had overruled the demurrers, Martin seized upon variations in the language of the pleadings to contend that the pleas were not responsive to the allegations and that the demurrers should therefore be sustained. The plaintiff's first count, for example, complained that the Georgia *legislature* had no authority to sell the lands in question, but the plea stated that the Georgia *governor* was legally empowered to sell the lands. After raising the same objection to the pleas to the second and third counts, Martin contended that by the special verdict on the fourth count and plea Georgia was never "seised in fee" of the lands and that at the time of the Revolution they devolved from the British crown to the United States.

In reply to Martin, Adams took up the entire day of March 2, and Harper spoke between two and three hours on March 3. After dismissing Martin's objections to the pleas as form without substance, they devoted the greater portion of their argument to demonstrating that title to the lands had belonged to Georgia from the time of its 1732 charter until the cession to the United States in 1802. They gave particular attention to explicating the Proclamation of 1763 to show that it was not intended to "disannex" Georgia's western lands. They cited numerous public acts that, so they asserted, explicitly or implicitly recognized the title to be in Georgia. Having good title, the Georgia legislature, Peck's counsel insisted, had full authority to sell the lands and convey a "fee simple" title even before the Indian title had been "extinguished." The Indian title was a mere right of "occupancy" for hunting purposes, not a legal possession in the sense of the English common law. Although it could sell the lands, the Georgia legislature could not revoke the grant once it was executed. The rescinding act of 1796, Peck's lawyers declared, was an exercise of judicial not legislative power and a violation of the Constitution's prohibition against impairing the obligation of contract. "A grant is a contract executed," they argued, "and it creates also an implied executory contract, which is, that the grantee shall continue to enjoy the thing granted according to the terms of the grant." They concluded by denying the judiciary's authority to inquire into possible legislative corruption, which in any event could not affect the rights of innocent purchasers.

Martin followed with the closing argument, which began on March 3 and continued through March 4, during which court adjourned two hours to attend the inauguration of President Madison. He reiterated his contention that the Proclamation of 1763 detached the western lands of Georgia and the other royal colonies and reserved them for the Indians. The British crown, not the states, had title to the lands and the right of preemption—that is, the right to purchase the lands occupied by the Indians. This right was ceded by the peace treaty to the United States.

Of his own speech to the Court, Adams chastised himself for being insufficiently "clear in my arrangement and method" and for being "dull and tedious almost beyond endurance." Commentators have criticized Martin's argument as "half-hearted and uninspired" and wholly ignoring the critical questions of whether bribery nullified the 1795 sale and whether the rescinding act violated the contract clause. To appraise Martin's performance on the basis of the case report might not do him justice. Although Martin held the floor for at least five or six hours over a period of three days, the reporter Cranch accorded Fletcher's counsel just slightly more than two out of ten printed pages devoted to the arguments. A possible explanation for this evident disproportion is that Adams and Harper may have provided Cranch with notes or memoranda of their arguments and that Martin did not.

However defective, Cranch's report appears to have faithfully reflected Martin's primary object, which was to persuade the Court that Georgia never possessed legal title to the Yazoo lands. Martin can hardly be faulted for focusing on the title question. This was indeed the principal issue, one that had received by far the greatest attention in the voluminous pamphlet literature on the Yazoo sale. The points arising from alleged legislative corruption and from the contract clause were subsidiary. To win his case, Martin with good reason believed that his best chance was to succeed on the broader issue of title. Martin's supposed lackluster representation of Fletcher has also been attributed to the lawyer's intoxication, which at one point reportedly forced the court to adjourn. No foundation exists for such a story. Had such an incident occurred during the 1809 argument, Adams surely would have recorded it in his diary.

On March 11, a week after the argument closed, Chief Justice Marshall delivered a brief opinion declaring that the circuit court had erred in overruling Fletcher's demurrer to Peck's first plea. The court accepted Martin's objection that the plea declaring that Georgia's *governor* was empowered to sell the lands was not a sufficient denial of the plaintiff's allegation that the *legislature* had no authority to sell them. The court decided the case "against us on a *defect in the pleadings*," a disappointed Adams wrote to his wife. "This is one of the *mysteries* of the Law, which I could not explain to you so as to make it intelligible. It has nothing to do with the real questions in the case."

In truth, the court's reversal on a technical point of pleading was a convenient cover for its reluctance to decide the merits of a case that had been so obviously arranged for the purpose. Even before argument commenced, Adams heard doubts expressed by the Court whether to hear the case, particularly noting that Justice Washington had "scruples about sitting." A few days after argument concluded, Adams reported conversations with both Marshall and Justice Livingston in which they intimated "the reluctance of the Court to decide the case at all, as it appeared manifestly made up for the purpose of getting the Court's judgment upon all the points. And although they have given some decisions in such cases, they appear not disposed to do so now." After reading his written opinion on March 11, Marshall, according to Adams, "added verbally, that, circumstanced as the Court are, only five judges attending, there were difficulties which would have prevented them from giving any opinion at this term had the pleadings been correct; and the Court the more readily forbore giving it, as from the complexion of the pleadings they could not but see that at the time when the covenants were made the parties had notice of the acts covenanted against; that this was not to be taken as part of the Court's opinion, but as a motive why they had thought proper not to give one at this term."

As matters stood on March 11, the case would have to go back to the circuit court and begin again, which likely meant a two-year delay in having the case reheard by the Supreme Court. Adams accordingly drew up an agreement, which he and Martin signed, that the parties would waive all exceptions to the pleadings and that the case would be "submitted to the Court, upon the Covenants contained in the plaintiff's declaration, and on the facts stated in the Special verdict." The Supreme Court consented to the agreement, which meant that it would not enter a formal judgment of reversal. The case remained on the Supreme Court's docket and was continued for further argument on the merits to the 1810 term. Adams had good reason to believe his client Peck would be victorious. After the court's opinion of March 11, Adams asked Chief Justice Marshall if "the Court had formed an opinion" on the title question, "to which he answered that on that and the right of the Legislature to sell, if the opinion of the Court had been against the defendant they would have given it."

Adams did not appear for the re-argument of *Fletcher*, having accepted a commission as the U.S. minister to Russia. His place as Peck's lawyer was taken by Joseph Story, a rising young legal talent and Republican politician from Salem, Massachusetts. He was fully conversant with the Yazoo business, having traveled to Washington on two previous occasions to lobby on behalf of the N.E.M. Land Co. Story had recently served a term in the U.S. House of Representatives, where his opposition to the embargo placed him at odds with the Jefferson administration. Within two years, following Justice Cushing's death, Story would take a seat on the U.S. Supreme Court, at thirty-two the youngest person ever to serve on that tribunal.

At the 1809 term several justices privately expressed reservations about deciding a case that was "manifestly made up for the purpose of getting the Court's judgment upon all the points." At the next term Justice Johnson publicly expressed his unwillingness to decide "a mere feigned case." Why did Chief Justice Marshall and his brethren ultimately agree to proceed with a case so artfully designed to elicit an advisory opinion? What considerations might have persuaded the justices to set aside their misgivings?

Fletcher v. *Peck* did meet the formal requirements of a "case or controversy." The parties were real persons, one of whom brought a common law action of covenant broken. Such an action between purchasers and sellers of Yazoo lands was not unknown. In 1798 a Connecticut superior court gave judgment for the defendants in an action for covenant broken brought against Phineas Miller and John C. Nightingale, who in 1795 had sold a large tract of Yazoo lands to New Haven purchasers. If the sale between Fletcher and Peck had taken place, say, in late in 1795 or early 1796, the case between them would have presented a clear legal dispute. The actual sale having occurred in 1803, the justices, as Marshall noted in 1809, "could not but see that at the time when the covenants were made the parties had notice of the acts covenanted against." They were perhaps willing to overlook this discrepancy, to accept the fiction that Fletcher entered into the sale contract oblivious of the rescinding act, because the pleadings presented a live issue appropriate for judicial decision. Critics of *Fletcher* contend that the case was a sham because there was no adversarial issue between the parties, each having an interest in the vindication of the Yazoo title. But the plaintiff's interest was to recover $3,000 and the defendant's interest was to resist this claim. This was essentially the same issue at stake in the numerous cases between buyers and sellers of Yazoo lands that had taken place earlier in New England. It is not implausible that Fletcher would prefer to get his money refunded rather than retain a deed that was of no immediate value and whose long-run value was uncertain even with a Supreme Court opinion upholding the title.

Justice Johnson overcame his scruples because of his "confidence" in the counsel who represented the parties, believing "they would never consent to impose a mere feigned case upon this court." This motive must have operated on the other justices as well, perhaps with John Quincy Adams, an exemplar of New England integrity, particularly in mind. Adams, Peck's original counsel, had supported the Yazoo claimants in the Senate, though without much enthusiasm, having no personal interest himself. His voluminous diary contains no hints that he harbored doubts about the authenticity of his client's case.

The justices were perhaps the more willing to take the case because otherwise the Yazoo claimants would be deprived of a forum in which to assert their rights at law. Indeed, other means of legal recourse in state and federal courts were effectively closed to them. Congress, as the claimants had often requested, might have referred the title question directly to the Supreme Court, but the justices likely would have resisted giving an advisory opinion under such circumstances. The advisory opinion they were being asked to give in *Fletcher* would at least have the virtue of accompanying the decision of an actual case or controversy. Such a decision they knew was bound to be controversial and particularly obnoxious to the sovereign pretensions of Georgia. But unlike the Cherokee cases of the 1830s, the Supreme Court would not in this instance find itself in the awkward and vulnerable position of having to enforce its judgment against a state. The only legal effect of a decision upholding the Yazoo title would be to deny Fletcher or his legal representatives the recovery of his damages, a judgment that required virtually no enforcement.

Conceivably, too, the chief justice and his colleagues believed they could break the impasse in Congress and advance a long-standing policy goal of the Jefferson and Madison administrations to effect a compromise with the Yazoo claimants. If so, they clearly misjudged the depth and tenacity of the opposition. As the event would show, the immediate effect of the Court's decision in *Fletcher* was to stiffen the resistance of the anti-Yazoo forces. It is unlikely, however, that the politically astute chief justice was under the illusion that the Court's legal pronouncement could or should resolve a question so deeply mired in politics. He for one did not want his Court to be perceived as intruding into the political sphere. Still, in *Fletcher,* the chief justice might well have seen an opportunity to make an important statement of constitutional law, just as he had done in 1803 in the politically charged case of *Marbury v. Madison.* In both cases the Court had virtually free rein to speak law without having to enforce its legal judgment. Such a motive for accepting the case of course could not be publicly acknowledged.

CHAPTER SIX

The Supreme Court Decides *Fletcher*; Congress Indemnifies Claimants

Second Argument and Decision, March 1810

When the Supreme Court convened for the 1810 term on February 5, the justices sat for the first time in their new courtroom designed by Benjamin Latrobe. Situated on the ground floor of the original north wing of the Capitol, this chamber would be the Court's home until 1860. As they waited for the second argument of *Fletcher v. Peck* and an anticipated favorable decision by the Supreme Court, the New England claimants were simultaneously pressing their case again in the halls of Congress. Two years earlier Massachusetts Governor James Sullivan's memorial on behalf of his state's Yazoo investors was rudely denounced by opponents of relief. At the same session the House overwhelming rejected a motion to allow the N.E.M Land Co.'s lawyer Joseph Story to speak on the House floor.

Now the N.E.M. Land Co. was back with yet another memorial, signed by the company's directors, one of whom was John Peck. So, too, was Story, the company's counsel, poised to argue its case and that of his client Peck (which were one and the same case) in both the legislative and judicial forums. The company may have believed that its political prospects were brighter under the recently inaugurated President Madison, who as a commissioner in 1803 had endorsed a plan to compromise with the purchasers under Georgia's act of 1795. One of the company's directors sent the president a copy of the latest memorial, assuring him that there was "indubitable proof" that the New England purchasers "were in no measure accessory" to nor did they have any knowledge of fraud alleged to have occurred in the Yazoo sale. The memorial rehearsed in abridged form arguments the company had made at great length in its "Vindication," presented to Congress five years earlier. Although it contained nothing new, the memorial clearly aimed to reiterate and bring into sharper focus the company's portrayal of its investors as innocent purchasers, without notice of fraud, many of whom had suffered severe financial reversal. Unlike the earlier "Vindication," which devoted many pages to denying that there was legal proof of the existence of fraud, the 1809 memorialists were content to say that fraud was "neither denied nor admitted," not knowing "facts enough to be prepared to do either." Even if fraud had been committed, this matter was "immaterial" to the rights of persons having no notice of the fact.

When the memorial was presented to the House in December 1809, a motion to refer it to the committee of claims provoked testy opposition from the anti-Yazoo troops, just as had happened with Governor Sullivan's memorial. In the absence of John Randolph, who did not take his seat until March 1810, George Troup of Georgia led the fight against compromise with corruption. He not only denied the claimants' assertion of ignorance but accused them of being "parties" to the corruption—"*participes criminis*"—as "original actors in it." After a short debate, the motion was narrowly approved, sixty to fifty-six. A majority of the affirmative votes came from Federalists, whose party was resurgent in New England owing to the administration's unpopular embargo policy. The memorial accordingly went to the committee of claims, where Story argued the company's case on February 16.

The day before, on February 15, Story joined Harper in representing Peck in the second argument of *Fletcher v. Peck*. Martin again served as counsel for Fletcher, whose death the preceding October was perhaps not yet known. The argument passed without comment or notice in the newspapers. Cranch's report wove together the arguments of 1809 and 1810 and merged those of Adams, Harper, and Story into a single argument "for the defendant in error." Since only one day was needed for rehearing the case in 1810, the lawyers confined themselves to briefly recapitulating arguments that had consumed four days at the 1809 term. They followed the same order, with Martin leading off for the plaintiff Fletcher, followed by Harper and Story for Peck, and Martin concluding. Having agreed to put aside the technical objections he had raised against the pleadings in 1809, Martin in 1810 again apparently focused his argument on the merits to denying that Georgia had title to the lands it had purportedly conveyed in January 1795. If the Court ruled against him on this issue (as Marshall had intimated it would at the preceding term), Martin in his meagerly reported argument gave no indication that he went beyond the pleadings to make the case that Peck's title was bad either on the ground that the sale was originally void because of legislative corruption or that the sale had been legally and constitutionally voided by the 1796 rescinding act. On Peck's behalf Harper and Story no doubt gave primary attention to establishing that Georgia had good title to the lands it sold in 1795, believing that if they prevailed on this question it would be easier to show that the title conveyed to their clients was still good notwithstanding corruption or the rescinding act.

On March 16 Chief Justice Marshall delivered the opinion of the Supreme Court. Sitting with him were Associate Justices Washington, Johnson, Livingston, and Todd. Again, as in 1809, only five of the seven judges were present. Todd had missed the 1809 term; Cushing had been present in 1809 but now ill health prevented him and Chase (who also missed the 1809 term) from attending. "The pleadings being now amended, this cause comes on again to be heard," said the chief justice—a slight misstatement, for he apparently forgot that counsel at the preceding term had agreed to waive exceptions to the pleadings in lieu of amending them. He then proceeded to decide the case on the original pleadings, which followed in succession the four counts in Fletcher's declaration, the "breach of covenant" assigned in each count, and Peck's plea. Each of the first three counts and pleas concluded with plaintiff and defendant joining in demurrer, leaving to the Court to decide the law on the matters raised in the pleadings. It was to Marshall's advantage to adhere to the dry language of the pleadings in fashioning an opinion that strove as much as possible to speak abstract law stripped of the impassioned politics of the Yazoo land sale.

The first count set forth as a breach that the Georgia legislature had no power to sell the lands that Peck had sold to Fletcher, which presented the question whether the 1795 sale act was void as repugnant to Georgia's constitution. This was perhaps the weakest point of the case against the sale's validity, and the Court had little difficulty in refusing to strike down the act. Such an exercise of judicial authority should "seldom, if ever," occur "in a doubtful case," Marshall said, noting that the "opposition between the constitution and the law should be such that the judge feels a clear and strong conviction of their incompatibility with each other." He might have added that judicial deference was peculiarly appropriate in a case in which the federal Supreme Court was being called upon to void a state law based on its reading of the state's constitution. The Court would feel no such inhibition when confronting the incompatibility between a state law and the federal Constitution.

Fletcher's second count alleged as a breach that the sale was void on the ground that the act was obtained by bribery of the Georgia legislators. Peck's plea, while not conceding that bribery had occurred, avowed that until after the Georgia Company's sale to James Greenleaf in August 1795 neither Greenleaf nor Peck and others claiming under Greenleaf had notice or knowledge of such bribery. In considering this count, the chief justice again adopted a stance of judicial restraint, expressing reservations about the judiciary's capacity to intervene in cases of legislative corruption. A court's competence to void a sale contract and annul rights of persons having no notice of corruption was questionable even in a case brought by the state itself, he said. Such a case would draw a court out of its comfort zone, presenting the perplexing if not insuperable difficulty of determining what degree of corruption was necessary before a court could intervene.

In considering this count, Chief Justice Marshall had no intention of drawing the Court into the particular circumstances of the 1795 Yazoo sale, outrageous as they were, nor was he required to do so. "This was not a bill brought by the state of Georgia, to annul the contract," he wrote. The Court's only duty was to decide the case "as made out in the pleadings," an action for breach of covenant on a deed for Georgia lands between two individuals; one party assigned as a breach that some members of the Georgia legislature were induced to vote for the sale act, which accordingly was "a mere nullity." But, insisted the chief justice, this "solemn question" of legislative corruption, could not "be brought thus collaterally and incidentally before the Court. It would be indecent, in the extreme, upon a private contract, between two individuals, to enter into an inquiry respecting the corruption of the sovereign power of a state." The pleadings allowed Marshall to steer clear of the notorious facts and contentious politics of Yazoo and deal with the issue of corruption in a way that was amenable to explication of principles applicable to this and other cases. These principles counseled against judicial inquiry into legislative motives even in so egregious a case as the Yazoo land sale.

The Court had little difficulty affirming the circuit court's rulings in Peck's favor on the first two counts. Fletcher's third count also recited the circumstances of legislative corruption as giving rise to the 1796 act rescinding the sale and asserting Georgia's title to lands conveyed in 1795. By this act, the count stated, Peck's title "was constitutionally and legally impaired, and rendered null and void." To this count, Peck repeated his plea to the second count, not admitting the bribery charges while affirming that in any event he and "the first purchaser" (Greenleaf) and "all intermediate holders" had no notice of corruption. By demurring to this plea, Fletcher admitted as fact that Peck was a purchaser without notice. The Court accordingly was not permitted to inquire into a matter that was hotly disputed in Congress, where the opponents of compromise loudly and repeatedly scoffed at the notion that the Yazoo purchasers were innocent, that they could claim to be unaware of the notorious circumstances of original sale. Most recently, Troup had denounced the New England claimants not only as having knowledge of the corruption but as participating in it. Again, the pleadings spared the Court from being drawn into a controversial political question.

Even without having to examine Peck's status as an innocent purchaser, Marshall acknowledged that the pleadings on this count raised questions of "importance and difficulty" that were "deeply felt by the court." His ensuing consideration of the legality and constitutionality of the rescinding act filled eight of the sixteen printed pages of his opinion. At the outset he framed the issue in a way that foretold how the Court would decide it. He placed the burden on those who would defend the validity of an act that in renouncing a sale tainted with corruption had in fact "annihilated" the rights of innocent purchasers. In this light the rescinding law "must be considered as a mere act of power which must find its vindication in a train of reasoning not often heard in courts of justice." To acknowledge the validity of this act, he implied, was in effect to concede that there were no limits to the legislative powers of the state governments. In stating the challenge confronting the Court in such stark terms, the chief justice left little doubt where the course of judicial duty lay.

Much of this section of the opinion consisted of a short disquisition on the nature and limits of legislative power, in which Marshall drew upon arguments that had been invoked against the rescinding act as a deprivation of vested rights. Critics, for example, had repeatedly denounced the Georgia legislature for flouting the maxim that no one should be judge of his own cause and for contravening the principle of separation of powers in deciding a judicial question. For his purposes, the chief justice was willing to concede that a legislature could act as a judicial tribunal, a concession apparently made on the basis of his knowledge that colonial legislatures had exercised judicial powers and some state legislatures continued to do so. If, however, a legislature assumed the role of judicial tribunal and claimed "the power of judging in its own case," still it could not or should not act with impunity, he said. There were "certain great principles of justice, whose authority is universally acknowledged, that ought not to be entirely disregarded." A legislature acting as a judicial tribunal should observe the same rules that governed the regular courts of justice; otherwise its decision was "a mere act of power in which it was controlled only by its own will."

To illustrate the point, Marshall likened this case to one in which a court of chancery heard a suit to set aside the original conveyance to the Georgia land companies as having been obtained by fraud. On clear proof of fraud, the court might decree that the conveyance be set aside as between the state of Georgia and the land companies. However, according to the well-established rules and principles of equity, such a decree could not disregard the rights of purchasers without notice of the fraud. "All titles would be insecure," he wrote, "and the intercourse between man and man would be very seriously obstructed, if this principle be overturned." In short, the Georgia legislature acting in the character of a judicial tribunal was bound by the rules of a court of chancery and "by the clearest principles of equity" to respect the rights of innocent purchasers.

If the Georgia legislature acknowledged no such restraints, then, said the chief justice, the rescinding act was an act of power—a power that could "devest any other individual of his lands" if the legislature so willed. It was far from his intention "to speak with disrespect" of the Georgia legislature, he said, but to identify the issue arising from the rescinding act as "a general question" and to treat it as such. Although such "powerful objections" as alleged against the Yazoo grant might not again occur, the principle behind the rescinding act, said Marshall, could "be applied to every case to which it shall be the will of any legislature to apply it. The principle is this; that a legislature may, by its own act, devest the vested estate of any man whatever, for reasons which shall, by itself, be deemed sufficient." The chief justice left no doubt as to what he believed to be at stake in this case. Georgia's rescinding act, for all its good intentions in punishing fraud and purging the state of the stigma of corruption, was a dangerous precedent, with dire implications for the security of private vested rights in the republican governments of the United States.

Chief Justice Marshall next considered the legislature's competence to revoke the titles of innocent purchasers and resume possession of the lands on the basis of the principle "that one legislature is competent to repeal any act which a former legislature was competent to pass; and that one legislature cannot abridge the powers of a succeeding legislature." Here he relied on another vested-rights argument that distinguished between "general legislation" and laws in the nature of contracts, a distinction perhaps most fully elaborated in the N.E.M. Land Co.'s "Vindication." As respected general laws, he acknowledged the legislature's absolute power of repeal. But when a law was "in its nature a contract, when absolute rights have vested under that contract, a repeal of a law cannot devest those rights." An act annulling vested rights "if legitimate" was "rendered so by a power applicable to the case of every individual in the community," said Marshall, again sounding a warning about the harmful consequences of a bad precedent.

This observation led Marshall to wonder whether there were inherent limits to legislative power as prescribed by natural law and

where were "they to be found" if property "fairly and honestly acquired, may be seized without compensation." The chief justice professed to be genuinely in doubt about whether an act transferring an
individual's property to the public was "in the nature of the legislative power." It was, he said, a question "well worthy of serious consideration." Applying the principle of separation of powers did not
yield a conclusive answer to this question. The legislature's "peculiar
province" was "to prescribe general rules"; applying those rules to
individuals "would seem to be the duty of other departments." Ultimately, Marshall had to concede the indeterminate power of the
legislature: "How far the power of giving the law may involve every
other power, in cases where the constitution is silent, never has been,
and perhaps never can be, definitely stated."

Although acknowledging that the validity of Georgia's rescinding
act "might well be doubted" if Georgia were regarded as "a single
sovereign power," the chief justice could not bring himself to pronounce that act void on the ground that it transcended the limits of
legislative power. But the case could not be considered as if Georgia
were "a single sovereign power." The state was "part of a large empire"; it was "a member of the American union" whose Constitution
was supreme law and imposed limits on the state legislatures. That
Constitution, said Marshall, declared "that no state shall pass any
bill of attainder, ex post facto law, or law impairing the obligation of
contracts." Having so far examined the case in the light of natural law
and vested rights without coming to any resolution, he now shifted
his focus to consider whether the case came "within this prohibitory
section of the constitution."

In the remaining few pages of the opinion, Chief Justice Marshall
expounded the contract clause for the first time, employing the rules
and methods of statutory construction to the text of the Constitution
in order to discover its intention. He adopted this technique in all his
constitutional cases, in the process setting American constitutional
law on a path in which its doctrines developed primarily by means
of judicial exposition of the Constitution's text. In subjecting the
Constitution to scrutiny in the same manner that judges examined
statutes, Marshall imparted to the Constitution the qualities of an

ordinary law, the kind of law that judges routinely interpreted in the regular courts of law. This "legalizing" of the Constitution became a central feature of American constitutional law.

For Marshall, construction—the process of discovering intention—above all meant paying close attention to the meaning of words. Words were to be understood in their natural or ordinary sense unless their context dictated a less common meaning. An interpreter might also refer to the subject matter and purpose of the particular provision to be expounded and if necessary regard that purpose in relation to the broader objects of the whole instrument. As much as possible, Marshall tried to make the Constitution expound itself, so to speak, by construing one provision in reference to another and in reference to the whole. He adopted this approach to explicate the meaning of "contract" as used in the clause prohibiting the states from passing bills of attainder, ex post facto laws, and laws impairing the obligation of contract.

Marshall's starting point was Blackstone's well-known classification of contracts as either executory or executed and the commentator's remark that an executed contract differed "in nothing from a grant." The Yazoo sale provided examples of both kinds of contracts, said the chief justice. The law under which the sale took place was an executory contract, in which the state of Georgia bound itself to convey the lands. This contract was subsequently executed by the conveyance from the governor to the land companies. The grant, or executed contract, nevertheless continued to be binding on the parties, being in effect an implied contract by the grantor not to reassert his right extinguished by the grant. "A party," he said, "is, therefore, always estopped by his own grant." These observations led Marshall to his first act of construction, which was to bring both executory and executed contracts within the reach of the contract clause. In this and in subsequent contract clause cases, the chief justice read much into the Constitution's use of "contract" as a general term, without any distinctions or qualifications to restrict its meaning. He shifted the burden of proof to those who would narrow the scope of the contract clause. To reinforce a broad construction, he pointed to the unreasonableness of excepting certain cases from its reach. "It would be strange," he said, "if a contract to convey"—an executory contract—"was secured by the constitution, while an absolute conveyance"—an executed contract—"remained unprotected."

If "a fair construction"—a favorite phrase—brought grants within the Constitution's protection, did it secure grants by a state as well as those between individuals? Although the words of the contract clause made no such distinction, to extend the clause's reach to contracts made by a state required a more intricate argument. In this second act of construction, Marshall began by invoking one of the Constitution's overarching purposes. "Whatever respect might have been felt for the state sovereignties," he said, the framers viewed with alarm "the violent acts which might grow out of the feelings of the moment." By adopting the Constitution and its restrictions on the state legislatures, the American people accordingly "manifested a determination to shield themselves and their property from the effects of those sudden and strong passions to which men are exposed." In a passage that neatly sums up a major theme of his constitutional jurisprudence, Marshall said the Constitution "contains what may be deemed a bill of rights for the people of each state."

Having summoned the Constitution's broad purposes to aid his construction, Marshall then abruptly shifted to examining the contract clause's immediate context, its juxtaposition with the prohibitions on bills of attainder and ex post facto laws. Here he found further confirmation that the framers did not intend to except state contracts from the contract clause's protection. If the power of the state legislatures over an individual's person and property "was expressly restrained" in the form of attainders or ex post facto laws, what reason could there be to allow the legislatures to seize a person's property by means of an act annulling his title to land? To read the general prohibition on laws impairing the obligation of contracts as exempting state contracts was to do "violence . . . to the natural meaning of words," said the chief justice. Before he was done, Marshall cited one more clue to intention, this one in a provision of the original Constitution that had since been removed. The jurisdiction of the U.S. courts originally included suits brought against the states, he said, without noting that this was actually the Supreme Court's construction of the jurisdiction clause in the case of *Chisholm v. Geor-*

gia (1793). If a state could be sued for violating its own contract, it was "scarcely to be conceived," said the chief justice, that the state's law nullifying that contract could be set up as a defense. Although this "feature" was "no longer found in the constitution," he said, alluding to the Eleventh Amendment (declaring that federal jurisdiction was not to be construed to extend to suits brought against the states), "it aids in the construction of those clauses with which it was originally associated."

Marshall was now prepared to say that there was no error in the circuit court's ruling in favor of Peck on the third count. Reverting to the language of the pleadings, he announced the Court's "unanimous opinion" that Georgia "was restrained, either by general principles which are common to our free institutions, or by the particular provisions of the constitution of the United States, from passing a law whereby the estate of the plaintiff in the premises so purchased could be constitutionally and legally impaired and rendered null and void." Such a statement of the Court's ruling seems oddly equivocal given the chief justice's preceding effort to demonstrate that the rescinding act clearly fell within the contract clause's prohibition. Did he mean to say that "general principles" were equally sufficient with the constitutional text to nullify the law? For Marshall the important thing was that the Court was unanimous in voiding the rescinding act whatever the precise basis of its decision. In his separate opinion (discussed below), Justice Johnson sharply disagreed with Marshall's construction of the contract clause, preferring to rely "on a general principle, on the reason and nature of things: a principle which will impose laws even on the deity." It seems clear that Marshall himself would have been satisfied to rest the decision on the contract clause. Presumably, he spoke for Justices Washington, Livingston, and Todd on this point, though it is possible that their silent acquiescence concealed doubts or disagreement.

The difference between the chief justice and Johnson (and perhaps other justices as well) was that the former preferred to read "general principles" into the text of the contract clause while Johnson believed the text did not support this reading. Both agreed that Georgia's rescinding act amounted to an uncompensated taking of property, a clear violation of a fundamental principle of law. For Johnson, this was sufficient to annul the act. Marshall, in treating a grant as an executed contract with a continuing obligation, made the rescinding act a constitutional infraction as well as a violation of a general principle of law. In the end it did not matter whether the Supreme Court based its decision on general principles or the Constitution because in cases like *Fletcher*, which originated in a federal court, the Supreme Court had broad jurisdiction to consider both general law and the Constitution. On the other hand, in cases coming from the state courts under section 25 of the Judiciary Act, the Supreme Court was restricted to deciding "federal" questions, such as whether a state law contravened the Constitution or a federal statute or treaty. The great advantage of Marshall's broad interpretation of the contract clause was that in cases appealed under section 25 the Supreme Court could treat the state's alleged violation of law as a constitutional question.

The remainder of the opinion, which took up the special verdict arising from Fletcher's fourth and last count, was anticlimax. The special verdict recited grants, treaties, and other public documents upon which the Court was to decide whether at the time of the sale title to the western lands was in the United States or in Georgia. Although this issue consumed much of the pamphlet literature on the Yazoo sale and also monopolized the argument of *Fletcher v. Peck*, the Court had little difficulty finding that Georgia had legal possession of and power to sell the lands. It rejected the plaintiff's principal argument, that the Proclamation of 1763 detached the western lands from the colonies and that during the war the lands were acquired by joint arms for the benefit of the United States. The Court, said Marshall, understood the Proclamation as a mere temporary suspension of settlement, not amounting "to an alteration of the boundaries of the colony." As to whether the western lands became a common national property or belonged to the individual states, that "momentous question" had been settled by the creation of the national domain by means of state cessions of western land claims. That "compromise" was "not now to be disturbed," said the chief justice.

In argument, a justice—undoubtedly Johnson—posed the question whether Georgia could convey a title in "fee simple" to lands occupied by Indian tribes. The Court majority sidestepped this issue, stating "that the nature of the Indian title, which is certainly to be respected by all courts, until it be legitimately extinguished, is not such as to be absolutely repugnant to seisin in fee on the part of the state." The Supreme Court would not fully confront the question of Indian title until 1823 in the case of *Johnson v. McIntosh*, though Justice Johnson did briefly consider the matter in his separate opinion in *Fletcher.*

Johnson's opinion has been described—not inaccurately—as a "dissent," although on the principal question he fully agreed with the Court's ruling invalidating Georgia's rescinding act. A Georgia newspaper noted that Johnson's "dissent" did "honor both to his head and heart." Interesting in its own right, Johnson's opinion helps to clarify Marshall's majority opinion, exposing its broader implications and potential problems. Rather than the contract clause, Johnson relied on standard vested-rights doctrine to deny that the Georgia legislature could revoke the Yazoo grant. Once this property was conveyed, the legislature "lost all control over" it. The property "vested in the individual" and became "intimately blended with his existence, as essentially so as the blood that circulates through his system."

Johnson dissented from what he regarded as a forced and overly broad reading of the contract clause, transforming it into a general protection of private rights from state interference. Although he agreed that the framers intended to provide such protection, he doubted whether the contract clause itself was designed to carry so much weight to accomplish this object. To extend that clause's embrace to grants, or executed contracts, was to enlarge the prohibition to one impairing "'the obligation and *effect* of contracts.'" A grant, he said, "by no means necessarily implies the continuance of an obligation beyond the moment of executing it." Johnson worried that Marshall's construction of the contract clause would bring within its scope many acts affecting contracts—for example, usury laws and statutes of limitation—that had always been considered proper exercises of state legislative powers. Where to draw the line between constitutional and unconstitutional acts would "be found a subject of extreme difficulty," he said. This problem fully revealed itself when the Supreme Court subsequently heard cases arising from state bankruptcy legislation. Faithfully adhering to his principles of construction, Chief Justice Marshall concluded, in the 1827 case of *Ogden v.*

Saunders, that the words of the contract clause made no distinction between bankruptcy acts affecting past contracts and those affecting future contracts and that both were prohibited. But this time he found himself in the minority and was compelled to register his dissent.

Justice Johnson also disagreed with the Court's holding on the first count, namely, that Georgia had "fee simple" possession of the western lands it sold in 1795. Relying on the technical meaning of that term, he doubted whether the state could convey a fee simple title that was subject to extinguishment of the Indian title. Georgia's interest in those lands, he contended, was nothing more than a preemptive right, "a power to acquire a fee-simple by purchase, when the proprietors should be pleased to sell it." Abraham Bishop had made the same point in *Georgia Speculation Unveiled*, dismissing the preemption right as "worthless." Thus, even as he upheld the Yazoo purchasers' title on one point, Johnson expressed doubts about that title on another. He was clearly troubled in deciding *Fletcher*, the more so because it had the aspect of "a mere feigned case."

The Aftermath of *Fletcher v. Peck*

The first public notice of the Supreme Court's decision occurred nearly two weeks after it was handed down. On March 28 the Washington *National Intelligencer* spread Marshall's opinion across the five columns of the first page and part of the second page. In April newspapers in Richmond, Raleigh, Milledgeville (Georgia), and Boston reprinted the opinion, and at least one (the Raleigh *Star*) included Johnson's opinion. The earliest response to *Fletcher v. Peck* occurred in Congress, which remained in session until May 1. After the N.E.M. Land Co.'s memorial had been introduced at the beginning of the session and referred to the House committee of claims, nothing further on the subject of Yazoo had occurred. Story, the company's agent, appeared before that committee on February 16, the day after he argued *Fletcher*. Sometime afterward the committee by its own request was discharged from further consideration because Congress was then preoccupied with British and French attacks on

American shipping. The memorial was back on the table, with the tacit understanding that it would be taken up at the next session. Story had returned home to Massachusetts.

Then, on April 17, Randolph surprised his House colleagues by moving that the memorial be again referred to the committee of claims for a report. "The House must be apprized," he said, "that a judicial decision, of no small importance, had, during the present session of Congress, taken place in relation to that subject." He feared that adjourning the session without examining the Yazoo question would signify "acquiescence" in the decision. He did not wish the House to give the slightest hint of approving a claim that "had been pressed upon the public with such pertinacity, with such art, with such audacity." He denounced the claimants as *the most nefarious combination of men* that ever obtruded themselves upon the patience of the house." The Supreme Court's decision, he added, "was made up on a false and feigned issue" and the defense against it was "either feebly conducted or *traitorously abandoned.*" Troup in like manner censured the decision as one "which the mind of every man attached to Republican principles must revolt at." The question, he darkly warned, "now lay between the Supreme Court and the Government of the United States, *to be decided eventually by the sword.*" When the claims committee chairman objected that not enough time remained for the committee to prepare a report, Randolph withdrew his motion and substituted another, that the company's memorial was "unreasonable, unjust, and ought not to be granted." This motion lost, forty-six for and fifty-four against, with twenty-eight Republicans, including a few from southern states, joining twenty-six Federalists to defeat the motion. Ever persistent, Randolph proposed another motion, "that the petitioners have leave to withdraw their petition," which after "a desultory debate" was postponed indefinitely. The memorial thus remained on the table.

In Boston, news of *Fletcher v. Peck* was hailed as forever putting "at rest any further discussion on the validity of the Title of the numerous sufferers in the Eastern States." The *Boston Patriot* optimistically expressed confidence that members of Congress, even those from Georgia, would "no longer hesitate to listen to" the claimants' petitions. At a meeting of the claimants under the Georgia grants held at the Concert Hall on April 16, a committee of five was appointed to devise a plan of how they "might most effectually avail themselves of the late important decision of the *Supreme Judicial Court of the United States.*" The *Patriot* advised the claimants to pursue the same strategy of compromise, seeking recompense in return for extinguishing their titles. The Supreme Court decision, the newspaper suggested, placed the claimants in a better bargaining position, for it was now "palpably" in the United States' "*Interest*" to meet their wishes. At the same time the paper cautioned that it was equally in the claimants' interest to accept an "*Indemnity*," even though the decision reached "to the whole extent of their purchase." The *Patriot* confidently predicted that Congress at its next session would "think it expedient and proper to effect" a compromise. If this fell short of a full indemnity, the claimants would at least have "an opportunity of displaying their Patriotism, and of sacrificing something to the Peace and Harmony of their Country."

Meanwhile, in the Mississippi Territory, the Supreme Court's opinion was producing turmoil and confusion among those who had purchased or intended to purchase public lands that had recently been opened for sale after the United States acquired them from the Cherokee and Chickasaw tribes. These lands lay in the Muscle Shoals region of present-day northern Alabama and thus overlapped with the tract sold by Georgia in 1795 to Zachariah Cox of the Tennessee Company. Even before the *Fletcher* decision, Michael Harrison had settled on lands he had purchased from Cox and was threatening to sue anyone purchasing within his claimed tract. Territorial officials expressed concern that Harrison's assertion of title would hinder sales of public lands and sought to have the federal government remove him as an "intruder" under the 1807 act "to prevent settlements being made on lands ceded to the United States, until authorized by law." They also endeavored to assure persons occupying those lands that Harrison's claim was "a fraudulent one, and unworthy of notice."

Publication of *Fletcher* emboldened Harrison to step up his activities, even competing with the government by selling out his claim. He and purchasers under him "industriously circulated" the opinion and used "all possible means" to persuade the public "that this decision completely confirms their title, in opposition to that of the United States." Their warnings to purchasers under the United States "to give immediate possession" caused "much uneasiness." Some who had purchased from the government also purchased from Harrison "to quiet their claim." The disruption resulting from Harrison's actions and the *Fletcher* decision was only temporary, however. Although in June 1810 few sales were recorded in the public land office, by the end of July the pace had picked up considerably. The "impression" made by *Fletcher* on the public mind was "now nearly done away," wrote a land office official, and the people were "generally quieted as to their titles."

The conflict over titles at Muscle Shoals was set forth in a report submitted by Secretary of the Treasury Gallatin to the House of Representatives, which was published as a pamphlet. The report attracted the attention of John Peck, the winning party in the Supreme Court case, prompting him to publish a "Cautionary Notice" addressed to "settlers and all persons contemplating making purchases of lands in the Mississippi Territory" that had been granted by Georgia in January 1795. Writing under a Boston dateline of June 20, 1810, Peck expressed his concern about the efforts of territorial officials (reported in correspondence with Gallatin) "to diffuse the most erroneous impressions, relative to the title of those individuals, who claim lands in the Mississippi territory under Georgia titles." To correct the "errour" he provided an extract of the *Fletcher* opinion in which the Court declared that the title conveyed by Georgia in 1795 could not be "constitutionally and legally impaired" by the rescinding act. He signed himself as "one of the principal owners of land in the Mississippi territory under the grants of the State of Georgia . . . whose title has been adjudged valid in the case aforesaid." To ensure greatest dissemination of his notice, Peck directed its insertion for "three weeks successively" in ten newspapers throughout the south. He assured the printers that he would pay their bills "to their order."

Armed with the Supreme Court's opinion and perhaps inspired by Harrison's example at Muscle Shoals, Peck apparently was ready to assert his title on the ground in the Mississippi Territory. If this was his aim, he was clearly acting as an individual, not as a director of the N.E.M. Land Co. The company had long since abandoned plans to obtain actual possession of its Mississippi lands in favor of obtaining an indemnity from Congress. Peck's win in the Supreme Court did not change this strategy and indeed raised hopes of a favorable settlement in the near term. Whatever he personally hoped to gain by the ruling in *Fletcher*, Peck was then facing financial pressures that in a few years would force him to sell his mansion in Newton and move to Kentucky. At the very time he was incurring the expense of publishing his "Cautionary Notice," Peck had not paid the fee of $250 he owed to Harper for representing him in the Supreme Court. Although this fee was in fact an expense of the N.E.M. Land Co., Peck "cheerfully accepted the draft & is fully competent to respond to it," wrote Story, who acted as go-between in this matter. Over the next two and a half years, a mortified Story applied repeatedly but was unable to collect despite Peck's assurances of payment. By September 1811 Story was proposing "to put the bill in suit," having "no doubt that the money will then come, as he unquestionably has property." Finally, in November 1812, Peck under threat of an execution produced the money, including an additional $15 in interest.

Well into the summer of 1810 *Fletcher v. Peck* stirred little attention in the press and no critical commentary. In late July the Richmond *Enquirer* published the first of two articles on the "Yazoo Fraud." The author professed astonishment "that so little notice has been publicly taken" of the Supreme Court's decision and reproached the press for having "slept amidst the perils of the country." But the danger was "no longer speculative or distant," he warned, calling attention to the meeting of the Yazoo speculators in Boston held "with the view of taking advantage of the opinion of the Court." Although the public was informed that the meeting had appointed a committee to report a plan, that report was "not published," the *Enquirer* writer noted, "because prudence, of course, suggested concealment." Since then, however, the speculators had thrown off secrecy and unveiled their plans "in the modest guise of" a private individual's "Cautionary Notice." The author of this "manifesto against the rights of the U.S." was John Peck, "the doughty defendant" in the recent case. It was time to sound the alarm, he warned, against "greedy speculators . . . marching in triumph over the prostrate ruins of public virtue," proclaiming the Supreme Court as "their friend" in a brazen attempt to claim the whole Yazoo country as "recompense" for their fraud. The author devoted a second number to attacking *Fletcher* as an obviously collusive and feigned case that did not, as Peck claimed, settle all the points in favor of the grants under the 1795 act. That decision, he pointed out, applied only to the special case of a purchaser without notice of fraud. Because the parties in their pleadings completely "relinquished" the issue of notice—another telling indication of collusion—the Supreme Court did not consider a question that figured prominently in the larger debate about compensating the Yazoo claimants.

It was left to "Camden," another *Enquirer* contributor, who in two numbers published in late September and early October 1810 took upon himself to fill the crucial gap resulting from the deftly drawn pleadings in the case between the two New England parties. The subject of notice had of course been sharply debated in Congress, where opponents of compromise fervently denied that there could be purchasers without notice in a sale so notoriously corrupt. Those who claimed ignorance of corruption attending the original sale, it was argued, failed to do due diligence, failed to read intrinsic signs of fraud in the original act such as the paltry consideration given for millions of acres. In any case, Yazoo opponents insisted, President Washington's message to Congress in February 1795 warning of harmful consequences arising from Georgia's sale constituted sufficient notice to potential buyers. "Camden" essentially recapitulated these arguments, putting them together in lawyerlike fashion with a learned discussion of the equitable doctrines of notice.

The relatively scant newspaper commentary prompted by *Fletcher v. Peck* did include a defense of the decision appearing in an October 1810 number of the Raleigh *Star*. The writer, "A Citizen of Lincoln," portrayed the Yazoo sale as a straightforward disposition of Georgia's western lands necessitated by the depleted condition of the state's treasury. Entirely ignoring the charge of corruption, he attributed the massive reaction against the sale to machinations of James Jackson, a politician of "unbounded ambition" who gained "unmerited sway over the uninformed people" of Georgia. In Congress, Jackson's ally John Randolph, "then in the zenith of his political career," managed through "his power of eloquence" and "altogether sophistical" arguments to induce a majority to oppose the Yazoo claimants. In this writer's narrative the Supreme Court stood forth as the champion of the wrongly maligned claimants. Its decision, he said, would "stand the test till law and virtue cease to govern our tribunals of justice." In a provocative reversal of the charge levied against the claimants' title, he asserted that *Fletcher* must convince the United States "that their title to those lands is founded in corruption and fraud."

In the aftermath of the Supreme Court's decision, the question remained what effect if any it would have in ending the long-standing impasse on the matter of compensating the Yazoo claimants. That another four years elapsed before Congress finally enacted legislation for this purpose indicates that the Court's influence in shaping public policy was at best limited and indirect. It should not be surprising that a case between two private individuals decided on narrow legal grounds was inadequate to the task of settling a question of such great public magnitude as the disposition of millions of acres of Yazoo lands. In the short run *Fletcher* served only to stiffen the resistance of the Yazoo opponents, who now raised the specter of hordes of claimants coming to Mississippi waving their titles and copies of the opinion to chase off settlers holding patents under the United States. Exaggerated as these fears were, the winning party in the Supreme Court appeared to give them a measure of plausibility when he published his "Cautionary Notice." John Peck's impetuous action must have chagrined his fellow N.E.M. Land Co. directors, concerned that it would antagonize even members of Congress favorably disposed to the company's claims and thus endanger the chances of compromise.

At the close of the previous session of Congress, the memorial of the N.E.M. Land Co. remained on the table, having survived a vote on a motion to reject it. No action on the memorial occurred at the third and last session of the Eleventh Congress, which convened in December 1810. The subject did come up briefly in the House when Troup, who by now had succeeded Randolph as the point man of the Yazoo opposition, offered a motion in response to reports of intruders in the Mississippi Territory. Calling attention to the 1807 law authorizing the president to remove by force persons on public lands claiming under other than U.S. titles, he moved to direct the secretary of the treasury to provide information about unlawful settlement in the territory and report what measures had been taken to remove intruders on the public lands. Troup did not pass up the opportunity to stoke fears about *Fletcher v. Peck*. If that decision were "acquiesced in," he warned, the people of the United States would be deprived of their right of "proprietorship of the soil" and the state of Georgia would be "defrauded" of the money the United States promised to pay out of the sales of those lands. If, however, the government resisted the decision, as Troup believed it should "to the last extremity," military force would be needed to remove a large body of Yazoo claimants who had taken possession in consequence of that decision. In his way, Troup viewed *Fletcher* in the same light as did Harrison, Peck, and "A Citizen of Lincoln." All appeared to concede a scope and authority to the decision far beyond its actual holding, as if it gave license to Yazoo claimants to enter on their Mississippi lands and eject settlers holding under the United States.

The House approved Troup's resolution on December 17. Secretary Gallatin submitted his report on January 9. It was Gallatin's report of the preceding year that had notified Congress of Harrison's attempts to assert his Tennessee Company title in the Muscle Shoals region. His second report appended correspondence with territorial officials relating Harrison's efforts to exploit the Fletcher decision but also showing that after a few months the confusion and anxiety over Yazoo intruders had largely dissipated. As matters stood at the end of 1810, it appeared that with respect to *Fletcher v. Peck* neither the great hopes of some Yazoo claimants nor the worst fears of their opponents would be realized.

Congress Adopts the Yazoo Indemnity Bill

The Eleventh Congress expired in March 1811 without taking action on the memorial of the N.E.M. Land Co. As optimistic as they were tenacious, the Yazoo claimants once again fixed their hopes of a favorable settlement on the meeting of a new Congress. The Twelfth Congress, which convened in November 1811, included seventy new members and saw the emergence of a younger generation of Republican leaders, among them Henry Clay of Kentucky, who was elected

Speaker of the House. At this Congress, however, war with Great Britain, declared in June 1812, monopolized the attention of the legislators, virtually assuring further delay in resolving the protracted issue of Yazoo claims. By the time it met for its second session in November 1812, the war on land was going badly for the United States, including an unsuccessful attempt to invade Canada. During the next four months the members engaged in lengthy debates on the army, navy, trade policy, finance, and other urgent matters pertaining to the prosecution of the war.

The matter of Yazoo claims did arise briefly and apparently unexpectedly at this session. It originated in a Senate committee's proposal to attach compensation for the Yazoo claimants to a bill to enable inhabitants of the Mississippi Territory to apply for admission as a state. After the House had passed the statehood bill in late November 1812, the Senate referred it to a select committee. This committee in mid-December reported amendments essentially adding three new sections to the original measure. These amendments allowed claimants under the Georgia act of 1795 to submit legal releases of their claims to the United States and pledged the United States, when a sufficient number of releases had been received, to indemnify the claimants according to the compromise terms proposed by Commissioners Madison, Gallatin, and Lincoln in their report of February 1803.

The Senate eventually postponed the Mississippi statehood bill and adopted the Yazoo compensation amendments as a separate bill. Seven years earlier, in 1806, the Senate had originated and adopted a compensation bill, only to see John Randolph successfully exhort the House to reject it outright the day it was received. When the 1813 bill was first read in the House on January 20, George Troup moved its immediate rejection as a measure originating in "hideous corruption" and containing "a principle destructive of republican government." Having previously denounced the Yazoo claimants as participants in the original corruption, Troup now accused them of diverting attention from this central issue by hunting up "in the law books of England" a maxim that suited their purposes and then making up a "feigned issue" for the Supreme Court's decision. The Georgia representative sounded a dire warning of corruption penetrating the federal legislature—the vital center of the government—through the medium of English law and the Supreme Court. In a way his listeners could scarcely misunderstand, Troup linked the Supreme Court with the law of an enemy nation bent upon destroying the free republican government of America. That the judges who issued this infamous decree went "unpunished" was because of the "mildness and moderation of our Government," he explained, taking care to "thank God it is so." If a court under a despotic monarchy gave a decision attacking the monarch, he added, the judges "would have perished." But in this country, having given a decision that shook "the foundations of the Republic," the Supreme Court justices "sleep in tranquillity."

Unlike Randolph in 1806, Troup did not succeed with his motion for immediate rejection, which lost by a close vote of fifty-nine to fifty-five. The compensation bill accordingly remained alive, and the House took it up on February 15. In a prepared speech, John A. Harper, a New Hampshire Republican, took the floor and held forth the remainder of the day. His address forcefully stated the case for the claimants as founded on the principles of "justice" and "sound national policy." While urging adoption of the bill on the basis of justice due to "innocent and suffering individuals" who purchased in good faith, Harper devoted the greater portion of his speech to showing that compromise with the claimants was in the best interests of the United States. In New England, for example, where there was widespread discontent with the federal government over the policies that led to war, a compensation act would be seen as a gesture of goodwill that would help restore that region's confidence in the administration. Not only would such an act promote national harmony, Harper argued, but for a trifling sum the United States would gain clear title to the Mississippi Territory, allowing the government to sell and settlers to buy public lands without the prospect of numerous and expensive lawsuits. This in turn would produce a steady increase in white settlement of the territory, enhance the commerce and prosperity of the entire trans-Allegheny region, and strengthen America's vulnerable southwestern frontier.

Harper also invoked *Fletcher v. Peck*, reminding his fellow Republicans that the Supreme Court majority in this case was composed of justices appointed by Jefferson, "'the Father of Democracy.'" He cautioned that it was both unwise and contrary to the Constitution "for the Legislative or Executive power to annul the decisions of the Supreme Judicature," pointing out that the history of the nation under the Constitution had so far revealed no instances of the national or state legislatures opposing "the judicial interpretation of the law." He called particular attention to President Madison's public declaration in 1809 of his legal duty to enforce a Supreme Court decree in the face of resistance by the governor of Pennsylvania. Harper exploited *Fletcher* not only to warn of its implied threat to the legality of U.S. land patents in the Mississippi Territory but also to underscore the great generosity and fair-mindedness of the claimants, who by agreeing to a compromise offered "to take less than one-eighth of what your own courts have declared to be their rights." No one rose to reply to Harper, an indication that the House was not inclined to enter a full debate on a controversial measure in the waning days of this Congress. After a motion to postpone further consideration carried comfortably, the bill was tabled, effectively killing it for the remainder of the Twelfth Congress.

Conspicuously absent from this day's proceedings was John Randolph, the Yazoo claimants' chief nemesis during the past ten years. Although he was still in the House, illness prevented his attendance for much of this session. Largely in consequence of his opposition to the war, Randolph had lost his House seat to a rival candidate in the recent elections. Having represented Virginia in the House since 1799, he would not return to the next Congress. Had he returned, this fearsome and intransigent foe of the Yazoo claimants most likely could not have prevented the adoption of a compensation bill. The opinions expressed in Harper's speech were gaining favor among growing numbers of Republicans beyond the northern and eastern states, where the claimants were concentrated, to include representatives from southern, southwestern, and western states. Among these were Thomas B. Robertson, Louisiana's first member of the House of Representatives, and new House members Bartlett Yancey of North Carolina and James Clark of Kentucky.

This shift within the Republican ranks toward a more positive view of compensation as just and sound policy that did not entail a sacrifice of republican principles became evident soon after the Thirteenth Congress convened for its second session in December 1813. As in the preceding Congress, the Senate acted first, when William Hunter, a Rhode Island Federalist, called up the memorial of the New England Mississippi Land Company, which had lain on the table since 1810. The memorial was referred to a select committee of five chaired by Hunter, who reported a bill in late January 1814 "to carry into effect" the commissioners' report of February 1803. This was essentially the same bill the Senate had adopted and presented to the House the previous year. In taking up the bill in 1814, the Senate modified the terms proposed by the commissioners: instead of allowing claimants to choose lands, interest-bearing stock certificates, or stock certificates without interest as the mode of indemnity, it permitted only the option of non-interest-bearing stock. The bill was approved on February 28 by a wide margin, twenty-four to eight. Its supporters, according to the *Daily National Intelligencer,* included many who had formerly "been decidedly adverse" to any accommodation with the Yazoo purchasers. The compensation bill provoked fierce resistance in the House, led by Troup, who on March 8 moved its rejection before it could have a second reading. In yet another impassioned address, the Georgian covered the whole ground of the Yazoo controversy in condemning a measure "originating in corruption." After holding forth at some length, he closed on a note of weariness, suggesting a lack of confidence that he would ultimately prevail: "But, sir, I am tired and disgusted with this subject. I hope the bill will be rejected." Troup's motion lost by nearly forty votes, and after a second reading the bill was referred to a select committee. Troup was named to the committee but declined to serve, leaving it heavily stacked with compromise supporters.

Thomas J. Oakley, a New York Federalist, presented the select committee's report on March 15, recommending adoption of the Senate bill without amendment. Not relying on the "strict legality" of the claimants' title, the report urged pragmatic attention to the nation's "permanent interests" in promoting speedy settlement of the Mississippi Territory while appealing to "equitable considerations" regarding the plight of third-party purchasers of Yazoo lands. Appended to the report were a number of documents relating to sales in the northern and eastern states, most importantly the Georgia Company's sale to James Greenleaf and the Georgia Mississippi Company's sale to the group that became the N.E.M. Land Co. This material evidently had some effect in persuading skeptical House members to view the New England claimants in a more favorable light, as themselves victims of the fraud that tainted the original sale of Georgia's western lands. Although this group included speculators who had bought at depreciated prices the claims of those forced to sell, most of the claimants, so it appeared, had purchased Yazoo lands in good faith and suffered financial hardship meriting relief. It helped, too, that the claimants demonstrated their readiness to relinquish their claims in return for an indemnity, as shown by their agents' written statements appended to the report. Benjamin Joy, for example, who represented the N.E.M. Land Co. and other companies and individuals in New England and New York with claims totaling nearly 25 million acres (about 70 percent of the entire Yazoo purchase), expressed "utmost confidence" that "every one of the claimants in New England" would accede to the compromise proposed in the Senate bill.

After the committee reported the bill, the House subjected it to intense scrutiny over five days. This was primarily a debate among Republicans, who continued to hold a large majority. Federalists, who held nearly all the New England seats, did, however, take a more active role at this session, believing (as Daniel Webster of New Hampshire noted) that they could "get the Democratic support." Oakley was the principal spokesman for the bill, ably assisted by Republicans Robert Wright of Maryland and William Lattimore, a nonvoting delegate from the Mississippi Territory. A member of the House since 1810, Wright had previously opposed compromise but at the preceding Congress had announced his conversion to settlement with the claimants.

Troup and other diehard Republicans continued to rail against compensating Yazoo purchasers even as they sensed that their efforts to defeat the bill would be unavailing. A new face in this group was Samuel Farrow of South Carolina, a sharp-witted lawyer who in his first and only term in Congress gave renewed energy to the anti-Yazoo forces. He derided the notion that the bill was designed to benefit "the poor, honest yeomanry of the East" who had become purchasers of Yazoo lands "innocent and ignorant of the fraud." To believe this, he said, was to "have a very contemptible opinion of the dexterity of speculators" who, knowing that a bill was likely to pass at this session, had bought up the shares of "those honest people" for "very trifling sums." He likened this speculation to that set off a generation earlier by the anticipated funding of the public debt, when speculators bought the greatly depreciated pay certificates of the "poor soldiers, whose toil and blood purchased your independence."

Troup's last great effort was a speech in support of his motion to postpone the bill indefinitely, "in which," the reporter noted, "he displayed that vehemence and zeal which usually characterizes his observations on this question." After an hour he sat down, appearing "to be exhausted by the effort of speaking." By this time Troup's allies were acknowledging "the total inability of any effort to stem the torrent now setting in favor of this measure." A newspaper correspondent reported that despite violent opposition "by a certain party in the House," the bill would "unquestionably pass" and the president would "not hesitate to sign it." The defeat of Troup's motion by eleven votes on March 24 foretold the final outcome. Two days later, on March 26, the House approved the Yazoo compensation bill, eighty-four to seventy-six. President Madison signed it on March 31.

For a decade Republicans under the sway of Randolph and Troup had prevented the passage of a compensation bill, unable to set aside their fears that such a measure would sanction a monstrous fraud and directly implicate their party—and the government itself—in corruption. It amounted to saying, said Troup, that the "free and virtuous people" of Georgia had no remedial power to set aside the fraudulent Yazoo sale act and divest the estate supposedly vested by that act. "This doctrine is too monstrous to be entertained by a moral people, who love liberty," he exclaimed; "it strikes at all virtue, at all morality—it overturns Republican Government." By 1814 such admonitions had less purchase among the party's rank and file, who increasingly adopted the view that compromise with the claimants was not a betrayal of republican principles. Republicans such as William Irving of New York and Robertson of Louisiana who now defended the compensation bill were no less fervent in expressing their "utter detestation" of the original fraud and disclaiming "any intention, either directly or indirectly, to give countenance to" it. Yancey of North Carolina spoke for many in his party in saying he would support the bill's passage "from a belief in its present expediency, and not from any view to sanction the original corruption of the Yazoo speculation." At the same time Republicans denied that the measure sanctioned fraud, insisting that it conferred no benefit on those guilty of perpetrating the fraud and that its purpose, said Robertson, "was to extend relief to innocent and uncontaminated sufferers, who, but for the compromise contemplated, would be involved in undeserved ruin, and to that ruin he would not consent to abandon them."

Republicans justified compensation not only as a benevolent measure to relieve suffering individuals but also as a binding duty to uphold the public faith—a faith that had been pledged repeatedly since 1802, if not explicitly then certainly by strong implication. As a matter of "plighted faith," said Senator John Taylor of South Carolina, "it is our duty to make the compromise." Senator William B. Giles of Virginia, formerly unfriendly to the Yazoo claims, said that Republicans were right to condemn the fraudulent sale with unabated disgust, but he now believed "with irresistible force" that the federal government was "precluded, by its own acts, from looking into that subject." The public faith was "unquestionably pledged," he continued. Was it "wise" or "politic," he asked, "to violate the pledged faith of the nation?" Representative Wright of Maryland reviewed the entire history of the Yazoo claims from 1795 through the Senate bill of 1812, from which he concluded that Congress should feel not only "justified" but "bound" to compensate innocent purchasers.

Arguments founded on justice and public morality merged with those that underscored the benefits of the bill in advancing great national interests at so little cost. Lattimore, the territorial delegate, was particularly concerned to make the House understand the importance of relieving the minds of Mississippi settlers anxious about their titles to public lands. If Congress failed to act, he warned, "the claimants will harass us by law, and ultimately evict us of our lands." Even if the claimants were complicit in corruption—which he denied but admitted for the sake of argument—why, he asked, should the people of Mississippi be "punished for their crime?"

The final debate on the Yazoo indemnity bill appeared to bear out the *Intelligencer* editor's supposition that *Fletcher v. Peck* helped to persuade formerly hostile or wavering Republicans to cast their votes in favor. Historian Henry Adams also attributed major importance to *Fletcher* in explaining why Congress, after ten years of "obstinately" resisting, finally conceded on the "Yazoo bill." To acknowledge the decision's influence is not to deny that Congress may well have settled with the claimants had the case never been brought. All the legal and constitutional arguments in support of compensation had been thoroughly aired and debated well before the case was heard. The Court's opinion added nothing new to these arguments, except perhaps to give central importance to the contract clause. *Fletcher*'s influence on Congress arose less from its legal and constitutional reasoning than from the weight of judicial authority it gave to the proposed political settlement with the claimants. Supporters of compromise used the decision to buttress their case that settling with the claimants had become an urgent national interest.

For their part, Yazoo opponents invoked *Fletcher* only to deny its authority in deciding whether Congress should indemnify the purchasers. They dismissed as groundless fears that a refusal to compromise, to give up 5 million acres, risked losing the whole 35 million acres. This "feigned" case between two New England speculators could not possibly affect "the right of the United States to the public property," argued Troup, because the government was "the guardian, the trustee of the public property" and "must of necessity determine" its "own rights of property." So long as the government remained faithful to this principle, he reassured the House, "all the decisions of all the judicial tribunals under Heaven cannot deprive you of a square acre of the public land."

Farrow, too, dismissed *Fletcher* as a legal nullity, denying that the Court "gave any decision on the great question before this House." The "special pleadings" in that case, he said, were deliberately and ingeniously designed "to keep the important question"—that is, the question of fraud—out of the Court's view. Unlike some critics, he did not accuse the Court of complicity in this feigned case, nor did he quarrel with the proposition that if Georgia's sale act of 1795 "was lawful, no subsequent act could rescind or impair contracts made under it." But he insisted that the sale was void from the outset by fraud, abundantly proved by the evidence presented in the commissioners' 1803 report. Just as the pleadings prevented the Court from inquiring into the crucial matter of fraud, so, too, they constrained the Court to accept as fact that the claimants were innocent purchasers having no notice of fraud. Here Farrow recapitulated the familiar anti-Yazoo arguments that the notorious circumstances of the sale as well as certain internal features of the deeds proved conclusively that the purchasers could not "have purchased, without some notice of the fraud practiced in the original transaction."

While Troup, Farrow, and other like-minded Republicans urged their fellow legislators not to let *Fletcher* dictate their votes, the bill's friends insisted on the contrary that the decision virtually required Congress to pass the bill—not as a solemn legal obligation but as a no less obligatory act of political expediency. Compromise advocates typically cited *Fletcher* to show that the claimants had a sound legal title to the Yazoo lands and that it would be folly not to accept their offer to surrender that title to the United States. Even conceding that the case was decided on a feigned issue, Senator Taylor inferred "that on a real issue, the decision would be the same." The day was not far distant, he added, when the "real issue"—in cases between parties claiming under the conflicting titles—would come before state and federal courts, where the Supreme Court's opinion would have its due weight. In the House, Wright, too, admitted that *Fletcher* had the appearance of a feigned case while acknowledging its force in establishing the validity of the claimants' title. After this decision, he warned, anyone who refused to accept a relinquishment of this title would "be deemed a madman."

Among those who spoke in support of compromise, only Senator Giles disavowed *Fletcher*, insisting that it would not affect his judgment of the question. Even if that decision "had been in a real, instead of a fictitious case," said Giles, he would not "acknowledge such decision, as a rule of conduct imposed upon him in his senatorial character." Indeed, he adopted the anti-Yazoo view that the question of title to the lands of the Mississippi Territory was beyond the competence of a judicial tribunal to decide because it was a question "affecting the sovereignty of the government." In making this point, Giles reflected thoughtfully on the nature of judicial and legislative power and the boundaries between them. Acknowledging the difficulty of drawing "the precise boundary" in cases where the jurisdictions of the legislature and judiciary were each "applicable," he said, there were some cases—of which this was one—in which the "lines of separation" were "so strongly marked" that they could "not be mistaken." Giles defined a court as "a tribunal of justice" to decide questions of property rights between individuals. A legislature, he explained, was both "a tribunal of justice in all cases" concerning the government's sovereignty and "a tribunal of policy." It prescribed "rules for the good of the nation," which courts explained and applied in cases brought before them. Courts, he continued, could not decide on matters touching "the sovereignty of the state, nor upon the policy of its measures." The case of the Yazoo claimants fell clearly within the province of the legislature, Giles reasoned, because the right to acquire territory was an attribute of sovereignty. A court of justice could no more adjudge the United States' right to the Mississippi Territory than it could its right to annex Louisiana.

After making his cogent case against the Supreme Court's intrusion into Congress's proper jurisdiction, Giles argued forcefully for the compensation bill as wise and good policy. Yet having said he was not "bound to obey" *Fletcher*, the Virginia senator did concede that the decision "was not without its effect in deciding upon the policy of the bill." It "would necessarily tend to strengthen" the claimants' confidence in their titles and make it more difficult for the United States to assert its title. The wiser course was to avoid a potential "unpleasant collision" between government departments, to allow them "to harmonise with each other, and in their respective spheres to co-operate for the general good." Giles's position was thus essentially no different from those who cited *Fletcher* to reinforce arguments for the policy and expediency of the compensation bill.

The "act providing for the indemnification of certain claimants of public lands in the Mississippi territory" required Yazoo claimants to release their claims to the United States by January 1, 1815. It authorized a board of commissioners consisting of the secretary of state, secretary of the treasury, and attorney general to decide on the legal sufficiency of the releases. As soon as the commissioners notified the president of sufficient releases amounting to "at least nine-tenths" of the lands claimed, non-interest-bearing stock certificates were to be issued, payable out of the proceeds of sales of public lands in the Mississippi Territory. The total amount was not to exceed $5 million and was to be distributed to claimants under the four original purchasing companies in proportion to the amounts each company paid to the state of Georgia in 1795. Thus claimants under the Georgia Company, which paid $250,000 of the total sale price of $500,000, were to receive stock not exceeding $2.25 million. Stock certificates could be used to pay for Mississippi public lands, provided that for every $100 paid, $95 was receivable in certificates and $5 in cash.

The act's final section declared that if any claimant under the Georgia act of 1795 refused to compromise, the United States was "exonerated and discharged" from such claim and no evidence of this claim could be pleaded or given in evidence "in any court whatever against any grant derived from the United States." This provision had been in the bill from the beginning and provoked unease even among steadfast champions of compromise. They were troubled by its naked assertion of coercion to deprive persons from pursuing their rights in courts of law—reminiscent, in certain respects, of Georgia's notorious 1796 rescinding law. There was no attempt to defend the section except on the ground of necessity, to foreclose all possibility of a legal challenge to the United States' title to the lands purchased under the compact with Georgia in 1802. The day before the House's final vote on the bill, William Gaston, a North Carolina Federalist, moved to strike out this section, denouncing it as an "arbitrary and despotic" exercise of legislative power. Congress, he said, was not "fettered as the Legislature of Georgia" by the contract clause but was "bound by the fundamental maxims of justice not to annihilate vested rights without the consent of those to whom they appertained." Earlier, Farrow had rebuked the compromisers for enacting a provision that if not unconstitutional was "repugnant to the first principles of civilized nations." Tellingly, Gaston announced his intention to vote for the bill even if his motion lost, convinced, he said, "that the public peace and the prosperity of an extensive territory demanded that a dangerous controversy should be quieted." No doubt many of those who cast their votes for the bill silently acquiesced in this sacrifice of principle to expediency.

In January 1815 Congress adopted a supplementary act relieving the cabinet officers from serving as commissioners and authorizing the president to appoint "three fit and disinterested persons" in their place. Appointed and confirmed on January 26, this new board, composed of Washington lawyers Francis S. Key, Thomas Swann, and John Law, immediately began examining and settling claims. A statement issued by the register of the Treasury in November 1818 showed a total of nearly $4.2 million awarded under the act to persons claiming under the four companies receiving grants from Georgia in 1795. This amount covered approximately 300 separate awards, mostly to named individuals.

The commissioners eventually approved payments of "Mississippi stock" to the trustees and individuals of the N.E.M. Land Co. of nearly $1.35 million. The company had submitted a deed of release to the United States on December 7, 1814, signed by the seven directors of the company, which still included John Peck of Newton, Massachusetts. Once a heavy investor in Yazoo lands, Peck was not on the 1818 list as an individual claimant. Most of the amounts awarded to the N.E.M. Land Co. were in the names of agents Benjamin Joy and Samuel Dexter. If in 1814 he still held any company scrip, Peck might have received an indemnity from the agents. In any event, he had disposed of all the vast holdings acquired in his own name. One of those tracts was the 15,000 acres he sold to the late Robert Fletcher in 1803. Fletcher, in turn, must have sold this tract along with the other properties he was forced to sell during his financially straitened last years. Rufus G. Amory, one of his lawyers in the suit against Peck, purchased Fletcher's Beacon Street house in Boston in 1808. It is possible that Amory also acquired Fletcher's interest in Georgia lands. The Boston lawyer subsequently obtained an indemnity of more than $25,000 under the 1814 act.

For most Yazoo claimants, the indemnity paid under the act of 1814 was a more or less satisfactory conclusion to a prolonged campaign to obtain some return on their investment in land speculation. Certain holders of N.E.M. Land Co. scrip, however, were not satisfied with the company's settlement with the commissioners. Instead of awarding the full amount appropriated by the act to indemnify the N.E.M. Land Co., the commissioners deducted $130,000 for unpaid promissory notes given by one of the original subscribers for his share in the company. They ruled that scrip issued by the company for the defaulting purchaser's share was bad and could not be indemnified under that act. One such holder of "tainted" scrip was Mary Gilman, John Peck's mother-in-law. In 1817 Gilman, a widow then living with Peck in Lexington, Kentucky, sued the N.E.M. Land Co., claiming $6,000 from the amount awarded by the commissioners to the company. The Supreme Court in 1819 upheld her claim, ruling that the whole company and not just individual scrip holders should bear the loss arising from the so-called tainted stock. This decision turned out to be the opening act of a long sequel to the N.E.M. Land Co.'s involvement in the Yazoo business that continued another half century.

Claiming that the commissioners had made a legal error in deducting $130,000—a claim that had support from the opinion in Mary Gilman's case—the company once again assumed its familiar role as a supplicant in the halls of Congress. It proved even more tenacious in pursuit of this deducted amount than it had been in procuring the 1814 indemnity act. Between 1822 and 1854 the company submitted no fewer than seventeen petitions and memorials, with supporting testimony that included affidavits of two of the commissioners acknowledging their error. Despite a number of favorable committee reports, the N.E.M. Land Co. failed to obtain Congress's approval of the claim. Still, the company persevered, taking its case to the newly established U.S. Court of Claims. That tribunal in 1864 also denied the claim, ruling that the commissioners' decision on the indemnity was final.

CHAPTER SEVEN

The Marshall Court and the Contract
Clause after *Fletcher*

Fletcher v. Peck was the Marshall Court's second major constitutional law pronouncement, coming seven years after *Marbury v. Madison.* These cases shared certain similarities. Both became landmarks of American law not for their particular outcomes but as precedents establishing constitutional principles and doctrines that could be applied with effect to future cases. In *Marbury* Chief Justice Marshall was able to transform a case in which the Court was powerless to enforce a party's legal right into a manifesto of judicial independence, most famously in proclaiming the judiciary's authority to invalidate laws deemed to be repugnant to the Constitution. In *Fletcher* the Court upheld Peck's title in his dispute with Fletcher, but this judgment did not put Peck or any other Yazoo purchaser in possession of his lands. The determination that Georgia's 1796 rescinding act violated the contract clause did not reverse a constitutional infraction that had occurred years earlier. Yet *Fletcher*, like *Marbury*, transcended its peculiar circumstances to become the foundation for the Marshall Court's effort to fashion the contract clause into an effective instrument to restrain the legislative powers of the states.

More broadly, *Fletcher* backed up the Supreme Court's assertion of its authority to adjudge the validity of legislative acts by the standard of the Constitution. Except for *Marbury*, which voided a section of a federal statute, the Marshall Court, beginning with *Fletcher*, directed its reviewing power exclusively to state laws. In striking down acts of state legislatures, the Court consolidated the practice of judicial review, so that it became a regular and continuously operating principle of the American constitutional system. It controlled state power in two classes of cases in which the Constitution imposed limits on the states. In one the Court voided a state law that was otherwise constitutional but conflicted with the constitutional exercise of a federal power. Such a law had to yield to the principle of national supremacy as expressed in the clause of the Constitution declaring the federal Constitution, laws, and treaties to be "the supreme Law of the Land." In these "federalism" cases the limits on state power were enforced by a broad reading of a federal power. Classic examples of this genre were *McCulloch v. Maryland* (1819), which struck down a Maryland law imposing a tax on the Bank of the United States, and *Gibbons v. Ogden* (1824), which invalidated New York's steamboat monopoly law.

Fletcher exemplified the other category of cases, in which the Marshall Court nullified state laws that infringed the private rights of individuals. These cases came within the Constitution's prohibitions and restrictions on the states as set forth in Article I, section 10, most importantly the clause prohibiting laws "impairing the Obligation of Contracts." In time, the contract clause would emerge as the Marshall Court's most potent weapon to restrain state interference with contracts and property rights, becoming in effect the constitutional expression of the doctrine of vested rights. Chief Justice Marshall signified his hopes and intentions for the contract clause by reading its general language broadly. He foresaw the clause's potential for protecting the people from the acts of their state governments, its promise to become the means by which the Constitution could operate effectively as a "bill of rights for the people of each state."

Fletcher was the first of a line of cases that expanded the scope of the contract clause to bring in a greater number and variety of cases than the framers of the Constitution could have anticipated—which is exactly what Chief Justice Marshall believed they intended. He placed the burden of proof on those who would restrict its meaning by excepting certain cases from its reach. His expansive reading of the contract clause encouraged parties aggrieved by what they believed to be unjust deprivation of their rights to bring their cases to the Supreme Court. Marshall, of course, did not intend the clause to be read literally to embrace all contracts or contractual circumstances and to proscribe every state regulation said to impair their obligation. The field of state legislative activity that was permissible or not permissible under the contract clause became clearer in a succession of adjudications that followed *Fletcher.*

In terms of constitutional doctrine, *Fletcher* was authority for the proposition that the contract clause applied to public contracts, including state land grants, as well as to private contracts. Its value as a precedent in this respect was evident two years later in *New Jersey v. Wilson.* The law challenged in this case was a New Jersey statute of 1804 repealing a tax exemption on land formerly held by a tribe of Delaware Indians, who in 1801 decided to move to New York and requested the state to sell the land on their behalf. The complainants were the purchasers of the former Indian lands. The tax exemption had been granted by the colonial legislature in 1758 in an act setting aside certain lands for the tribe. After New Jersey's high court upheld a tax assessment for taxes on the land, the purchasers appealed to the Supreme Court under section 25 of the Judiciary Act. In both courts the case turned on the single question whether the state law repealing the tax exemption was repugnant to the contract clause of the Constitution.

The case was submitted to the Supreme Court on a state of facts without argument. In a brief opinion delivered in March 1812, Chief Justice Marshall cited *Fletcher's* holding that the contract clause extended to public as well as private contracts. Thus the only question to consider was whether a contract existed in this case and whether it was impaired by the state law. Marshall held that the colony's promise of a tax exemption, given in return for the Indians relinquishing their claims to a large portion of New Jersey, contained "[e]very requisite to the formation of a contract." The tax exemption privilege, "though for the benefit of the Indians," was "annexed . . . to the land itself," he continued. The subsequent purchasers succeeded to this right conferred by the original contract, which was "certainly impaired by a law" annulling "this essential part of it."

The state court judges insisted that the tax exemption "was never in legislative contemplation distinct from *Indian possession,*" that nothing in the 1758 colonial statute indicated an intention to bind future legislatures from taxing the land after the Indians vacated it. The repealing law of 1804 accordingly did not impair any obligation of contract. Marshall and the Court thought otherwise, though conceding that New Jersey in its act for selling the Indian lands could "have insisted on a surrender of this privilege as the sole condition on which a sale of the property should be allowed." This concession considerably diminished the decision's restriction on a state's sovereign power of taxation.

New Jersey v. Wilson essentially reaffirmed Fletcher without advancing interpretation of the contract clause. In both cases the contract in question was a legislative grant and the impairment was a legislative act revoking the grant. Although the New Jersey case, unlike *Fletcher*, was devoid of references to general law, in both the infraction amounted to a taking of a vested right of property.

Marshall Court commentators have identified the "takings analogy" as an important feature of the early contract clause cases. Although the federal government was prohibited by the Fifth Amendment from taking private property without compensation, there was no such express constitutional prohibition on the state governments. Because the Supreme Court in contract cases coming up from the state courts was restricted solely to the constitutional question, the contract clause accordingly emerged to embrace such takings violations by the states, allowing the Court to discard reliance on extraconstitutional general principles. How this process ultimately worked out became clear in the next important contract clause case, *Dartmouth College v. Woodward* (1819).

The case arose from the religious and political factionalism of early-nineteenth-century New Hampshire, culminating in a series of acts passed by the Republican-controlled legislature that fundamentally revised Dartmouth College's 1769 charter. This legislation essentially transformed the college into a state institution, which henceforth was to be known as Dartmouth University. Claiming that these laws constituted an unlawful deprivation of property rights, the college trustees sued in the state court. Their lawyers carefully constructed the case to challenge the state laws as infringing vested rights and the New Hampshire constitution and also as contrary to the contract clause of the U.S. Constitution. In this way a loss in the state court could be appealed to the federal Supreme Court.

The New Hampshire Superior Court, as expected, ruled against the trustees in November 1817. Once the case came to the Supreme Court, the justices were restricted by the provisions of section 25 to the sole issue of whether the New Hampshire acts violated the contract clause. When the case was argued at the 1818 term, this jurisdictional restraint did not deter Daniel Webster, principal counsel for the trustees, from devoting the great preponderance of his argument to stating the case as essentially a taking of private property and giving it to another. This was a deprivation of vested rights, he contended, which the New Hampshire legislature was prohibited from doing either by inherent limitations on legislative power or by specific restrictions found in the state constitution. The case was left undecided at this term because some justices had not formed an opinion and those who had "do not agree," noted Chief Justice Marshall.

Some justices might have been uncertain about whether the college's case could be made under the contract clause. Webster clearly believed that framing the issue as an unlawful deprivation of vested rights put the case on more solid ground. Joseph Story, one of the undecided justices, seemed to agree, expressing regret (after the case was decided) that "we were so stinted in jurisdiction in the Supreme Court, that half the argument could not be met and enforced." Story had recently delivered the majority opinion in *Terrett v. Taylor* (1815), holding that the Virginia legislature could not divest the title of the Episcopal Church to its glebe lands. Not "stinted in jurisdiction" because the case originated in a federal court, Story based his decision denying that a legislative grant of land was revocable on broad principles of natural justice and vested rights, barely alluding to the contract clause. In an attempt to avoid the jurisdictional limitations imposed by section 25 on the Dartmouth College case, Webster during the interval between terms commenced new actions in Story's federal circuit court. These cases were quickly certified to the Supreme Court in time to be argued with the expected rehearing of *Dartmouth College v. Woodward* at the 1819 term.

Chief Justice Marshall confounded these expectations when he announced at the beginning of the term that the Supreme Court had come to a decision in the college case. By a vote of five to one the Court upheld the Dartmouth trustees, holding that the college's charter was a contract protected by the Constitution. Marshall gave the opinion of the Court, with Washington and Story giving concurring opinions. All three justices adhered to the jurisdictional constraints and resolved the case strictly within the confines of the contract clause without resorting to extraconstitutional vested rights principles. Story, it is true, could not refrain from censuring the New Hampshire acts as contrary to the principles that restrained legislative power from infringing legally vested rights. But he then promptly conceded that the application of these "perfectly correct" principles did not "properly belong to the appellate jurisdiction of this Court in this case."

Building on *Fletcher*, Marshall constructed a case that extended the reach of the contract clause to embrace grants of corporate charters and made the result appear to flow inexorably from the earlier precedent. He assumed without argument that a corporate charter like a land grant was a grant of property by public authority and thus constituted a contract. This point was not seriously disputed even by the college's opponents, who contended that Dartmouth's charter was a grant of political power, not of private property rights, and therefore was not a contract meant to be protected by the Constitution. The chief justice agreed that the contract clause was never intended "to restrain the states" from regulating their governmental institutions and conceded that the clause was restricted to contracts concerning private property. A crucial inquiry therefore was the nature of the Dartmouth charter, whether it created a public corporation for public purposes or a private corporation for the exercise and enjoyment of purely private rights.

Closely examining the charter, the chief justice found that Dartmouth College originated as a private "eleemosynary" (charitable) corporation and retained that character despite the application of its funds to broad public purposes such as education. The private rights conferred by the charter were those of the corporation itself, a legal device for perpetuating the property rights of the original founders and donors. While conceding that protection of corporate rights might not have been contemplated by the framers of the Constitution, Marshall insisted that the Court ought to be guided by the contract clause's intention as manifested by its words. "It is not enough to say that this particular case was not in the mind of the convention when the article was framed, nor of the American people when it was adopted," he said. "It is necessary to go farther, and to say that, had this particular case been suggested, the language would have been so varied as to exclude it, or it would have been made a special exception." This rule of construction formed the core of Marshall's interpretation of the contract clause, allowing him to exploit its general language to give it a comprehensive reach and to place the burden of proof on those who would restrict its meaning by excepting certain cases from its reach.

In *Fletcher*, Chief Justice Marshall had strongly intimated his preference for constitutional text over general principles in deciding the case, but its jurisdictional latitude allowed him to give seemingly equal prominence to both sources. Although as section 25 cases *New Jersey* and *Dartmouth* compelled the judges to stick to the language of the Constitution, Marshall rendered that restriction virtually meaningless by showing that the constitutional text itself provided broad protection for the vested rights of property. Indeed, his expansive reading of the contract clause made it possible for the Supreme Court to rely on the Constitution alone in adjudicating cases involving vested property and contract rights no matter whether the case began in a state or a federal court. This had important consequences for the future of judicial review in the United States.

Chief Justice Marshall in particular perceived that the Supreme Court's ability to exercise judicial review—a practice still in its formative stage—would be enhanced by having the written text of the Constitution as the sole standard for determining the validity of a legislative act. He was not alone among judges who were dubious about pronouncing a law void as contrary to natural justice or general principles of law. As Justice Iredell had observed in *Calder v. Bull* (1798), a court could not pronounce a law void "merely because it is, in their judgment, contrary to the principles of natural justice. The ideas of natural justice are regulated by no fixed standard; the ablest and the purest of men have differed upon the subject." General principles of law, too, provided a scarcely less vague standard than natural justice by which to measure the legitimacy of legislation. Marshall's great achievement was to infuse the contract clause with ample vested rights doctrine, so that invoking its principles as an independent ground of decision was no longer necessary. In this way, judicial exposition of the Constitution's text, as exemplified in *Dartmouth*, became the Supreme Court's established mode of exercising its authority to review legislation.

Dartmouth announced a principle of constitutional law that applied not only to charitable corporations such as private colleges but also to business corporations. By creating a wide scope for unfettered entrepreneurial activity, the principle suited the requirements of a burgeoning capitalist economy. Yet the decision by no means gave a blank check to corporations and was not intended to strip the states of their regulatory authority over the economy. As Story noted in his concurring opinion, states in granting corporate charters could reserve the power to alter or repeal them, just as Marshall had conceded in *New Jersey* that states could reserve the right to repeal tax exemptions. In preserving the charter of a small new England college, Marshall and his brethren sought to fulfill the Constitution's overriding intention to provide for the security of private rights. New Hampshire's laws radically transforming Dartmouth College appeared to be a classic manifestation of the vulnerability of private rights to the fluctuating policies of republican legislatures. Anxiety about the precariousness of such rights in a republic had done much to bring into being a new federal constitution in 1787. This "republican" concern rather than the future welfare of American business enterprise was uppermost in the minds of the Supreme Court justices in *Dartmouth*.

Two weeks after *Dartmouth*, the Supreme Court decided another important case arising under the contract clause case, *Sturges v. Crowninshield*, which considered the constitutionality of state bankruptcy laws. A financial and business panic and onset of a severe economic depression gave urgency to the case, for the extent to which the states could respond to the crisis hinged on the Supreme Court's resolution of the issue. Bankruptcy laws were challenged as running afoul not only of the contract clause but also of the clause empowering Congress to establish "uniform laws on the subject of Bankruptcies." There was no federal bankruptcy law at the time.

Laws for the relief of debtors had been enacted by American legislatures since the colonial period. The most common of such laws released the debtor from imprisonment on assigning his assets to creditors, leaving future assets still liable for his debts. Some states had also adopted laws that not only released the debtor from prison but also released him from future liability for his debts, enabling him to get a fresh start free from the crushing burdens of past obligations. Although the former were usually called "insolvent" acts and the latter "bankrupt" acts, these terms were applied interchangeably to both kinds of legislation.

Supreme Court justices on circuit had given sharply divergent opinions about the constitutionality of such laws. In 1814 Judge Washington applied the contract clause to strike down a Pennsylvania statute discharging the debt that operated retrospectively on an existing contract. In voiding the act, he put more emphasis on its conflict with what he unequivocally declared was Congress's exclusive power under the Constitution to pass bankruptcy laws. By contrast, Judge Livingston in 1817 just as forcefully rejected the exclusive power doctrine in upholding a New York law subsequently overturned in *Sturges*. He also denied that laws discharging a debtor from future liability, whether retrospective or prospective, came within the purview of the contract clause. Such laws, he contended, should be presumed constitutional from the long practice of enacting them in New York and other states without any complaint that they impaired the obligation of contract.

Sturges arose from the failure to pay two promissory notes given in March 1811 by Crowninshield, a Boston merchant, then residing in New York City, to Sturges of New York. This was just the sort of private contract between two persons that there was no doubt the Constitution was intended to protect. Crowninshield subsequently obtained a discharge under New York's insolvency law, adopted in April 1811, and moved back to Boston, where his business flourished. In 1816 Sturges sued Crowninshield in the U.S. circuit court at Boston. This court adjourned the case to the Supreme Court on a pro forma certificate of division, presenting the questions of whether the bankruptcy power was concurrent or exclusively vested in Congress and whether the New York act of 1811 impaired the obligation of contract.

In his opinion for the Court, Chief Justice Marshall rejected the exclusive power construction, noting the "inconvenience" of preventing the states from acting in cases not reached by federal law. In any event, there was no federal bankruptcy law, so it would be unreasonable to prevent state legislation on the subject. "It is not the mere existence of the power, but its exercise," he said, "which is incompatible with the exercise of the same power by the states."

On the second question Marshall again employed his spacious interpretation of the contract clause to void the New York law as impairing the obligation of contract. As in *Dartmouth*, he countered the objection that the contract clause did not embrace the particular case, that bankruptcy laws were not on the minds of the Constitution's framers in 1787, and that the contract clause was directed only at the mischiefs complained of at the time. The chief justice rejected so restrictive a view, decrying as "dangerous in the extreme to infer from extrinsic circumstances, that a case for which the words of an instrument expressly provide, shall be exempt from its operation." He subjected Article I, section 10, to a close analysis to show that the contract clause was not directed at particular laws but intended to guard against the manifold and unforeseen ways that republican legislatures might undermine or destroy the sanctity of contracts. That clause, he said, was "intended to establish a great principle, that contracts should be inviolable." By investing the contract clause with such an exalted purpose, Marshall set the bar high for those seeking to exempt a particular case from its operation.

To project the appearance of unity, the Supreme Court's usual course was to issue a single opinion delivered by the chief justice. Dissenting and even concurring opinions were discouraged as diminishing the Court's authority. The opinion in *Sturges* masked how badly divided the justices were on the reach of the contract clause to prohibit state bankruptcy laws. Marshall evidently was able to get a majority to sign on to his opinion only by confining it "to the case actually under consideration." In short, its authority extended only to laws that operated retrospectively on existing contracts, though nowhere did the chief justice expressly limit the contract clause to this class of cases.

Left open in 1819 was whether the contract clause applied to a prospective law, discharging a debtor from liability on a contract subsequent to the law's enactment. The Supreme Court confronted this question directly in *Ogden v. Saunders*, decided at the 1827 term. The case arose from bills of exchange payable to Saunders and accepted for payment by Ogden. This transaction occurred in 1806; soon after, not having paid Saunders, Ogden entered debtor's prison and was released in 1808 after obtaining a discharge under New York's insolvent law. Saunders sued Ogden in the federal court of Louisiana in 1814 and obtained a judgment in 1819. Ogden took an appeal to the Supreme Court, where the case languished on the docket. The Court heard three days of argument at the 1824 term but was unable to reach a decision at this and the next two terms. Three more days of argument followed at the 1827 term before the Court announced its decision. This time Chief Justice Marshall was unable to cobble together a majority to agree on a single opinion. Indeed, on a vote of four to three upholding the constitutionality of the 1801 New York law, he found himself in the minority. Reviving a practice not used since before the Marshall Court, the four majority justices—Washington, Johnson, Smith Thompson, and Robert Trimble—delivered seriatim opinions. For the first and only time during his long tenure as chief justice, Marshall delivered a dissenting opinion in a constitutional case.

In argument the meaning of "obligation of contract" emerged as the key point on which the constitutionality of prospective bankruptcy laws (those in existence at the time of the contract) hinged. One side contended that the obligation of contract was a legal obligation arising from the laws in force when the contract was made and the remedies provided by those laws for enforcing the contract's performance. Bankruptcy laws fell into this class of legislation, not differing in principle from laws against usury, gambling laws, statutes of frauds, statutes of limitation, or any other ordinary regulation of contract. The other side denied that the obligation of contract originated in municipal law (the internal law of a sovereign state) but sprang from a binding natural law. Municipal law, it was argued, did not enter into or form part of a contract but rather acted upon it after it was broken to provide various remedies. Correctly understood, obligation, founded in natural law, inhered in the contract and was distinct from the remedy given by municipal law to enforce it. A state's power to modify the remedy could not extend to impairing or destroying the obligation.

In excepting prospective bankruptcy laws from the reach of the contract clause, the majority did not deny that the obligation of contract derived from natural law. Washington, for example, conceded this was the obligation acknowledged in compacts among sovereign nations or in contracts made on a desert island. But he denied that the framers intended this to be the exclusive meaning of the phrase, contending that they also meant to include the municipal laws of the state where the contract was formed. Natural law obligation, he said, was to be understood as strictly subordinate to the obligation defined by municipal legislation. In their various ways the other three majority justices agreed that a state had authority to regulate, modify, or control the operation of universal law within its jurisdiction. State laws created a civil obligation that in respect to private contracts superseded natural law, and it was this civil obligation that the Constitution was meant to protect. To concede a state's power to outlaw usury and gambling contracts, to adopt statutes of frauds and limitation, was to "surrender" the whole argument, said Johnson, for it admitted "the right of the government to limit and define the power of contracting, and the extent of the creditor's remedy against his debtor."

In his dissent, in which he also spoke for Story and Duvall, Marshall wholeheartedly embraced the view that the contract clause barred state bankruptcy laws that discharged the debt no matter whether they were retrospective or prospective. He made clear at the outset that he was defending a constitutional principle that left no room for compromise. Given his previous pronouncements that the Constitution protected public as well as private contracts, executed as well as executory contracts, it is difficult to conceive how the chief justice could have admitted a distinction between retrospective and prospective bankruptcy laws. The whole thrust of his construction had been to demonstrate the comprehensive scope of the contract clause, to show that it was not directed at particular laws but embodied a general principle of the sanctity of contracts. In what was to be his last major exposition of the contract clause, Marshall reiterated his deeply held convictions about its meaning and the principles of construction for determining its intention.

Most striking in the *Ogden* dissent was the extent to which natural law principles informed his contract clause jurisprudence. He read into that clause a manifest intention to infuse a natural law understanding of the obligation of contract, denying categorically that obligation was a civil obligation created by municipal law. This was a fundamental error, he contended, for the act of making a contract occurred independently of society and government. Contract preceded legislation, which therefore could not be the source of the right to contract. Municipal law could not create the obligation, Marshall pointed out, but could only act upon an intrinsic, preexisting obligation. True, in forming society, individuals surrendered natural liberty for civil liberty protected and enforced by government, but he denied that the natural obligation of contract was thereby converted into a civil obligation. Individuals surrendered not the right to contract but only the right to coerce its performance.

Marshall's opinion was intellectually elegant, proceeding from premise to conclusion with a relentless logic that exposed the flaws of every opposing argument and met every objection to his own. Yet in the end his argument foundered on the attempt to maintain the distinction between a legislature's acknowledged remedial power over contracts and its power to enact a prospective bankruptcy law that discharged the contract—a power prohibited by the Constitution because it impaired the obligation of contract. The chief justice steadfastly resisted the conflation of remedy and obligation, asserting that there was a material distinction between statutes of fraud, usury, and limitation and a law that discharged a debt. But Marshall's case was too abstract and theoretical for a majority unable to discern a practical difference between the two kinds of laws. If, for example, acts of limitation could void once-obligatory contracts, did they not impair their obligation? Indeed, so strong was the resemblance between such acts and the New York bankruptcy law under consideration that Johnson professed to "have seen no distinction between the cases that can bear examination."

In *Ogden* Marshall had to confront the consequences of what

Johnson called "a severe literal construction" of the contract clause, giving it an ever-expanding scope that threatened to suck into its vortex a large mass of state legislation dealing with contracts. Johnson had foreseen the problem in *Fletcher*, warning that such a construction would make it extremely difficult to draw a line between constitutional and unconstitutional acts. With impeccable logic and reasoning, the chief justice stuck by his principles of constitutional construction even if it meant sacrificing the majority he was usually able to command. This unwavering stance seems at odds with the image of a moderate, pragmatic jurist, willing to compromise for the sake of a unified Court. Apart from Court unity, there were sound policy reasons for upholding state bankruptcy laws. In the absence of national legislation on the subject, state laws providing for the relief of "honest debtors" along with reasonable protection for creditors would encourage commercial enterprise and promote economic growth. That he refused to bow to expediency in this case was a measure of the strength of his conviction that the principle of the sanctity of contract embodied in the contract clause was the vital essence of the Constitution. As in other cases, a Madisonian fear that this principle was vulnerable to republican legislative majorities lay behind Marshall's contract clause jurisprudence.

With this rebuff of the chief justice's argument that prospective bankruptcy laws impaired the obligation of contract, the Marshall Court had reached the limit of its application of the contract clause to void state laws. *Green v. Biddle* (1823), decided four years before *Ogden*, was the last time the Court invalidated a state law as impairing the obligation of contract. The contract in this case was not between two persons or between a state and a private party but a compact between Virginia and Kentucky by which the latter separated from the former in 1789, three years before Kentucky became a separate state. Under this compact the rights to lands within the Kentucky district derived under Virginia laws before the separation were to remain valid and secure under the new state's laws and to be determined by the laws of Virginia then existing.

As a favorite object of speculation, Kentucky lands were a confusing mass of overlapping and disputed claims, often involving absentee owners and settlers. Settlers staked out claims and made improvements, only to be subsequently ousted by one with a superior title. To provide relief for such ousted occupants, Kentucky enacted laws stating that occupying claimants were entitled to compensation for improvements and not liable for rents during the period of their uncontested occupancy. *Green* was a suit between an absentee owner and an occupant that began in the U.S. Circuit Court of Kentucky. It came to the Supreme Court by certificate of division on two questions, one of which was whether Kentucky's occupying claimant laws of 1797 and 1812 were constitutional. The case was first argued in 1821, when the six sitting justices (Washington was absent) unanimously decided that the laws were unconstitutional. In his opinion for the Court, Story interpreted the 1789 compact as a binding promise that future Kentucky laws would protect the rights of owners of Kentucky lands obtained under Virginia law before the separation. Without explicitly referring to the contract clause, he said that a Kentucky law diminishing those rights was "a violation of the compact, and is consequently unconstitutional." Examining the two acts, he had little difficulty determining that they "materially" impaired the owner's rights in the land.

This decision was highly unpopular in Kentucky, setting off angry protests accusing the Supreme Court of gratuitously denying the state's sovereign authority to enact its own land laws. Because no counsel had appeared on behalf of the claimant, the Court granted a rehearing of *Green*, which took place at the 1822 term. However, in 1823, the Court, speaking through Justice Washington, affirmed its earlier decision striking down the Kentucky laws. This ruling only intensified the outcry in Kentucky, provoking one of the state's senators to propose a sweeping restriction on the Supreme Court's power to review state and federal laws. The second decision particularly rankled, for it was believed to have been made by a minority of three of the seven justices—Story, Washington, and Duvall. Chief Justice Marshall did not sit, apparently because of his family's interest in Kentucky lands, and Livingston and Todd were absent because of illness. Johnson delivered a separate concurrence, though his opinion (as did his *Fletcher* concurrence) had aspects of a dissent.

The Court was clearly uneasy about having to decide such a delicate case. In concluding his opinion, Washington confided his wish that the result could have been "favorable to the validity of the laws." Story, too, privately "felt a solicitude" about the decision. Both, however, had no doubt that the opinion stated the correct view of the law and Constitution. Johnson, noting the "intrinsic difficulties" of the case, declined to give an opinion on the constitutional question, insisting that he was bound to conduct such an inquiry only in an appeal from a state court. Troubled by a construction of the 1789 compact that would cut deep "into the sovereign powers of Kentucky," Johnson could not admit "that it was ever the intention" of the Constitution's framers or of the parties to the compact "that Kentucky should for ever be chained down to a state of hopeless imbecility." In the end, however, he ruled that the claimant could not have judgment against the Virginia owner under Kentucky's occupying claimant laws, a decision he based on the rules of practice in the federal courts.

Green and *Ogden* illustrated how the contract clause could draw the Supreme Court into awkward and perplexing difficulties in attempting to draw the line between acceptable and prohibited state activity. Although the justices in the former case were in full agreement that Kentucky's occupying claimant laws impaired the interests of nonresident Virginia owners, none could deny that Kentucky had a legitimate interest in protecting the interests of occupants who improved the tract from which they were later ousted. As counsel for the occupants observed, "a new proprietary interest" had emerged since the compact "not foreseen nor provided for." Invoking the contract clause to uphold one party's property rights could thus be seen as depriving the other party's rights.

Perhaps somewhat chastened by *Green*, the Marshall Court in *Ogden* and in succeeding contract cases upheld the challenged state law. The Court, to be sure, had always recognized that states retained ample authority to regulate contractual arrangements, as Marshall himself acknowledged in his insistent attempt to maintain a distinction between customary remedial laws and a law discharging a debt. If the Court was now more inclined to defer to state regulatory authority, it was also because the kinds of cases the justices confronted were different from the early contract cases. In *Fletcher*, *New Jersey*, *Dartmouth*, and the bankruptcy cases, the issue could more easily be framed as a taking of property, a deprivation of vested rights. These cases were perceived to embody the kind of legislative abuse that Madison and other founders complained about at the time of the Constitution and that gave rise to the contract clause. The later cases did not conform so well to the vested-rights model. Rather than a relatively straightforward impairment of a contractual right, these cases presented a more complicated dispute between different property interests, each claiming protection or vindication. In such cases, the Court was not disposed to construe the contract clause as barring the state's regulation or resolution of the conflict.

The one case in which the late Marshall Court did strike down a state act regulating the economy, *Craig v. Missouri* (1830), arose not under the contract clause but under the clause of Article I, section 10, prohibiting the states from issuing "bills of credit." The Court by a bare majority ruled that loan office certificates issued under a Missouri law were in fact bills of credit and barred by the Constitution. In an opinion reminiscent of his early contract cases, Marshall argued for a broad reading of the prohibitory clause, citing its general language as comprehending "the emission of any paper medium, by a state government, for the purpose of common circulation." But this construction of the ban on paper money proved to be a much less effective restraint on state legislation than the contract clause. In 1837, two years after Marshall's death, the Supreme Court under Chief Justice Taney held in *Briscoe v. Bank of Kentucky* that notes issued by a state bank were not bills of credit in the sense meant by the Constitution.

None of the late contract cases was of major importance. In 1831 the justices had an opportunity to revisit the question whether a Kentucky land law was void for impairing rights based on the state's 1789 compact with Virginia. This time Johnson for the Court had little difficulty upholding the law and distinguishing this case from *Green*. The Court also rejected contract clause challenges to Pennsylvania statutes that substantially modified its land laws. In the first case, decided in 1829, Washington dismissed the plaintiff's reliance on *Fletcher* as authority for voiding laws divesting a vested right. "It is no where intimated in that opinion," he wrote, "that a state statute, which divests a vested right, is repugnant to the *constitution of the United States*." It was thus not enough to show that a right had been divested but it had to be shown that there was a contract whose obligation had been impaired. Story reiterated this point in 1834 in the second Pennsylvania case, stating that the Court had "no right" to void a state act as contrary to the Constitution merely because "it devests antecedent vested rights of property." In another 1834 case Story declared that state acts dissolving a corporation could not "in any just sense" be considered as impairing the obligation of the company's contracts.

The Marshall Court's greater solicitude for the rights of the states during its last decade has been attributed at least in part to political opposition to the federal judiciary, including attempts to abolish appeals from state courts under section 25. Yet in sustaining state laws against contract clause challenges, the Court was able to reach this result without sacrificing principles laid down in the earlier cases. A good illustration was *Providence Bank v. Billings* (1830), the principal contract case of the late Marshall Court period and the only one in which the chief justice himself gave the opinion. This was an arranged case to try the constitutionality of a Rhode Island law of 1822 imposing a duty upon licensed persons and corporations within the state. The Providence Bank, chartered by the state legislature in 1791, refused to pay the tax, prompting a lawsuit in which the corporation contended that the law was repugnant to the contract clause of the Constitution. A state court decision against the bank was confirmed pro forma in 1828 by the Supreme Judicial Court of Rhode Island, clearing the way for a section 25 appeal to the Supreme Court. Counsel for the bank presented an elaborate argument invoking the constitutional principles of limited legislative power, protection of private property, and "inviolability of vested rights" as ratified by a long line of judicial decisions, including *Fletcher, New Jersey, and Dartmouth*. Like other corporate charters, the bank's charter was a contract protected by the Constitution, and the state tax, so the argument ran, impaired the obligation of this contract, for the taxing power could be exercised to destroy the bank.

In a brief opinion, Chief Justice Marshall rejected this argument, finding no express or implied promise of an exemption from taxation in the bank's charter. "The state, then, has made no express contract which has been impaired by the act of which the plaintiffs complain,"

he said. He went on to say that the power of taxation was so fundamental, "founded in society itself" and residing "in government as a
part of itself," that a state was not required to reserve this vital power
in granting a corporate charter. The taxing power could be abused,
he conceded, but the Constitution "was not intended to furnish the
corrective for every abuse of power which may be committed by the
state governments." Representation and elections provided "the only
security, where there is no express contract." The chief justice easily
distinguished the earlier contract cases and admonished the bank's
counsel for making incorrect "inferences drawn from general expres-
sions" in opinions addressed to a different issue.

In *Providence Bank* Marshall examined the bank's charter closely
and, finding nothing in its words indicating an exemption from taxation, said that "it would be going very far to insert it by construction."
The next year, in 1831, the Marshall Court heard arguments in another corporate charter case that would prove to be of transcendent
importance in the field of contract clause jurisprudence: *Charles River
Bridge v. Warren Bridge*. At issue in this case was a Massachusetts act
of 1828 authorizing construction of a new bridge over the Charles
River connecting Boston and Charlestown. This new bridge was to
be built near the older Charles River Bridge, a toll bridge chartered
in 1785, and would eventually revert to the state and become a free
bridge. In the face of this threat to its lucrative business, the Charles
River Bridge proprietors sued to prevent construction of the Warren
Bridge, contending that the 1828 act impaired the obligation of its
charter. After the state's highest court ruled against them, the Charles
River Bridge proprietors brought a section 25 appeal to the Supreme
Court.

Despite hearing the case over five days in 1831, the justices were
unable to reach a decision during Marshall's four remaining years
as chief justice owing to absences, vacancies, and a close division of
opinion. Neither side could obtain four votes, which by Court practice had become the minimum needed to decide constitutional cases.
The case was finally reargued at the 1837 term, presenting in stark
terms a clash between different property interests hinted at in recent
contract clause cases. On the one side were older established property rights represented by the Charles River Bridge proprietors; on

the other were emergent entrepreneurial rights of ownership represented by the Warren Bridge proprietors. The Supreme Court's decision in favor of the Warren Bridge served notice that the contract clause would not be construed to hamper state efforts to promote internal improvements such as turnpikes, canals, and railroads. In his opinion Chief Justice Taney said that corporate charters must be read strictly as not conveying implied privileges such as the exclusive right to collect tolls. Story, in dissent, argued the contrary, that the older company's charter granted just such a privilege. Despite a common assumption that he shared Story's view, Marshall, it has been credibly argued, appears to have endorsed the constitutionality of the Warren Bridge's charter since the case's first hearing in 1831. Among various facts and circumstances supporting this argument was Marshall's strict reading of the bank's charter in *Providence Bank* to sustain Rhode Island's tax on the bank. Chief Justice Taney quoted this opinion approvingly in *Charles River Bridge*, remarking that the two cases were "in principle precisely the same."

Charles River Bridge was the last Marshall Court contract clause case and the first decided by the Taney Court. Commentators then and later read this decision as significantly undermining Chief Justice Marshall's grand project to make the contract clause an effective barrier against state interference with property rights. Careful study, however, has shown that the case's outcome was consistent with the Supreme Court's previous decisions and apparently even had the sanction of the late chief justice himself. During the next three decades the Taney Court (1836–1864) interpreted the contract clause to accord greater latitude to the states in regulating economic policy, but its modifications developed logically from its predecessor's jurisprudence. In numerous cases the Taney Court confirmed and consolidated principles established under Chief Justice Marshall. It did not hesitate to invoke the contract clause, striking down more than twice as many state laws as did the Marshall Court, though the proportion of such cases was about the same. The contract clause, wrote Taney in 1843, "was undoubtedly adopted as a part of the Constitution for a great and useful purpose. It was to maintain the integrity of contracts, and to secure their faithful execution throughout the Union." The language was less lofty—Marshall would have substituted "inviolability" for "integrity"—but expressed essentially the same point about the contract clause's importance.

During the Taney era the reach of the contract clause received closer definition, giving birth to principles and doctrines that became enshrined in constitutional law. *Charles River Bridge*, for example, established the principle of strict construction of public grants, building upon Marshall Court precedents, notably *Providence Bank*. In another case, decided in 1848, the Court upheld a Vermont statute in which the state exercised its sovereign power of eminent domain to acquire a previously chartered toll bridge and compensate its owners so the state could build a public highway. From this case emerged the doctrine that eminent domain was paramount to the contract clause, that a state in granting a charter did not part with its power to take property for public use and provide just compensation. No such Marshall Court case raised this issue, though Johnson in *Green v. Biddle* expressed the wish that Kentucky had found some other way to aid its occupying claimants, evidently suggesting that the state could have resorted to eminent domain to compensate the owner and provide relief to the occupant. After the Civil War the Supreme Court dismissed a contract clause challenge to a Mississippi law revoking a charter to conduct lotteries. This decision gave official recognition to the principle that, as with eminent domain, a state could not surrender its "police power" to protect the health, safety, and morals of its citizens. Intimations of the police power doctrine can be traced back to the original controversy over Georgia's 1796 rescinding law, which was defended as a measure necessary to preserve the republican character of the people.

The contract clause retained its high standing in American constitutional law throughout the nineteenth century and into the twentieth. Originating in the framers' goal of preventing the state legislatures from committing the kinds of abuses against private rights that characterized the 1780s, the prohibition against impairment of contracts emerged under Chief Justice Marshall to provide broad protection for the vested rights of property. During the remainder of the nineteenth century the contract clause evolved into the Supreme Court's principal weapon to exercise supervisory power over state regulations of the economy. Despite restrictions on its scope, the contract clause continued to thrive as an instrument of judicial review through the turn of the century. By then, however, it had already begun a steady decline in importance, moving from the center to the "margins of modern constitutional law." A pivotal case that both signified and hastened the contract clause's fall from grace was a Supreme Court decision in 1934 upholding a Minnesota law permitting state courts to postpone mortgage foreclosures. In this case the police power exception was enlarged to permit states to grant debtor relief during periods of economic crisis. The implications of this highly controversial decision were not immediately apparent, but since then the Supreme Court has rarely upheld a contract clause challenge to a state law.

The reasons for the contract clause's long downward trajectory are complicated and subject to much scholarly debate. Perhaps after many years of exhaustive litigation and adjudication the contract clause simply died of natural causes. As the accretion of various principles and doctrines more or less settled its meaning, the contract clause became an increasingly barren field of litigation, particularly because the adjudicative trend was toward limiting its reach. Parties came to perceive less advantage in relying on the contract clause to protect against state interference with their interests. Moreover, the adoption of the Fourteenth Amendment in 1868 provided a new constitutional weapon of great potential. The amendment's first section prohibits the states from depriving "any person of life, liberty, or property, without due process of law." With its far more comprehensive scope to safeguard property rights and contractual freedom, companies preferred to rely on the due process clause when going to court. Due process through the Fifth Amendment was also a tool to contest federal economic regulations, which increasingly posed a more serious threat than those originating in the states—yet another cause of the contract clause's shrinking share of litigation. A more general explanation for the demise of the contract clause (which would also apply to the due process clause as a protection for economic liberty) is that it was the victim of a broad political shift in the early twentieth century that favored judicial deference to government efforts to set economic policy. The "marked eclipse" of the contract clause, a leading constitutional scholar has written, occurred simultaneously "with the rise of a political climate supportive of the regulatory and welfare state."

Although the contract clause has become virtually obsolete, the modern Supreme Court exercises far greater supervision over state laws than was conceivable in Marshall's day. The open-ended due process clause gives the Court vast discretion to bring state legislation under its scrutiny. Moreover, countless more state laws have been brought under review by the process of "incorporation," in which the first eight amendments of the Bill of Rights have been held to apply to the state as well as federal governments. For more than a century after its adoption, the Bill of Rights was almost universally assumed to be a restriction on the powers of Congress. The Marshall Court in *Barron v. Baltimore* (1833) gave official sanction to this view in declining to hear a case under the Fifth Amendment. It is well to bear in mind that until after the Civil War, the contract clause provided the only protection (other than the state constitutions) for private rights against infringement by the state legislatures. Given the limited scope of its jurisdiction, the Marshall Court succeeded to a remarkable degree in fashioning the contract clause into an effective instrument of judicial review and so fulfilled the original Constitution's potential to be "a bill of rights for the people of each state."

In its leading aspects, constitutional law under Chief Justice Marshall strove to preserve the Constitution's delicate equipoise between the general and state governments. In the compound system of a national republic superimposed on state republics, the chief justice believed the states' centrifugal tendency to resist regulation by a central government posed the greater danger to the breakdown of constitutional stability. Acting on this premise, he adopted a broad construction of the Constitution with respect both to the powers granted to the federal government and to the restrictions and prohibitions on the state governments. Broad construction served the complementary purposes of promoting the energetic and efficient operation of the federal government while enforcing the Constitution's abridgments of state sovereignty.

Marshall's expansive interpretation of the Constitution sprang naturally from his premise about the precarious nature of the constitutional settlement of 1787. Broad construction was also the natural default mode for a court that had the unique opportunity to read the Constitution in virtually pristine form, to parse its text directly unburdened by a gloss of accumulated law. The chief justice understood that in the largely virgin field of constitutional law his court took on the grave responsibility of being the first to decide the meaning of the Constitution. It would make the precedents that became the starting point for subsequent judicial inquiry. Given a chance at the outset to shape the Constitution into an effective check on the states, Chief Justice Marshall in *Fletcher v. Peck* construed the prohibition against impairing the obligation of contract in an enlarged sense, as applying to a broad category of cases, including those not in contemplation at the time the provision was adopted. In *Fletcher* and subsequent contract cases, Marshall relied on a "plain meaning" or "natural sense" reading without resorting to extreme literalism. Yet his expansive interpretation was never intended to be unqualified, to foreclose modification or even restriction of the contract clause's scope by subsequent adjudications. It placed a substantial burden on those seeking to take certain cases out of the prohibition but did not prevent astute lawyers and jurists from successfully rising to the challenge. Indeed, the process of giving the contract clause a more precise delineation began with the Marshall Court and mostly with the chief justice's approval.

No doubt the desire to project an image of the Supreme Court as a tribunal that decided matters of law and refrained from intruding on the political sphere cautioned against pushing broad construction too far. Justice Johnson had sounded an early warning in *Fletcher* that the Court would be drawn into cases of ever more complexity where the line between admissible and inadmissible state laws was not easily discernible. After *Ogden* in 1827 the Marshall Court was inclined to adopt a more circumspect if not skeptical attitude toward contract clause challenges to state legislation. It was more sensitive to the risk posed by these cases of being perceived as the arbiter of public policy rather than as a court of law.

Little trace remains of the Marshall Court's expansive interpretation of the contract clause in modern Supreme Court jurisprudence.

Although *Fletcher v. Peck's* principal holding—that states as well as individuals are bound by their own contracts—is still part of the law of the land, it has become so attenuated as virtually to cease operating as a restraint on the states. Yet the enduring significance of the Marshall Court's contract clause jurisprudence and indeed of the entire body of its constitutional adjudications extends beyond its particular rulings in the early nineteenth century. The lasting influence of the Marshall era on American constitutional law is to be seen in the flourishing state of judicial review, an instrument that continues primarily to enforce constitutional prohibitions against acts of the state legislatures. The very enterprise of judicial review—of constitutional law—had its beginnings in the Marshall Court's contract clause cases. These cases provided the occasion and opportunity for the Supreme Court to present itself as the peculiar guardian of the Constitution, as the authoritative expounder of the nation's fundamental law. In deciding them Chief Justice Marshall applied the rules and methods of common law interpretation and statutory construction to the text of the contract clause, effectively demonstrating that the Constitution had the attributes of an ordinary law whose meaning could be determined by courts in the process of adjudication. Under Chief Justice Marshall enforcement of the Constitution came to be entrusted to the judiciary department and constitutional law developed by means of judicial exposition of the Constitution.

CHRONOLOGY

February 1785	Georgia legislature adopts act erecting Bourbon County, embracing settlements along the Mississippi south of the Yazoo
February 1788	Georgia legislature authorizes delegates to cede western lands on certain conditions
July 1788	Congress rejects Georgia's offer to cede western lands
December 1789	Georgia legislature sells 25 million acres of western lands to South Carolina Yazoo Company, Virginia Yazoo Company, and Tennessee Yazoo Company for $208,000; grants never issue because companies did not meet two-year deadline for payment
November 1794	Georgia legislature convenes in temporary capital at Augusta
December 20, 1794	Georgia legislature passes bill to sell western lands to four companies headed by James Gunn and others
December 29, 1794	Governor George Mathews vetoes sale bill
January 7, 1795	Governor Mathews signs revised sale bill, authorizing sale to Georgia Company, Georgia Mississippi Company, Upper Mississippi Company, and Tennessee Company; sale price is $500,000 for total acreage estimated to be 21.4 million acres (later determined to be about 35 million acres)
May 1795	Convention to revise Georgia constitution convenes at Louisville; considers petitions and grand jury presentments condemning the sale of the state's western lands; adjourns without taking action on the sale. Refers question to next meeting of legislature
June–July? 1795	George Blake and William Williamson of Georgia meet in Boston to discuss sale of Georgia Mississippi Company tract

August 1795	Senator James Jackson resigns seat and launches anti-Yazoo crusade; publishes "Letters of Sicilius"
August 22, 1795	Georgia Company sells most of its Yazoo lands to James Greenleaf, who sells most of this off between August and November
September 1795	Covenant between Williamson and Blake for purchase of Georgia Mississippi tract
Fall 1795	Jackson leads the anti-Yazoo forces to a decisive victory at the polls, with many newly elected legislators pledged to declare the 1795 sale act null and void
December 1795	Georgia Mississippi Company conveys its tract of 11.38 million acres to Williamson and Amasa Jackson as coagents to sell the lands
January 1796	Georgia legislature convenes in Louisville
February 13, 1796	Williamson and Jackson deliver deed to Georgia Mississippi Company's tract to group of investors styled New England Mississippi Land Company; John Peck one of the original subscribers to the company
February 13, 1796	Georgia legislature passes rescinding act
February 15, 1796	Members of the legislature assemble in State House square for public burning of the Yazoo sale act of January 1795
March 16, 1796	Copy of rescinding act received in Boston
February 3, 1797	Publication of Robert G. Harper's *The Case of the Georgia Sales on the Mississippi Considered*
August 1797	Jedidiah Morse publishes *American Gazetteer,* including *A Description of the . . . Georgia Western Country* (later published as separate pamphlet)
October–November 1797	Abraham Bishop's *Georgia Speculation Unveiled* published
October 30, 1797	Royall Tyler's *The Georgia Spec; Or, The Land in the Moon* performed in Boston
April 1798	Congress passes act for amicable settlement of limits of Georgia and authorizing establishment of government in Mississippi Territory

October 1799	In *Derby v. Blake* Supreme Judicial Court of Massachusetts declares Georgia's rescinding act void
May 1800	Congress passes supplemental act to that of April 1798; authorizes U.S. commissioners to receive compromise proposals from private claimants to Mississippi lands
April 24, 1802	U.S. and Georgia agree to compact that cedes western lands to U.S. for $1.25 million; stipulates that the U.S. might within one year set aside 5 million acres to satisfy claims not previously recognized
February 16, 1803	U.S. commissioners present report to Congress; says Yazoo claimants title "cannot be supported" but recommends "compromise on reasonable terms"
March 1803	Congress passes act regulating grants of land and providing for disposal of U.S. lands in Mississippi Territory; allows Yazoo claimants to submit compromise proposals to commissioners
May 18, 1803	Robert Fletcher files suit against John Peck in U.S. Circuit Court, Boston; case "continued by consent," June 1803–October 1806
February–March 1804	House debates John Randolph's resolutions excluding compensation for claimants under 1795 grants; postpones bill for settling land claims and authorizing commissioners to settle with claimants
November 30, 1804	New England Mississippi Land Company presents memorial to House
January 18, 1805	House Committee on Claims reports resolution authorizing commissioners to settle with claimants to Mississippi lands
January 29–February 2, 1805	Claims committee resolution touches off acrimonious debate in House
February 5, 1805	Bill presented to House embodying resolution of January 18; passes to second reading but Congress adjourns March 3 without taking action

January 1806	Senator John Quincy Adams presents petitions of New England claimants to Senate
March 1806	Adams drafts bill to indemnify claimants if they release claims to U.S.; Senate passes bill of March 28 but Randolph's opposition persuades House to reject it on March 29
October 1806	Pleas and special verdict filed in *Fletcher v. Peck*; Judge Cushing gives judgment for Peck
January 1807	House by large majorities rejects motions to refer latest Yazoo petition to committee
March 1807	Congress passes act "to prevent settlements being made on lands ceded to the United States, until authorized by law"; provides for forfeiture of titles of "intruders"
June 1807	*Fletcher v. Peck* commences anew in U.S. Circuit Court, Boston, apparently because of failure to prosecute writ of error after 1806 judgment
October 1807	Judge Cushing again gives judgment for Peck in U.S. Circuit Court; writ of error issued in November to take case to Supreme Court
January 1808	Memorial of Gov. James Sullivan of Massachusetts seeking relief for Yazoo claimants presented to Congress; touches off angry debate
February 10, 1808	Joseph Story, counsel for the N.E.M. Land Co., petitions to speak at the bar of the House; motion to admit him defeated by large majority
February 13, 1808	Appeal of *Fletcher v. Peck* filed in Supreme Court
March 1–4, 1809	Luther Martin opens case of *Fletcher v. Peck* on behalf of plaintiff Fletcher, followed by John Quincy Adams and Robert G. Harper for Peck; Martin closes
March 11, 1809	Supreme Court rules for Fletcher on technical point of pleading; after parties agree to waive objections to pleadings, case remains on docket for rehearing at next term
December 1809	N.E.M. Land Co. memorial presented to House and referred to committee on claims

February 15, 1810	*Fletcher v. Peck* reargued by Martin, Harper, and Story (replacing Adams)
February 16, 1810	Story appears before committee on claims on behalf of N.E.M. Land Co.
March 16, 1810	Chief Justice Marshall delivers Supreme Court's opinion in favor of Peck
April 17, 1810	In House, Randolph and George M. Troup denounce *Fletcher*; Randolph's motion to reject N.E.M. Land Co. memorial defeated
June 20, 1810	Peck publishes "Cautionary Notice," with extract of *Fletcher* opinion
December 17, 1810	Troup warns House of dire consequences of acquiescing in *Fletcher*
June 1812	Congress declares war on Great Britain
January 19, 1813	Senate passes Yazoo compensation bill
January 20, 1813	Troup in House unsuccessfully moves rejection of bill; again denounces *Fletcher*
February 15, 1813	House takes up compensation bill; John A. Harper of New Hampshire delivers major speech in favor; House postpones further consideration
January 1814	In Senate, William Hunter of Rhode Island calls up N.E.M. Land Co. memorial, which had lain on table since 1810; presents bill for compromise on principles of commissioners' report of February 1803
February 28, 1814	Senate passes indemnity bill, twenty-four to eight
March 26, 1814	After five days of intense debate, House passes bill, eighty-four to seventy-six; President Madison signs into law on March 31
1815	Commissioners under indemnity act begin to hear and settle claims
February 1819	Supreme Court decides *Brown v. Gilman*
1822–1854	N.E.M. Land Co. petitions Congress for recovery of sum disallowed by commissioners under the indemnity act
October 1864	U.S. Court of Claims rejects N.E.M. Land Co.'s claim

BIBLIOGRAPHICAL ESSAY

Note from the Series Editors: The following bibliographical essay contains the major primary and secondary sources the author consulted for this volume. We have asked all authors in the series to omit formal citations in order to make our volumes more readable, inexpensive, and appealing for students and general readers. In adopting this format, Landmark Law Cases and American Society *follows the precedent of a number of highly regarded and widely consulted series.*

For half a century after its publication, C. Peter Magrath, *Yazoo: Law and Politics in the New Republic: The Case of* Fletcher v. Peck (Providence, RI: Brown University Press, 1966), was the only book-length account of this seminal case. At just over a hundred pages of text and another hundred pages of documents and notes, *Yazoo* is a lively and insightful study that continues to instruct students of American constitutional history and law. That this truly excellent book is no longer in print (though copies in limited number can be purchased online) is perhaps sufficient reason for offering my own contribution to the subject.

My work is based on essentially the same documentary record used by Magrath, no significant new source material having come to light since he wrote. Our points of difference, such as they are, arise mainly from somewhat different perspectives. Magrath, a political scientist before he entered higher education administration, wrote under the influence of interest-group theory that was predominant in the scholarship of the 1950s and 1960s. His treatment of the Yazoo controversy tends to make it a precursor of modern American politics, while as a historian I am inclined see this episode as reflecting unresolved issues arising from the establishment of a federal republic under the Constitution. These different points of view are scarcely noticeable and do not intrude upon the primary goal I share with Magrath: to provide an accessible narrative of the great Yazoo land sale and its political and constitutional repercussions.

Before Magrath's *Yazoo*, the most authoritative—and still valuable—survey of the subject was Charles H. Haskins, "The Yazoo Land Companies," *Papers of the American Historical Association* 5, pt. 4 (1891): 61–103, an early work by the great medievalist. More recently, Julius Goebel Jr. and Joseph H. Smith, eds., *The Law Practice of Alexander Hamilton: Documents and Commentary*, vol. 4 (New York: Columbia University Press, 1980), 356–425, provided a thorough scholarly investigation of "The Georgia Lands Controversy." The editors contend for the influence of Hamilton's 1796 opinion on Marshall's subsequent exposition of the contract clause. Among numerous other general accounts of Yazoo, I found Horace H. Hagan, "Fletcher vs. Peck," *Georgetown Law Journal* 16 (1927): 1–40, to be particularly worthy. Also valuable for its extensive reliance on original sources is Thomas P. Abernethy, *The South in the New Nation 1789–1819* (Baton Rouge: Louisiana State University Press, 1961), 136–168.

Virtually all the printed original source material pertaining to Yazoo is available online, to which I have enjoyed free access through the Swem Library of the College of William and Mary. The following databases have been indispensable: "A Century of Lawmaking for a New Nation: U.S. Congressional Documents and Debates" (http://memory.loc.gov /ammem/amlaw); "America's Historical Imprints" (www.infoweb.news bank.com); "America's Historical Newspapers" (www.infoweb.newsbank .com); and HeinOnline (www.heinonline.org).

"A Century of Lawmaking" is the entry point for the two most important sources on which I have relied. The first is the *Annals of Congress*, published under its formal title as *The Debates and Proceedings in the Congress of the United States*. Its forty-two volumes cover the 1st Congress through the first session of the 18th Congress, from 1789 to 1824. The second is the *American State Papers*, thirty-eight volumes containing the legislative and executive documents of Congress during the period 1789 to 1838. This collection is divided into ten classes. I have relied almost exclusively on two volumes of "Public Lands" (Class VIII), covering 1789 to 1815. I will provide more specific references to these sources at the appropriate points below.

The various series of "America's Historical Imprints" cover American publications from 1639 through 1819. Its titles have been integrated into the catalogs of subscribing libraries. Many of these titles are also available (with better quality images) by way of "Sabin Americana, 1500–1926" (www.galenet.galegroup.com). The search capability of these online databases has proved invaluable, particularly in researching newspapers in "America's Historical Newspapers."

HeinOnline makes available an extensive set of legal sources, including *United States Reports*, the official reports of all Supreme Court cases since 1789. In addition to providing access to federal and state case law, this database contains a large collection of titles under the rubric of "Legal Classics." Its collection of U.S. congressional documents also includes the *Annals of Congress*, which is more easily navigable than that provided by "A Century of Lawmaking."

The following survey is organized more or less according to the order in which the subjects are considered in the body of the work. An excellent brief introduction to American land speculation is Jamie Bronstein, "Land Speculation," in *Encyclopedia of the New American Nation*, ed. Paul Finkelman (New York: Charles Scribner's Sons, 2005). A. M. Sakolski, *The Great American Land Bubble: The Amazing Story of Land-Grabbing, Speculations, and Booms from Colonial Days to the Present Time* (New York: Harper Brothers, 1932), is still the classic work. For a concise and perceptive consideration of colonial land speculation, see Bernard Bailyn, *The Peopling of British North America: An Introduction* (New York: Knopf, 1986), 65–85. Shaw Livermore, *Early American Land Companies: Their Influence on Corporate Development* (New York: Octagon Books, Inc., 1968), originally published in 1939, is still the standard work on its subject. See also Archibald Henderson, *Dr. Thomas Walker and the Loyal Company of Virginia* (Worcester, Mass.: American Antiquarian Society, 1931). On George Washington's land acquisitions, see Joel Achenbach, *The Grand Idea: George Washington's Potomac and the Race to the West* (New York: Simon and Schuster, 2002), and John Ferling, *The Ascent of George Washington: The Hidden Political Genius of an American Icon* (New York: Bloomsbury Press, 2009).

Several specialized studies have deepened my understanding of land speculation: Stephen Aron, "Pioneers and Profiteers: Land Speculation and the Homestead Ethic in Frontier Kentucky," *Western Historical Quarterly* 23 (1992): 179–198; Jonathan Bean, "Marketing 'the Great American Commodity,'" *Ohio History* 103 (1994): 152–169; and Kristofer Ray, "Land Speculation, Popular Democracy, and Political Transformation on the Tennessee Frontier, 1780–1800," *Tennessee Historical Quarterly* 61 (2002): 161–181.

For Henry Adams's description of the Georgia's western territory, see Henry Adams, *History of the United States of America during the Administration of Thomas Jefferson and James Madison*, 2 vols. (New York: Library of America, 1986), 1: 205–206. One of the grantee companies published a promotional pamphlet containing copious extracts from Hutchins's *Historical Narrative*. See *Grant to the Georgia Mississippi Company . . .* (Augusta, GA: John Smith, 1795). See also Jedidiah Morse, *A Description of the Soil, Productions, Commercial, Agricultural and Local Advantages of the Georgia Western Territory . . .* (Boston: Thomas & Andrews, 1797). On the "Yazoo line," see Absalom H. Chappell, *Miscellanies of Georgia, Historical, Biographical, Descriptive, &c.* (Columbus, GA: Thomas Gilbert, 1874), 76–79.

The authoritative study of Georgia politics in the early national period is George R. Lamplugh, *Politics on the Periphery: Factions and Parties in Georgia, 1783–1806* (Newark: University of Delaware Press, 1986). My understanding of Yazoo in its Georgia context has benefited immeasurably from this book. Lamplugh has recently published a sequel, *Rancorous Enmities and Blind Partialities: Factions and Parties in Georgia, 1807–1845* (Lanham, MD: University Press of America, 2015). The same author's articles, including "John Wereat and Yazoo, 1794–1799," *Georgia Historical Quarterly* 72 (1988): 502–517; "James Gunn, Georgia Federalist, 1789–1801," *Georgia Historical Quarterly* 94 (2010): 313–341; and "'Oh the Colossus! The Colossus!': James Jackson and the Jeffersonian Republican Party in Georgia, 1796–1806," *Journal of the Early Republic* 9 (1989): 315–334, have been collected and published as *In Pursuit of Dead Georgians: One Historian's Excursions into the History of His Adopted State* (iUniverse, 2015). Still useful nineteenth-century histories of Georgia are William Bacon Stevens, *A History of Georgia, from Its First Discovery by Europeans to the Adoption of the Present Constitution in 1798*, 2 vols. (Philadelphia: E. H. Butler, 1859); Chappell, *Miscellanies of Georgia* (cited above); and Albert James Pickett, *History of Alabama, and Incidentally of Georgia and Mississippi*, 2 vols. (Charleston, SC: Walker and James, 1851). George White, *An Accurate Account of the Yazoo Fraud* (Marietta, GA: "Advocate" Printing Office, 1852), is a succinct (and decidedly anti-Yazoo) account by a nineteenth-century Episcopal clergyman and amateur historian. An even briefer account is in the same author's *Statistics of the State of Georgia . . .* (Savannah, GA: W. Thorne Williams, 1849), 48–54.

For the legislative proceedings concerning the sale of 1795, see *State of Facts: Shewing the Right of Certain Companies to the Lands Later Purchased by Them from the State of Georgia* ([Philadelphia], 1795), appendix VII, 51–64. The Georgia Company's articles of agreement were appended to the report of the commissioners submitted to Congress in February 1803. This report also reproduced extracts from the journals of the Georgia House and Senate recording the votes of January 2 and 3, 1795, showing the names of those voting for and against the bill. See *American State Papers, Public Lands*, 1:127–129, 130–131. For examples of Yazoo defenders who conceded that Georgia legislators probably acted corruptly while denying the relevance of the corruption charge, see the speeches of Erastus Root and James Holland in 1805, *Annals of Congress*, 14:1095–1096, 1141.

President Washington's message to Congress in February 1795 enclosing the sale act is in *American State Papers, Indian Affairs*, 1:551–558. This prompted a brief debate in Congress, followed by another on the bill to obtain a cession of Georgia's claims within present Indian boundaries. See *Annals of Congress*, 4:851, 1253–1268, 1277–1280.

On James Jackson, Thomas U. P. Charlton's eulogistic *Life of Major General James Jackson* (Augusta, GA: Randolph, 1809) appeared a few years after the protagonist's death. A reprint of this work contains some of Jackson's letters, including one written just after the passage of the sale act (Atlanta: Noonan, 1897), 206–208. The standard modern biography is William Omer Foster, *James Jackson: Duelist and Militant Statesman* (Athens: University of Georgia Press, 1960). Jackson's newspaper essays as Sicilius were subsequently published as a pamphlet, *The Letters of Sicilius, to the Citizens of the State of Georgia . . .* (Augusta, GA: John Smith? 1795). Jackson's vivid "Sketch of the Yazoo Speculation," written no earlier than 1803, is in Lila M. Hawes, ed., "Miscellaneous Papers of James Jackson, 1781–1798, Part II," Georgia Historical Quarterly 37 (1953): 152–156. *The Letters of a Farmer to the People of Georgia . . .* (Charleston, SC: W. P. Young, 1796) was a reply to Sicilius.

On the proceedings of the Georgia legislature that enacted the rescinding law, see *Journals of the House of Representatives of the State of Georgia Journals* (Augusta, GA: John Smith, 1796). The rescinding act was one of many Yazoo documents that the U.S. House ordered to be printed in 1809: *Sundry Papers in Relation to Claims, Commonly Called the Yazoo Claims* (Washington, DC: A. and G. Way, 1809), 13–26. The text is also reproduced in *American State Papers, Public Lands*, 1:142–144. On the 1798 constitution, see *The Constitution of the State of Georgia . . .* (Louisville, GA: A. M'Millan, 1798).

Biographical information on James Greenleaf can be gleaned from secondary works such as Sakolski and Livermore. Bob Arnebeck, *Through a Fiery Trial: Building Washington, 1790–1800* (Lanham, MD: Madison Books, 1991) has frequent references to Greenleaf as a speculator in Washington lots. A schedule of Greenleaf's purchase from the Georgia Company in August 1795 and his subsequent conveyances are in *American State Papers, Public Lands*, 2:745–746. Much useful information about conveyances of land derived from titles under the Georgia sale, including the seller, buyer, and date of the transaction, is to be found in James Madison's report to Congress in February 1805, "Evidences of Title Derived from the State of Georgia," in *American State Papers, Public Lands*, 1:201–228.

The Georgia Mississippi Company's sale to the group of Boston investors that became the New England Mississippi Land Company is abundantly documented in the following sources: George Blake's statement, March 12, 1814, in *American State Papers, Public Lands*, 2:746–748; Brown v. Gilman, 17 U.S. (4 Cranch) 255 (1819); *Deposition of Edward Stow, in relation to the Claim of the New England Mississippi Land Company [Thomas L. Winthrop and Others] on the United States*, a twelve-page pamphlet printed for a committee of Congress. Stow, Peck's brother-in-law, gave his deposition in Boston in March 1840. See also *Articles of Association and Agreement, Constituting the New-England Mississippi Land Company* [Boston, 1796?]. These articles were also printed with amendments in 1797, 1798, and 1814.

On John Peck, see "Robert Maynard Peck, Midshipman & John Peck, Boy," an online article posted on the website *ContientalNavy.com: The History and People of the Continental Navy* (http://continentalnavy.com/?s=peck). Information about Peck's portrait by John Johnston, now in the National Gallery of Art, is in Ellen G. Miles, *American Paintings of the Eighteenth Century* (Washington, DC: National Gallery of Art; New York: Cambridge University Press, 1995), 109–110. For Peck's notices as a broker and as agent for the Boston Mill Corporation, see *Boston Independent Chronicle*, February 14, September 2, 1793, February 7, 1805. The sale of Peck's "elegant country seat" was advertised in the *Boston Daily Advertiser*, May 2, 1814.

Firsthand accounts of the speculative fever that struck New England include Timothy Dwight, *Travels in New England and New York*, ed. Barbara Miller Solomon, 4 vols. (Cambridge, MA: Harvard University Press, 1969), 1:158–161; François-Alexandre-Frédéric, duc de La Rochefoucauld-Liancourt, *Travels through the United States of North America* . . . , 2 vols. (London: R. Phillips, 1799), 1:144; 2:175–177, 600, 608–617; William Priest, *Travels in the United States of America* . . . (London: J. Johnson, 1802), 132. For unscrupulous practices by sellers, see the article "Of Georgia Lands—*Cautionary*," *Boston Columbian Centinel*, March 16, 1796. A notice of the play by Royall Tyler was reprinted from a Boston paper in the Philadelphia *Aurora General Advertiser*, November 6, 1797. *Greenleaf's New York Journal*, March 8, 1796, reprinted the mock obituary notice from a Boston paper. Weld's "caution" notice was printed in the *Boston Columbian Centinel*, March 30, 1796.

The cases of Dexter and others against Payne and others and those of Nightingale and Miller against the Bishops and others are discussed in Goebel and Smith, eds., *Law Practice of Alexander Hamilton*, 4:376–377, 388–417. See also *Connecticut Courant*, March 26, 1798; *Boston Columbian Centinel*, March 17, 1798; *Connecticut Journal*, March 29, 1798; *Norwich Packet*, March 6, 1799; *New-York Evening Post*, June 30, 1802. *Derby v. Blake* is reported in 226 Mass. 618 (Sup. Jud. Ct., Mass., 1799), reprinted from the *Boston Columbian Centinel*, October 9, 1799. See also George Blake's 1814 statement, *American State Papers, Public Lands*, 2:747–748. For opinions doubting the legality of the rescinding act, see *Connecticut Courant*, March 7, 1796, and a letter written by one of Hamilton's clients soon after Hamilton drew up his opinion. An excerpt of this letter, along with the several drafts of Hamilton opinion, can be found in Goebel and Smith, eds., *Law Practice of Alexander Hamilton*, 4:405, 425–431.

On the organizational activities of the New England claimants, see notices of meetings in the *Massachusetts Mercury*, August 23, 30, 1799, and *Boston Columbian Centinel*, Nov. 11, 1801. Minutes of meetings and other papers, including a draft of a memorial to the president, are in the New England Mississippi Land Company Records, Hargrett Library, University of Georgia. In 1797 three pamphlets on Yazoo appeared: Robert G. Harper, *The Case of the Georgia Sales on the Mississippi Considered* . . . (Philadelphia: Benjamin Davies, 1797); Jedidiah Morse, *A Description of the Soil, Productions, Commercial, Agricultural and Local Advantages of the Georgia Western Territory* . . . (Boston: Thomas & Andrews, 1797); Abraham Bishop, *Georgia Speculation Unveiled; in Two Numbers* (Hartford, CT: Elisha Babcock, 1797); *Georgia Speculation Unveiled, Second Part* (Hartford, CT: Hudson & Goodwin, 1798). Harper's pamphlet was reprinted in 1799 and again in 1814 in *American Law Journal* 5 (1814): 354–457. A facsimile of Bishop's first two numbers was published by University Microfilms, Ann Arbor, Michigan, in 1966. Magrath, *Yazoo*, 140–148, 151–171, reprints excerpts of Harper's pamphlet and the first two numbers in full of Bishop's pamphlet.

The attorney general's report of April 1796 and a subsequent committee report are in *American State Papers, Public Lands*, 1:28–59, 70–71. The proceedings and debates in the Senate and House on the bill for establishing the Mississippi Territory are in *Annals of Congress*, 7:489–490, 511, 514–515, 1278–1284, 1298–1312. For the act as adopted in April 1798, see *U.S. Statutes at Large*, 1:549–550. On the "diffusion" theory of ameliorating slavery, see Lacy Ford, "Reconfiguring the Old South: 'Solving' the Problem of Slavery, 1787–1838," *Journal of American History* 95 (2008): 105–109.

For Gov. Winthrop Sargent's efforts to block the N.E.M. Land Co.'s attempts to settle the Mississippi Territory, see Dunbar Rowland, ed., *The Mississippi Territorial Archives, 1798–1804* (Nashville, TN: Brandon Printing, 1905), 59–60, 61–65, 68. The New England claimants' 1798 memorial was printed as *To the President of the United States* (1798; Early American Imprints, Series 1, no. 34179). The act empowering U.S. commissioners to look into private claims in Mississippi is in *U.S. Statutes at Large*, 2:69–70. For Georgia's 1802 cession, see *American State Papers, Public Lands*, 1:113–114. Payson Jackson Treat, *The National Land System 1785–1820* (New York: E. B. Treat, 1910), 355–366, is a helpful account of the cession.

The notice urging New England claimants to submit their title papers was inserted in the *Boston Columbian Centinel*, June 26, 1802. The commissioners' report of February 1803 is in *American State Papers, Public Lands*, 1:120–144 (137–139, for the appended propositions of the claimants, January 1803). The act of March 1803 is in *U.S. Statutes at Large*, 2:229–235.

Lindsay G. Robertson, "'A Mere Feigned Case': Rethinking the *Fletcher* v. *Peck* Conspiracy and Early American Legal Culture," *Utah Law Review* (2000): 249–265, argues that *Fletcher* should be understood in the context of a legal culture that was more tolerant of legal fictions and feigned issues. The writ of attachment, pleadings, and docket entries for *Fletcher v. Peck* as heard in the U.S. Circuit Court are in Record Group 21, Records of the U.S. Circuit Court for the District of Boston, National Archives at Boston. After the case was decided in 1807, the proceedings were printed as *Copy of the Record in the Case, Robert Fletcher vs. John Peck: Decided at the Circuit Court of the United States for the First Circuit, held at Boston* [October 20, 1807] (Boston: Munroe, Francis and Parker, 1808).

Information about Robert Fletcher has been gleaned from Daniel F. Secomb, *History of the Town of Amherst, Hillsborough County, New Hampshire* . . . (Concord, NH: Evans, Sleeper, and Woodbury, 1883), 589–590; *The Boston Directory* . . . (Boston: Edward Cotton, 1807), 70; *The Farmer's Cabinet* (Amherst, NH), June 10, 1806 (sale of "late Homestead of Robert Fletcher Esq. in said Amherst,–consisting of a large dwelling House"); *Merrimac Intelligencer* (Haverhill, MA), October 28, 1809 (death notice); Norman W. Smith, "The Amherst Bubble," *Historical New Hampshire* 20 (1965): 28.

Biographical information about the lawyers for Fletcher and Peck was obtained from William T. Davis, *Bench and Bar of the Commonwealth of Massachusetts*, 2 vols. (New York: Da Capo Press, 1974); William Sullivan, *The Public Men of the Revolution* . . . (Philadelphia: Carey and Hart, 1847); Clifford K. Shipton, *Sibley's Harvard Graduates*; vol. 17: *The Classes 1768–1771* (Boston: Massachusetts Historical Society, 1975). Jane H. Kamensky, *The Exchange Artist: A Tale of High-flying Speculation and America's First Banking Collapse* (New York: Viking, 2008), a biography of Andrew Dexter, has much information about his father Samuel Dexter and Perez Morton. Papers relating to Morton's agency for the N.E.M. Land Co. are in the New England Mississippi Land Company Records, Hargrett Library, University of Georgia.

David Johnson, *John Randolph of Roanoke* (Baton Rouge: Louisiana State University Press, 2012), is the most recent biography of the eccentric Virginian. See also Hugh A. Garland, *The Life of John Randolph of Roanoke* (New York: D. Appleton, 1850) and William Cabell Bruce, *John Randolph of Roanoke 1773–1833*, 2 vols. (New York: G. P. Putnam's Sons, 1922). Notable for its penetrating insights is Robert Dawidoff, *The Education of John Randolph* (New York: W. W. Norton, 1979). For Jefferson's views on Yazoo, see Dumas Malone, *Jefferson the President: First Term, 1801–1805* (Boston: Little Brown, 1970), 452–453 (also 444, for contemporary descriptions of Randolph).

For the debates in Congress, 1803–1808, see *Annals of Congress*, 13:1039–1040, 1099–1122, 1131–1168 (Eighth Congress, first session); 14:1023, 1024–1033, 1034–1042, 1064–1080, 1100–1108), 1121–1126, 1173–1174, 1178 (second session); 15:46, 48, 165, 181, 184, 192, 208, 906–921 (Ninth Congress, first session); 17:1277–1296, 18:1601–1613, 18:2255–2258 (Tenth Congress, first session) (1808).

The N.E.M. Land Co.'s 1804 memorial and vindication were printed as *Memorial of the Agents of the New England Mississippi Land Company to Congress, with a Vindication of Their Title at Law* (Washington: A. & G. Way, 1804). The memorial (without the vindication), the report of the committee of claims of January 1805, and memorials presented to the Senate in 1806 are in *American State Papers, Public Lands*, 1:191–192, 197–200, 234–236.

The diaries of John Quincy Adams are an invaluable source for the Senate during his service in that body. See Charles Francis Adams, ed., *Memoirs of John Quincy Adams, Containing Portions of His Diary from 1795 to 1848*, 12 vols. (Freeport, NY: Books for Libraries Press, 1969 reprint), 1:381, 389, 390–91, 392, 403, 404–405, 408–409, 414, 417, 418, 423, 424, 452–453. The original diaries are available online: *The Diaries of John Quincy Adams: A Digital Collection* (Boston: Massachusetts Historical Society, 2005) (http://www.masshist.org/jqadiaries). A copy of Adams's bill concerning the Georgia claimants was obtained from the Massachusetts Historical Society (*Online Adams Catalog*, Record Number 11974, March 7, 1806). Also valuable is Everett Somerville Brown, ed., *William Plumer's Memorandum of Proceedings in the United States Senate 1803–1807* (New York: Macmillan, 1923), 462–463.

A valuable supplementary source for the March 1807 debate on the bill to prevent settlements was provided by the Washington correspondent for the *United States' Gazette* (Philadelphia), March 6, 1807. For the act as passed, see *U.S. Statutes at Large*, 2:445. A copy of Governor Sullivan's memorial was printed in the *New-York Herald*, February 3, 1808.

On the first Supreme Court, see William R. Casto, *The Supreme Court in the Early Republic: The Chief Justiceships of John Jay and Oliver Ellsworth*

(Columbia: University of South Carolina Press, 1995). The best modern biographies of Marshall are Jean Edward Smith, *John Marshall: Definer of a Nation* (New York: Henry Holt, 1996) and R. Kent Newmyer, *John Marshall and the Heroic Age of the Supreme Court* (Baton Rouge: Louisiana State University Press, 2001). An excellent short biography is Francis N. Stites, *John Marshall: Defender of the Constitution* (Boston: Little Brown, 1981). These works have superseded the classic biography, Albert J. Beveridge, *The Life of John Marshall*, 4 vols. (Boston: Houghton Mifflin, 1916–1919). Charles F. Hobson, *The Great Chief Justice: John Marshall and the Rule of Law* (Lawrence: University Press of Kansas, 1996), is a biographical study focusing on Marshall's political and constitutional thought. My understanding of how Marshall took judicial review down the path of judicial exposition of the Constitution is indebted to Sylvia Snowiss, *Judicial Review and the Law of the Constitution* (New Haven, CT: Yale University Press, 1990).

The Supreme Court under Marshall is comprehensively treated in two volumes of the Oliver Wendell Holmes Devise History of the Supreme Court of the United States: George Lee Haskins and Herbert A. Johnson, *Foundations of Power: John Marshall, 1801–15* (New York: MacMillan, 1981), and G. Edward White, *The Marshall Court and Cultural Change, 1815–35* (New York: MacMillan, 1988). Johnson subsequently wrote a one-volume history, *The Chief Justiceship of John Marshall, 1801–1835* (Columbia: University of South Carolina Press, 1997). For a brief overview see Charles F. Hobson, "The Marshall Court 1801–1835: Law, Politics, and the Emergence of the Federal Judiciary," in *The United States Supreme Court: The Pursuit of Justice*, ed. Christopher Tomlins (Boston and New York: Houghton Mifflin, 2005): 47–73. This volume also includes capsule biographies of all the justices.

James W. Ely Jr., *The Contract Clause: A Constitutional History* (Lawrence: University Press of Kansas, 2016), updates and supersedes Benjamin Fletcher Wright Jr., *The Contract Clause of the Constitution* (Westport, CT: Greenwood Press, 1982), originally published in 1938. Warren B. Hunting, *The Obligation of Contracts Clause of the United States Constitution* (New York: AMS Press, 1977), originally published in 1919, reads Marshall's contract decisions as according with eighteenth-century ideas about natural law. Edward S. Corwin, "The Basic Doctrine of American Constitutional Law," *Michigan Law Review* 12 (1914): 247–276, reprinted in Alpheus T. Mason and Gerald Garvey, eds., *American Constitutional History: Essays by Edward S. Corwin* (New York: Harper & Row, 1964), 25–45, is a classic essay on the centrality of the doctrine of vested rights. Gordon S. Wood, "The Origins of Vested Rights in the Early Republic,"

Virginia Law Review 85 (1999): 1421–1445, explains how the reaction against the excesses of republican legislatures in the 1780s promoted the rise of an independent judiciary entrusted with the protection of private rights. On Madison's veto, see Charles F. Hobson, "The Negative on State Laws: James Madison, the Constitution, and the Crisis of Republican Government," *William and Mary* Quarterly 36 (1979): 215–235.

Adams's diary is the best source for his service as Peck's lawyer in 1809, not all of which is covered in the printed edition. See John Quincy Adams diary 27, 1 January 1803–4 August 1809, 374–388, 392, *The Diaries of John Quincy Adams: A Digital Collection* (Boston: Massachusetts Historical Society, 2005) (http://www.masshist.org/jqadiaries). The entries for March 1–March 11 are in Adams, ed., *Memoirs of John Quincy Adams*, 543–547. Paul S. Clarkson and R. Samuel Jett, *Luther Martin of Maryland* (Baltimore: Johns Hopkins Press, 1970), is the standard biography. For the arguments and opinion, see *Fletcher v. Peck*, 10 U.S. (6 Cranch), 115–124, 125–127. Adams expressed his disappointment with the opinion in his letter to Louisa Catharine Johnson, March 12, 1809, Adams Family Papers, Massachusetts Historical Society. The agreement he drew up and signed with Martin, dated March 15, 1809, is in Fletcher v. Peck, Appellate. Case No. 311, Record Group 267, National Archives. Adams mentioned this agreement in his diary entries of March 13 and 14 (not in the printed edition). For the 1798 Connecticut case of covenant broken, see Goebel and Smith, eds., *Law Papers of Alexander Hamilton*, 4:412–413.

The opinions of Marshall and Johnson are in *Fletcher v. Peck*, 10 U.S. (6 Cranch) 127–143, 143–148. For an annotated text of Marshall's opinion, see Charles F. Hobson, ed., *The Papers of John Marshall*, vol. 7 (Chapel Hill: University of North Carolina Press, 1993), 225–241. The proceedings and debates of the Eleventh Congress, second session (1809–1810) are in *Annals of Congress*, 20:729–738; 21:1881–1883. The N.E.M. Land Co.'s memorial presented at this session was published under the title *To the Honorable, the Senate and House of Representatives of the United States: The Memorial of the Directors of the New-England Mississippi Land Company, Citizens of the State of Massachusetts* (n.p., n.d.: Early American Imprints, Series 2, no. 32240 [misdated 1814]). For Story's appearance before the committee of claims, see William W. Story, *Life and Letters of Joseph Story*, 2 vols. (Boston: Little Brown, 1851), 1:196–197.

Marshall's opinion in *Fletcher* was printed in these newspapers: *Washington National Intelligencer*, March 28, 1810; *Richmond Enquirer*, April 3, 1810; *Raleigh Star*, April 5, 12 (Johnson's opinion), 1810; *Boston Patriot*, April 21, 1810. Troup's remarks in Congress on April 17, not reported in

Annals of Congress, were recorded by the Washington correspondent for the *Boston Patriot*, April 28, 1810. The meeting of claimants in Boston was reported in the *New-England Palladium*, April 20, 1810, and *Boston Patriot*, April 21, 1810.

For documents on the turmoil in the Mississippi Territory, see Clarence Edwin Carter, ed., *Territorial Papers of the United States*, vol. 6: *The Territory of Mississippi, 1798–1817* (Washington, DC: U.S. Government Printing Office, 1938), 20–21, 25–26; *Letter from the Secretary of the Treasury, Transmitting a Report . . .* (Washington, DC: Roger C. Weightman, 1809); *American State Papers, Public Lands*, 2:209–218. Peck's notice appeared in the *Washington National Intelligencer*, July 23, 1810. The correspondence between Story and Harper concerning Peck's legal fee is in Howell J. Heaney, ed., "The Letters of Joseph Story (1779–1845) in the Hampton L. Carson Collection of the Free Library of Philadelphia," *American Journal of Legal History* 2 (1958): 69–71. For newspaper commentary on *Fletcher*, see *Richmond Enquirer*, July 27, August 3, September 28, October 5, 1810; *Raleigh Star*, October 4, 1810. Troup's comments in the House in December 1810 are reported in *Annals of Congress*, 22:414–415.

The Mississippi statehood bill presented to the Twelfth Congress, second session (1812–1813), and amendments added by the Senate are printed in Carter, ed., *Territorial Papers . . .* , 6:332–334, 341–342. The Senate's Yazoo compensation bill and amendments added by the House were printed as *A Bill to Carry into Effect the Report Made to Congress in February, One Thousand Eight Hundred and Three . . .* ([Washington, DC: 1813]; Early American Imprints, Series 2, no. 30138) and *Amendments Proposed by the Committee on the Public Lands . . .* ([Washington, D.C.: 1813]; Early American Imprints, Series 2, no. 30014). See also *Annals of Congress*, 25:856–860, 1066–1074 (Harper's speech).

On the adoption of the Yazoo compensation bill in 1814 by the Thirteenth Congress, see *Annals of Congress*, 26:572, 612, 629, 630–31, 643; 27:1838–1848, 1873–1875, 1883–1890, 1893–1912, 1917–1922, 1923–1924; *American State Papers, Public Lands*, 2:740–743, 743–748 (for the memorial of the N.E.M. Land Co. and the Oakley committee's report); *A Bill to Carry into Effect the Report Made to Congress in February, One Thousand Eight Hundred and Three . . .* ([Washington, DC: 1814]; Early American Imprints, Series 2, no. 33172); *U.S. Statutes at Large*, 3:116–120 (1814 act), 192–193 (1815 supplementary act). The speeches of Taylor and Giles, not published in *Annals of Congress*, were printed in *The Senator* (Washington, DC), March 5, 1814. For the Treasury statement of 1818, see *American State Papers, Finance*, 3:281–283. Treat, *National*

Land System, 366, notes the efforts of the N.E.M. Land Co. to recover the money deducted by the commissioners and the company's ultimate defeat in the Court of Claims. For the decision, see *New England Mississippi Land Co. v. The United States*, 1 Ct. Cl. 135 (1864). G. Edward White, *The Marshall Court and Cultural Change*, abridged ed. (New York: Oxford University Press, 1991), 595–673, is a magisterial examination of the Marshall Court's contract clause cases. Also valuable is James W. Ely Jr., "The Marshall Court and Property Rights: A Reappraisal," *John Marshall Law Review* 33 (2000): 1023–1061. The rise and decline of the contract clause is ably analyzed in James W. Ely Jr., "Whatever Happened to the Contract Clause?," *Charleston Law Review* 4 (2010): 371–394. The substance of these articles has been incorporated into Ely's recently published *The Contract Clause*.

INDEX

Jackson, Amasa, 58
Jackson, James, 71, 93
    commissioner to negotiate
        Georgia cession, 77
    death of, 105
    Facts in Reply, 103
    and Georgia constitution of
        1798, 54
    leads anti-Yazoo campaign, 5,
        42–47, 48–51, 161
    "Letters of Sicilius," 43–46
    rivalry with Gunn, 42
    in Senate, 41, 70, 102–103
Jackson, John G., 98–100
Jay, John, 84, 111–112
Jefferson, Thomas
    as president, 8, 71, 77, 93, 94,
        112, 113, 117–118, 120,
        166
    and Yazoo, 98
Johnson, William
    opinion in *Fletcher*, 153,
        155–156, 190
    opinion in *Green v. Biddle*, 191,
        192, 197
    Supreme Court justice, 117–118,
        120, 136, 140, 141, 145, 187,
        188, 189, 193
Johnson v. McIntosh, 17, 155
Joy, Benjamin, 135, 168, 175
judicial review, 98, 112, 116–117,
    126
    as check on state legislatures,
        177–178, 197–198, 199,
        201
    contract clause and, 1–2, 9–10,
        201
    scope of, 183–184
Judiciary Act of 1789, 87, 110–111
    section 25, 111, 154, 179, 181,
        183, 194, 195
Judiciary Act of 1801, 8, 114
Judiciary Act of 1802, 114, 115

Kentucky, 15–16, 21, 22, 190–192,
    193
Key, Francis S., 175

land companies, 14–23
land speculation, 4, 11–23
Latrobe, Benjamin, 143
Lattimore, William, 168, 170
Law, John, 175
Lee, Charles, 66, 72
"Letters of Sicilius," 43–46
Lincoln, Levi, 77, 94, 164
Livingston, Brockholst
    Supreme Court justice, 118,
        120–121, 136, 139, 145, 153,
        185, 191
Loyal Company, 14, 16
Lyon, Matthew, 94, 95, 101

Macon, Nathaniel, 94
Madison, Dolley, 136
Madison, James
    and contract clause, 127
    critique of legislative power, 10,
        124–126
    favors Yazoo compromise, 98–99
    president, 107, 118, 136, 137,
        143, 166, 169
    U.S. commissioner on Yazoo
        claims, 77, 94, 164
Magrath, C. Peter, 3
Marbury, William, 114, 116
Marbury v. Madison, 1, 114–117,
    133–134, 142
    compared with *Fletcher*, 177
Marshall, John
    chief justice, 1, 8–9, 110,
        113–119, 136, 139, 140–142
    expounds contract clause, 128,
        150–154, 178, 182–183, 186,
        188–190, 194–195, 199–201
    and natural law, 121–123,
        149–150, 189

opinions in *Fletcher v. Peck*, 138–139, 145–155
rules rescinding act unconstitutional, 147–153
and scope of judicial review, 183–184
understanding of contract, 121–123
and vested rights, 128, 129, 133–134
Marshall, Thomas, 22
Martin, Luther, 136–138, 139, 144–145
Massachusetts, 19–20, 106–107
Mathews, George, 74, 75
as Georgia governor, 33–34, 40, 49–50, 56
McCulloch v. Maryland, 178
Milledge, John, 73, 77
Miller, Phineas, 62–63, 66, 71, 140
Mississippi Company, 15
Mississippi River, 3, 14, 15, 23, 24, 26, 28, 30, 34, 63, 73
Mississippi Territory, 83, 92, 96, 158–159, 162–163, 164, 165
act to establish, 6, 72–74
N.E.M. Land Co. attempts to colonize, 6, 74–77
Mitchill, Samuel L., 94
Morris, Robert, 4, 16, 20–21, 56–57
Morse, Jedidiah, 67–68
Morton, Perez, 89–90, 95
Moultrie, William, 27
Moultrie v. Georgia, 29, 82
Muscle Shoals, 25, 26, 27, 28, 29, 158–159, 163

Natchez District, 24, 26, 73
Native Americans
title to lands, 69, 137, 154–155
See also Cherokee tribe; Chickasaw tribe; Choctaw tribe; Creek tribe

natural law, 129, 132, 133, 187–188
Marshall and, 121–123, 149–150, 189
New England
sale of Yazoo lands in, 5–6, 56–64
Yazoo claimants, 3, 64–65, 75–77, 157–158, 175–176
New England Mississippi Land Company (N.E.M. Land Co.), 3
attempts to colonize Mississippi lands, 6, 74–77
disputes award under indemnity act, 175–176
hires Adams to represent Peck, 135
purchases Georgia Mississippi Company grant, 5–6, 56, 57–58, 64, 82, 168
pursues Yazoo claims, 6–8, 64–65, 75–77, 95–96, 143–144, 156–157
"Vindication," 96, 132–133
New Jersey v. Wilson, 2, 179–180
Nicholson, John, 56–57
Nightingale, John C., 62–63, 71, 140
North American Land Company, 21, 56–57
North Carolina, 22–23
Northwest Ordinance, 17, 74, 126
Northwest Territory, 4, 17, 18–19

Oakley, Thomas J., 167–168
O'Fallon, James, 28–29
Ogden v. Blackledge, 134
Ogden v. Saunders, 2, 123, 155–156, 187–190
Ohio Company, 14, 16
Ohio Company (postrevolutionary), 18–19
Ohio River, 15, 16, 17, 21, 24, 25

Yazoo, *continued*
New England claimants, 3,
64–65, 75–77, 157–158,
175–176
pamphlets attacking and
defending, 66–71
and Republican Party, 8, 9, 71,
92, 93–94, 95–96, 166–172
Yazoo lands
Georgia cedes to United States,
3, 76–78
sale of 1789, 23–29
sale of 1795, 2–3, 4–5, 29–36,
37–40
sales in New England, 56–64
U.S. claim, 6, 30, 40–41,
66–68, 67, 72, 75, 76, 131,
137, 154
"Yazoo line," 24–25
Yazoo River, 24–25, 26, 73